Social Problems

Recent Sociology Titles from W. W. Norton

Code of the Streets by Elijah Anderson

The Cosmopolitan Canopy by Elijah Anderson

Essentials of Sociology, 4th Edition by Anthony Giddens, Mitchell Duneier, Richard P. Appelbaum, and Deborah Carr

You May Ask Yourself: An Introduction to Thinking like a Sociologist, 3rd Edition by Dalton Conley

The Real World: An Introduction to Sociology, 3rd Edition by Kerry Ferris and Jill Stein

Introduction to Sociology, 8th Edition by Anthony Giddens, Mitchell Duneier, Richard P. Appelbaum, and Deborah Carr

Mix it Up: Popular Culture, Mass Media, and Society by David Grazian

The Contexts Reader, 2nd Edition edited by Douglas Hartmann and Christopher Uggen

When Sex Goes to School by Kristin Luker

Inequality and Society by Jeff Manza and Michael Sauder

Doing Race by Hazel Rose Markus and Paula M. L. Moya

Readings for Sociology, 7th Edition edited by Garth Massey

Families as They Really Are edited by Barbara J. Risman

Sociology of Globalization by Saskia Sassen

The Sociology of News, 2nd Edition by Michael Schudson

The Social Construction of Sexuality, 2nd Edition by Steven Seidman

The Corrosion of Character by Richard Sennett

Biography and the Sociological Imagination by Michael J. Shanahan and Ross Macmillan

A Primer on Social Movements by David Snow and Sarah Soule

Six Degrees by Duncan J. Watts

More than Just Race by William Julius Wilson

American Society: How it Really Works by Erik Olin Wright and Joel Rogers

For more information on our publications in sociology, please visit wwnorton.com/soc

Social Problems

Second Edition

JOEL BEST

W. W. NORTON & COMPANY

NEW YORK   LONDON

W. W. Norton & Company has been independent since its founding in 1923, when William Warder Norton and Mary D. Herter Norton first published lectures delivered at the People's Institute, the adult education division of New York City's Cooper Union. The firm soon expanded its program beyond the Institute, publishing books by celebrated academics from America and abroad. By midcentury, the two major pillars of Norton's publishing program—trade books and college texts—were firmly established. In the 1950s, the Norton family transferred control of the company to its employees, and today—with a staff of four hundred and a comparable number of trade, college, and professional titles published each year—W. W. Norton & Company stands as the largest and oldest publishing house owned wholly by its employees.

The text of this book is composed in Berkeley Book
with the display set in Scala Sans.
Book design by Margaret Wagner.

Editor: Karl Bakeman
Editorial assistant: Rebecca Charney
Project editor: Kate Feighery
Production manager: Benjamin Reynolds
Composition: Jouve—Brattleboro, VT
Manufacturing: Maple-Vail—York, PA

Library of Congress Cataloging-in-Publication Data

Best, Joel.
  Social problems / Joel Best. — 2nd ed.
    p.cm.
  Includes bibliographical references and index.
  ISBN 978-0-393-91863-2 (pbk.)
  1. Social problems. I. Title.
  HN28.B45 2013
  361.1—dc22

                        2011050942

W. W. Norton & Company, Inc., 500 Fifth Avenue, New York, N.Y. 10110
www.wwnorton.com

W. W. Norton & Company Ltd., Castle House, 75/76 Wells Street,
London W1T 3QT

2 3 4 5 6 7 8 9 0

Contents

Figures   vii

Boxes   ix

A Note to the Reader   xiii

Acknowledgments   xv

1   The Social Problems Process   3

2   Claims   29
   CASE STUDY • MAKING CLAIMS ABOUT PROBLEM ANIMALS
   AND ANIMAL PROBLEMS   61

3   Activists as Claimsmakers   64
   CASE STUDY • MOBILIZING AGAINST HOMOPHOBIC
   BULLYING   93

4   Experts as Claimsmakers   96
   CASE STUDY • THE AUTISM EPIDEMIC AND DISPUTES OVER
   EXPERTISE   123

5 The Media and Claims *127*
   CASE STUDY • Reporting about Risk *157*

6 Public Reaction *160*
   CASE STUDY • Public Reactions to Immigration *187*

7 Policymaking *190*
   CASE STUDY • Health Care as a Policy Challenge *218*

8 Social Problems Work *221*
   CASE STUDY • Loan Applications and Financial
            Collapse *251*

9 Policy Outcomes *255*
   CASE STUDY • Technological Change and Policy
            Outcomes *283*

10 Claims across Space and Time *286*
   CASE STUDY • Sexual Trafficking across
            Space and Time *315*

11 The Uses of the Constructionist Stance *318*

Glossary *331*

References *339*

Index *353*

Figures

1.1 Basic Natural History Model of the Social Problems Process *19*

1.2 Resources and Rhetoric Affect Each Stage of the Social Problems Process *24*

2.1 The Structure of Social Problems Claims *31*

2.2 Dynamics Shaping Claims *58*

3.1 Claimsmaking by Outsider and Insider Claimsmakers *65*

3.2 Activists' Concerns in Making Effective Claims *90*

4.1 Experts' Role in the Social Problems Process *121*

5.1 The Media's Role in the Social Problems Process *155*

6.1 The Public's Role in the Social Problems Process *185*

7.1 Kingdon's Policy Stream Model *199*

7.2 Policymaking in the Social Problems Process *216*

8.1 Social Problems Workers in the Middle *225*

9.1 One Social Problems Process Can Inspire Others *265*

10.1 Bases for Comparison among Social Problems Processes *291*

11.1 Basic Model of the Social Problems Process *319*

11.2 Interactions in the Social Problems Process *322*

Boxes

1.1 A Weighty Disagreement 7

1.2 Pluto: A Planetary Problem? 13

2.1 The Basic Recipe: Grounds for Viewing College-Educated White Males' Job Losses as a Social Problem 34

2.2 Claiming Closure 39

2.3 Disputes within the Apparent Agreement about Food Security 42

2.4 Targeting Disney 47

2.5 Expanding Trauma's Domain 50

2.6 Competing Constructions of the Lives of Homicide Victims 52

3.1 Framing the Grotesque 69

3.2 Shifting Frames for Women's and Children's Victimization 74

3.3 Forging Alliances across Social Movements 77

3.4 Foundations Redirect Activism for Forest Preservation 79

3.5 Allies, Opportunities, and Abortion 84

3.6 Why Isn't the Gun Control Movement Stronger? 91

4.1 Medicalizing Opposition by Using the Label *Phobia* 100

4.2 The Various Meanings of Genetic Information 105

4.3 The Path toward Scientific Consensus *108*

4.4 Think Tanks and Officials *115*

4.5 Officials, Hedgehogs, and Foxes *117*

4.6 Are Experts Enough? *120*

5.1 Turning Events into News *131*

5.2 When Do Reporters Find Activists Newsworthy? *135*

5.3 How New Are New Media? *140*

5.4 Covering Conditions, Rather Than Problems *143*

5.5 Crimes Become Iconic *145*

5.6 Infotainment and Shame *151*

6.1 Wording Survey Questions about Climate Change/Global Warming *164*

6.2 How Citizens Make Sense of News *166*

6.3 Telling Stories about 9/11 *171*

6.4 Don't Take a Card, Any Card *175*

6.5 Worrying about Spiked Drinks *179*

6.6 Joking about Disasters *182*

7.1 Legislators' Understandings of Sex Crimes *194*

7.2 Waiting for the Next Policy Wave *197*

7.3 Does Congress Listen? *205*

7.4 Agreeing on a Frame Isn't Enough *207*

7.5 Constructing Abu Ghraib as an Isolated Incident *212*

7.6 The Undeclared War on Traffic Fatalities *215*

8.1 Weather Forecasting as Social Problems Work *226*

8.2 How Police on the Beat View Compstat *229*

8.3 Managing Dignity in Nursing Homes *236*

8.4 Human Resource Workers Shape Policy *238*

8.5 New Identities for Drug Addicts? *240*

8.6 Managing the Abortion Experience *248*

9.1 Alcohol, Risks, and Pregnancy *260*

9.2. When Should Pathologists Identify Abuse as a Cause of Death? *263*

9.3 Holding Colleges Accountable for Crime on Campus *268*

9.4 Do Sex Offender Policies Work? *274*

9.5 Commissions Explain Disasters *277*

9.6 Participation as an Outcome of Social Programs *281*

10.1 Religion, Democracy, and Israeli Social Issues *293*

10.2 Sexual Harassment Attracts Attention in Japan *298*

10.3 Social Movements' Selective Memories *301*

10.4 Cycles Can Have Ironic Consequences *305*

10.5 Taking a Long View of Social Movements
and Press Coverage *308*

10.6 Forecasting Future Problems *312*

A Note to the Reader

Many, many books titled *Social Problems* have been published in the past hundred years. Their tables of contents look a lot alike: they begin with a brief discussion of the nature of social problems, then consider a list of different problems. Each chapter presents more or less up-to-date information about a particular social problem: there is a chapter about crime, another about racism, and so on. If your parents, grandparents, or even great-grandparents read a social problems textbook, that book almost certainly fit this pattern.

This is not your parents' social problems textbook.

The chapters in this book do not deal with different problems. Instead, each chapter deals with a different stage in the *social problems process*—the process by which particular problems become a focus of concern. Why do we worry about, say, the risks of breast implants in one year, road rage in another, and identity theft in still another? This book seeks to explain how and why attention to different issues rises and falls.

If you're a student who's been assigned to read this book, it probably already seems long. All I can say is that it could have been a lot longer. Lots of people have written about the rise and fall of social problems; hundreds of studies have been published on the topic, particularly since the 1970s. But I have decided to cite relatively few sources. Often where I've cited one source, I could have cited dozens. In general, I have chosen to cite sources that appeared relatively recently. In addition, because this book is intended as an introduction to thinking about social problems, I have tried to hold jargon to a minimum. If you go on to read more of what sociologists have written on the topic—and I hope that this book will get you interested enough to do just that—you will find that other authors have explored the ins and outs of studying social problems in far more detail, and that they have developed many specialized terms and concepts to help us think about the social problems process. However, my goal is not to summarize everything that has been written about what I call the constructionist approach to social problems. Rather, I want to give you a basic framework for understanding this approach. This book is intended to help you become a more critical thinker; it provides some tools that can help you better analyze what you read and hear about social problems.

Acknowledgments

I particularly want to thank Karl Bakeman, Norton's editor for sociology. Over the years, I have been approached by several publishers who said they wanted me to write a book about social problems. I had a standard response: "You don't want to publish the book I want to write, and I don't want to write the book you want to publish." That was enough to discourage everyone—except Karl. I appreciate his willingness to take a chance on the book I wanted to write.

I also want to thank Kathe Lowney, who read the entire manuscript and gave me a lot of good advice. I also benefited from the comments of the other reviewers: Alison Alkon, University of California, Davis; Nancy Berns, Drake University; Vincent Carter, Emory University; Tracy Citeroni, Mary Washington University; Joseph E. Davis, University of Virginia; Stephanie Decker, University of Kansas; Jen Dunn, Southern Illinois University at Carbondale; Heather Feldhaus, Bloomsburg University; Jessica Greenebaum, Central Connecticut State University; Scott Harris, St. Louis University; Ann Herda-Rapp, University of Wisconsin–Marathon County; Jim Holstein, Marquette University; Pam Hunt, Kent State University; Michelle Jacobs, Mira Costa College; Ellis Jones, University of California, Davis; Jeanne Mekolichick, Radford College; Bryce Merrill, University of Colorado at Boulder; David Meyer, University of California, Irvine; Dorothy Pawluch, McMaster University; Gina Petonito, Miami University–Ohio; Meredith Redlin, South Dakota State University; Theodore Sasson, Middlebury College; Stu Shafer, Johnson County Community College; Ira Silver, Framingham State University; and Loreen Wolfer, University of Scranton.

The second edition benefited from comments and advice from Nancy Berns, Drake University; Eric Best, University of Delaware; John Barnshaw, University of South Florida; Dave Ermann, University of Delaware; John E. Glass, Colin College; Jerry Jacobs, University of Pennsylvania; Joanna Kempner, Rutgers University; Kathe Lowney, Valdosta State University; David Meyers, University of California, Irvine; Barret Michalec, University of Delaware; Lynne Moulton, State University of New York, Brockport; Victor Perez, University of Delaware; Dave Schweingruber, Iowa State University; Shelli Walker, University of Colorado; and Robyn White, Northwest Arkansas Community College.

Finally, I want to thank the other folks at Norton who helped me pull the book together. In particular, Romaine Perin did the copyediting on the second edition.

Social Problems

1

The Social Problems Process

The title of this book identifies its subject: social problems. But what are *social problems*? If asked, most people have no difficulty listing some examples: crime, suicide, racism, sexism, terrorism, global warming. Most people have a commonsense notion of what the term means, but actually defining the concept turns out to be much trickier.

Suppose we agree that suicide and global warming are both social problems. What, exactly, do the two have in common? They seem very different: we usually think of suicide as an extremely personal act, committed by individuals who feel isolated and in despair, whereas global warming involves physical climate change across a whole planet. What sort of definition can cover both individual acts and global transformations?

TWO WAYS TO DEFINE SOCIAL PROBLEMS

Social Problems as Harmful Conditions: The Objectivist Outlook

The usual answer is to define social problems as conditions that somehow harm society. For example, another recent book that shares the title of this book, *Social Problems*, offers this definition: "A social problem is a social condition or pattern of behavior that has negative consequences for individuals, our social world, or our physical world" (Leon-Guerrero, 2011, p. 8). In other words, some conditions have the characteristic of causing "negative consequences" that makes them social problems. Although the precise wording of their definitions varies, most books on the topic characterize social problems as harmful conditions.

This approach to defining social problems is sometimes called **objectivist** because it tries to couch the definition in terms of objectively measurable characteristics of conditions. Once we define social problems as harmful conditions, we can look around until we spot a harmful condition and then identify it as a social problem. Most books titled *Social Problems* have chapters devoted to crime, racism, and other conditions that presumably have been objectively determined to be harmful.

Objectivist definitions seem fine—until we start to think about them. Then some problems with the objectivist approach become obvious. The first difficulty is that conditions that might be deemed harmful aren't always identified as social problems. Take sexism. Virtually all the books titled *Social Problems* and published in the United States in recent decades discuss sexism; it is widely understood to be a social problem. And yet, although social arrangements that discriminate against females have had a very long history, often they have been taken for granted, viewed as normal and natural—not at all a problem. Even today, many people around the world believe that their religions or traditions justify—even require—such discriminatory social arrangements. In fact, even American books about social problems published before 1970 rarely mentioned sexual discrimination. Only in recent decades has the term *sexism* emerged to refer to a form of discrimination seen as analogous to racism (which already was widely understood to be a social problem).

If we ask people to explain why racism is a social problem, they are likely to emphasize justice or fairness. It is, they will explain, unjust to discriminate against people simply because they belong to a particular race. Some may add that racism also harms society in that victims of racial discrimination are blocked from making all of the contributions they might make to the larger society, so that not only are those victims harmed, but the larger society is damaged because it misses out on what the victims could contribute; moreover, society is harmed further because racial tensions create conflict that makes the society less productive and harmonious. In other words, it is easy to argue that racism is a harmful condition and should be recognized as a social problem.

Obviously it is possible to make analogous arguments about sexism—that it is unfair, blocks women from fulfilling their potential, fosters conflict, and therefore harms the larger society. Thus, by objective standards, we might assume that racism and sexism should both be seen as social problems, although we know that—at other times or in other places—people have treated both racist and sexist practices as normal, even as the way things ought to be.

Note, however, that we might make essentially the same arguments about discrimination based on height. Studies show that taller people have various advantages; for example, they are more likely to be hired and more likely to be promoted. Thus, short people can be seen as victims of height discrimination (Rosenberg, 2009). Such discriminatory treatment also might be considered unfair, and ultimately harmful to society in much the same ways that racism and sexism are harmful. By objective standards, then, shouldn't "heightism" also be considered a social problem?

The first difficulty with objectivism becomes apparent: although we might argue that racism, sexism, and heightism all have analogous effects on society, as social problems these three forms of discrimination have not received anything like the same degree of attention. Racial discrimination has long been understood to be a serious social problem; sexism has only recently been added to the list of significant social problems; and heightism rarely receives mention as a social problem. As far as I know, no book about social problems includes a chapter about height discrimination. The different treatment of these three forms of discrimination makes it difficult to argue that there is an evenly applied objective standard for identifying what is or is not a social problem.

A second challenge to objectivism is that the same condition may be identified as a social problem for very different reasons; that is, people may disagree about why a certain condition is harmful. For example, some commentators argue that contemporary society discriminates against people who are overweight; heavier people find it more difficult to get jobs, are the objects of scorn, and so on. In this view, weight discrimination, like racial, gender, or—yes—height discrimination, should be considered a social problem because it is unjust and blocks some individuals from opportunities. More recently, however, attention has focused on obesity itself as a social problem. Here the argument is that heavier people are less healthy, and that obesity costs society many millions of dollars in additional health care expenditures. Critics taking this view consider obesity a social problem not because it leads to discrimination, but because it harms individuals and is a drain on societal resources (see Box 1.1).

Note that, although both arguments suggest that there is a social problem related to weight, they make very different claims: the former suggests that discrimination against overweight people is unfair (presumably, this position might lead to suggestions that society ought to become more tolerant of weight differences and that such discrimination should be discouraged); the latter views obesity itself as a source of harm (and would presumably lead to calls to reduce obesity). This example reveals a second problem with the objectivist view of social problems: very different—even contradictory—objective standards may be used in identifying a condition as a social problem.

Box 1.1   A Weighty Disagreement

Many Americans are heavy. Is this a social problem? If so, what exactly is the nature of this problem? Is it a discrimination/civil rights problem? Or is it a medical/public health problem?

The fat acceptance movement (led by the National Association to Advance Fat Acceptance) argues that weight is a form of diversity. In its view, fat people (to use the term the movement favors) are stigmatized; they are ridiculed and face discrimination in the workplace and elsewhere. Fat acceptance activists argue that this is a civil rights issue, that discrimination based on weight is no more justified than racial or gender bias. They point to research suggesting that people cannot control—and therefore should not be blamed for—their weight.

In contrast, many medical authorities and government officials warn that increases in Americans' average weight constitutes an "obesity epidemic." They note that higher weight increases one's risks of heart disease and other medical problems, and that this has consequences, not only for the affected individuals who suffer more health problems, but for the larger society, which must bear the increased costs of medical treatment. In this view, obesity is a public health issue, analogous to smoking, and policies are needed to encourage citizens to maintain healthy weight.

These different views on obesity illustrate that even people who agree that a particular condition is a social problem may disagree about the sort of social problem it is.

Source: Saguy & Riley, 2005.

A third problem with objectivism has already been suggested: our lists of social problems include wildly diverse phenomena. They usually range from problems affecting particular individuals, such as suicide or mental illness, to global trends, such as overpopulation, globalization, or global warming. Any objective definition that tries to cover such a broad range of topics must be fairly vague, and speak in only the most general terms about harm, undermining well-being, or anything else. Although objectivists argue that social problems are harmful conditions, they don't specify what constitutes harm. Instead, harmfulness becomes a big conceptual umbrella, covering a huge array of phenomena, ranging from, say, the pain experienced by those who knew someone who committed suicide, through all of the economic and ecological costs that might be incurred as global temperatures rise. In practice, then, objective definitions of social problems turn out to be so vague as to be almost meaningless.

For all of these reasons, it is quite difficult to devise an objective definition of social problems that can distinguish between the things that people consider social problems and the things that they don't. So let's ask the question again: what, exactly, do suicide and global warming have in common? Once we think about it, we realize that there is really only one quality that all of the diverse phenomena considered social problems share: they are all considered social problems. The point is not so much that some conditions cause harm, but that people think of some conditions as being harmful.

Social Problems as Topics of Concern: The Subjectivist Outlook

Imagine two societies with arrangements that discriminate against women; in one, people consider these arrangements normal and natural; in the other, some people consider these arrangements wrong. From the point of view of the first society's members, sexism is not a social problem; some members of the second society, though, do regard sexism as a social problem. Of course, people's views may change. In recent decades, Americans have come to view social arrangements that treat men and women differently as problematic, so even though sexism was formerly not considered a social problem, it has become one.

We might think of this as a **subjectivist** approach, in that it defines social problems in terms of people's subjective sense that something is or isn't a problem. If people don't think that height-ism is a social problem, then it isn't one; but if height discrimina-tion began receiving a lot of concerned attention, heightism could become a social problem. If people consider both suicide and global warming to be social problems, then both are.

Once we start thinking about social problems in terms of subjec-tive judgments, we realize that people often disagree about what should be considered social problems. We might expect people of above-average height to dismiss arguments that height discrimina-tion should be considered a social problem, and those of below-average height to be more receptive to those claims. Similarly, the views of individuals outside a society may differ from those of its members. When Americans criticize sexism in other countries, they are identifying a social problem, even if most of the occupants of those countries disagree. Remember, there is no objective standard that lets us declare, "X is a social problem, but Y is not." Rather, whether a condition is a social problem depends on different peo-ple's points of view—and they won't always agree.

In this view, social problems will come and go as people's subjec-tive judgments change. Announcements of discoveries of a new dis-ease or a new environmental threat can vault previously overlooked conditions onto people's lists of social problems. Other social prob-lems fade away. For example, during the 1950s many commentators worried that young Americans were apathetic, but apathy stopped being considered a social problem during the 1960s, when campus demonstrations led critics to charge that students had become too concerned, too involved in political activity.

From the subjectivist outlook, it is not an objective quality of a social condition, but rather the subjective reactions to that con-dition, that make something a social problem. Therefore, social problems should not be viewed as a type of social condition, but as a *process* of responding to social conditions. Thus, we can define social problems as efforts to arouse concern about conditions within society. Or, to quote one influential definition, social problems are "the activities of individuals or groups making assertions of grievance and claims with respect to some putative conditions" (Spector & Kitsuse, 1977, p. 75). In other words, the study of social problems should focus not on conditions, but on claims about conditions.

At first glance, this approach may seem wrongheaded. If we're interested in, say, poverty, then shouldn't we be studying poverty as a condition? We might try to measure the number of poor people, determine the causes of poverty, and so on. In other words, shouldn't we adopt a more objectivist approach and focus on the condition of poverty, rather than on claims about poverty? Of course, it is possible to study poverty and other social conditions, and there is nothing wrong with doing so. But that has nothing to do with studying poverty *as a social problem.*

Studying poverty as a social problem requires asking how and why people came to consider poverty problematic. After all, poverty has been around for a long time; throughout history, many people in many societies have taken poverty for granted, seeing it as necessary, normal, even just. Some societies with very large populations of poor people have not viewed poverty as a social problem. In contrast, in the United States and many other modern societies, the widespread view is that poverty should be considered a social problem, and that we ought to do something about it. Studying poverty *as a social problem* requires studying how that view emerged and spread.

In other words, efforts to find a workable definition of social problems based on the objective characteristics of social conditions have proved futile. Thinking systematically about social problems requires adopting a subjectivist approach that focuses on the process by which people identify social problems. That process involves what sociologists call *social construction.*

SOCIAL CONSTRUCTION

By **social construction**, we mean the way people assign meaning to the world. People use language; language is essential to our understanding of the world that surrounds us (just try thinking without using words). One of the principal accomplishments of infancy and early childhood is learning to recognize, understand, and use words. Through language, we learn to categorize the world, to understand that some things are edible (*food*) while others are dangerous and must not be eaten (*poison*), and so on. This is obviously a social process: we do not invent our language; rather, we learn to use the language of our parents and the other people around us. The meanings of their words—their categories for classifying the world—are the ones that we learn. Children grow up speaking English, or French, or whatever language the people in the group around them speak, and they learn to assign that group's meanings to the world.

Language is flexible: as people learn new things about the world, they devise words with new meanings. In this way, people continually create—or construct—fresh understandings about the world around them. Because this is a social process, sociologists refer to it as *social construction* (Berger & Luckmann, 1966).

Sociologists do not view social construction as a completely arbitrary process; it is constrained by the physical world within which people find themselves. We can imagine all sorts of ridiculous meanings that people might, in theory, construct. For instance, an imaginary society might, in theory, teach its young that rocks are edible, or that people can fly by flapping their arms, but this is hardly likely. Although this could happen, it probably wouldn't, because those lessons would prove worthless, even dangerous. In general, the meanings people construct need to make sense of the world they inhabit.

The point is not that people could assign ridiculous meanings to the world, but rather that they must assign some meanings to at least some of their surroundings. Probably every human society throughout history has categorized people as either male or female. The distinction is relatively clear-cut: we can look at virtually any newborn infant and confidently declare that it falls into one category or the other. If this doesn't seem to be a social process, remember that a tiny fraction of infants (about one in every thousand) are born with anomalous sexual organs that do challenge the simple male/female classification, and societies have to decide how to deal with those cases (Preves, 2003). These individuals, once called her-maphrodites, but now termed *intersex*, pose challenges to simplistic male-female categories. There are various solutions: Many Native American societies defined these individuals as having a special status as *berdaches*—a sort of third sex outside the standard male/female divide. By contrast, in contemporary America surgeons often "correct" the anomalies, to give the infant either a male or a female appearance, and foster an unambiguous gender identity.

This example reminds us that even something as apparently straightforward as sorting people into males and females is a social process of constructing meanings. Note, too, that the precise mean-ings assigned to these categories—the qualities attributed to males or females—vary from one society to another. Both the two-category male/female classification and the specific qualities associated with each category are instances of social construction. All meanings, including how we designate planets in the solar system and all other elements in the physical world, are socially constructed (see Box 1.2).

Sociologists sometimes illustrate social construction by pointing to problems that seem ridiculous. These examples offer a sort of analytic leverage: they lay bare the process of social construction. Witch hunts are a favorite historical example; UFO abductions and satanic ritual abuse offer more contemporary cases. Critics might argue that there is no convincing evidence that witches, UFOs, or child-abusing satanists exist (ignore, for the moment, those people who remain convinced that these are real phenomena). Therefore,

---

Box 1.2 Pluto: A Planetary Problem?

For decades, schoolchildren learned that there were nine planets, but that changed in 2006, when astronomers demoted Pluto from the list, reclassifying it as a *dwarf planet*. Pluto is unlike the other planets in several ways: (1) It is much smaller. (2) It has a different composition; the four inner planets (Mercury, Venus, Earth, and Mars) are basically rocks, and the four giant planets (Jupiter, Saturn, Uranus, and Neptune) are composed of gas, but Pluto is basically a big lump of ice. (3) It has a less circular, more elliptical orbit than the other planets, so sometimes it is closer to the Sun than Neptune is. And (4), unlike the other eight planets, whose orbits fall more or less along a single plane, Pluto has an orbit that is at an angle to that plane.

No one denies that Pluto exists; the question is whether it makes more sense to classify it as a planet or as belonging to a different category. When Ceres—the largest asteroid—was discovered in 1801, it was initially considered a planet, but astronomers dropped that classification once they realized that there were many asteroids. Now Ceres joins Pluto in the new category of dwarf planet. These examples remind us that *planet* is a social construction, a category that people use to assign meaning to the world. Our words are social products: we create them and teach them to one another. Because we understand our world through language, sociologists view all knowledge as socially constructed.

Source: Tyson, 2009.

---

the sociologists declare, witchcraft, UFOs, and satanic blood cults are clearly social constructions.

This conclusion is true, but its implication is quite false. UFO abductions are a social construction, in the sense that this term was created and disseminated by people. But the implication—that only unprovable claims are socially constructed—is wrong. Poverty is just as much a social construction as UFO abductions are.

The term *poverty* is another category that people have created to make sense of the world. Just as some people have drawn attention to UFO abductions, others have campaigned to raise concern about poverty (during the 1960s, for example, President Lyndon Johnson declared "war on poverty"). Saying that poverty is a social construction does not mean that poverty doesn't exist, that it somehow doesn't occur in the real world; obviously some people have much less money than others. But the words we choose to describe those people (*impoverished*, for instance, rather than *wretched* or *depraved*—terms that were once used to describe the poor), how we explain their condition, and what we recommend doing about it are meanings that people create and use. In that sense, poverty—like everything else we know about—is a social construction.

Once we recognize that social problems are social constructions, and that what the conditions constructed as social problems have in common is precisely that construction, then it becomes apparent that social problems should be understood in terms of a **social problems process**. That is, the study of social problems should focus on how and why particular conditions come to be constructed as social problems. How and why did poverty—or UFO abductions—emerge as topics of interest and concern at particular moments, and in particular places? Why do people decide that something needs to be done about some conditions, and how do they decide exactly what should be done? This approach to studying social problems is called **constructionist**, and it is the perspective adopted in this book.

THE BASIC FRAMEWORK

The constructionist approach requires understanding a few basic terms. These will reappear throughout the chapters that follow. The first is **claim**. Constructing a social problem involves a process of **claimsmaking**: someone must bring the topic to the attention of others, by making a claim that there is a condition that should be recognized as troubling, that needs to be addressed. For constructionist sociologists, social problems are defined in terms of this claimsmaking process, because it is claimsmaking—and only claimsmaking—that all social problems have in common.

Note that claims may be supported by very different sorts of evidence: someone making claims about poverty might present poverty statistics, photographs of poor people, or all manner of other evidence; claims about UFO abductions tend to rely on first-person accounts by people who say they recall having been abducted. Whether other people find a claim convincing is a separate issue. At one extreme, we can imagine a claim that no one finds convincing: picture a man standing on a street corner warning passersby that invisible, undetectable aliens from planet Zorax have infested the very air that they're breathing. This may be a claim, but if everyone who hears it dismisses or ignores it, it will have no impact. The social problems process requires not only that someone make a claim, but that others react to it.

The people who make claims are, of course, **claimsmakers**. They are the ones who seek to convince others that something is wrong, and that something should be done about it. Obviously not all claimsmakers are equal: we tend to treat some claims more seriously, simply because they seem more plausible, or because they are promoted by people we respect—experts, officials, and so on. Successful claims spread, so that they become the subject of media coverage and debates over public policy.

These few concepts—claim, claimsmaking, and claimsmaker—provide a foundation upon which we can build a more elaborate analysis of the social problems process. Throughout this book, we will distinguish between claims and the conditions about which claims are being made. We will refer to **troubling conditions**—that is, the conditions that become subjects of claims. The word *troubling* focuses our attention on people's subjective reactions: a condition is troubling if it bothers someone. Note that it isn't necessary for everyone to accept the claim; some people may consider UFO abductions troubling, even though others regard such claims as fantastic. We can consider both poverty and UFO abductions troubling conditions, regardless of whether we agree that they both exist.

Adopting a subjectivist stance can seem confusing at first. In particular, two sorts of confusion arise. We have already discussed the first: people sometimes wrongly imagine that *social construction* refers only to imaginary, nonexistent phenomena. Again, this is wrong—all human knowledge is socially constructed through our language, which means that all social problems are socially constructed.

The second source of confusion is that we must acknowledge that sociologists are themselves engaged in social construction. Like all other people, sociologists must use language to make the world meaningful; they devise their own categories—such as *claims* and *claimsmakers*—that they use to classify the world. This book, for instance, can be understood as a set of sociological claims about the social problems process.

Some people worry that, if sociology is one more social construction, we can't really have confidence in sociological knowledge. The response, of course, is that we can have exactly the same sort of confidence in sociology that we have in our other sorts of knowledge. When we encounter claims in everyday life—when someone gives us a compliment, politicians ask for our votes, or advertisers try to sell us their products—we neither accept everything we hear at face value nor assume that it is all meaningless. Rather, we learn to evaluate claims, to look for evidence, and so on. Similarly, sociologists can offer support for their arguments, and this book will try to suggest the nature of that support. (For more detailed discussions of various theoretical and methodological aspects of the constructionist approach, see Harris, 2010; Holstein & Gubrium, 2008; Holstein & Miller, 2003a; Loseke, 2003).

THE PLAN OF THE BOOK: THE NATURAL
HISTORY OF SOCIAL PROBLEMS

To understand the approach that this book takes toward social problems, it may help to begin with a familiar example from U.S. history: the 1960s civil rights movement against segregation. After World War II, the southern states retained customs and laws maintaining racial segregation: African Americans were blocked from voting; intermarriage was illegal; whites and blacks attended different schools; and other institutions were segregated, so that the races ate in different restaurants, sat in different sections on buses, and used racially separate restrooms and drinking fountains. Organized protests against this system of segregation became more common; in particular, the 1955–56 bus boycott in Montgomery, Alabama, brought national attention to the leadership of the Reverend Martin Luther King Jr.

By the early 1960s, there were numerous civil rights organizations— including King's Southern Christian Leadership Conference (SCLC), the Congress of Racial Equality (CORE), and the Student Non-violent Coordinating Committee (SNCC, pronounced "snick")— leading marches, boycotts, freedom rides, voter registration campaigns, and other sorts of protests. Television news programs showed dramatic scenes of police beating and arresting protesters, and public opinion—particularly outside the South—increasingly sympathized with the civil rights campaign. In 1963, the great March on Washington called for congressional action, and Congress eventually passed the Civil Rights Act of 1964 and the Voting Rights Act of 1965. By the end of the 1960s, segregation in the South had generally lost its legal standing, although of course other forms of racial inequality remained.

We can use the story of the civil rights movement's campaign against segregation to illustrate a more general phenomenon: the natural history of a social problem. The term **natural history** refers to a sequence of stages that tends to appear in lots of different cases. Figure 1.1 diagrams the natural history of the social problems process.

This natural history identifies six stages: claimsmaking, media coverage, public reaction, policymaking, social problems work, and policy outcomes. The figure sketches a general framework. Describing a natural history helps us organize our thinking about a typical social problems process, although not every instance of social problems construction will fit this model. In fact, other sociologists have offered different natural histories of the social problems process (see Blumer, 1971; Spector & Kitsuse, 1977). Figure 1.1 is a simplified diagram intended to give an overview of what is actually a much more complicated process. In later chapters, we will expand this diagram to consider some of those complexities, but this version gives us a starting point.

Stage One: Claimsmaking

The first stage in Figure 1.1 concerns claimsmaking. During this stage, claimsmakers make claims; that is, they argue that a particular troubling condition ought to be recognized as a social problem, and that someone ought to do something about that problem. In the case of the civil rights movement, the claimsmakers were the social movement activists and demonstrators who protested against the system of racial segregation. We can distinguish between claimsmakers and their claims. *Claims* are arguments, efforts to persuade others that something is wrong, that there is a problem that needs to be solved. For example, the civil rights movement claimed that racial segregation was wrong, that it was unjust, and violated the basic American belief in equality. The social problems process always begins with claims, so we will begin this book by exploring various aspects of claims in Chapter 2.

Typically we think of claimsmakers as **activists**, members of social movement organizations such as the civil rights movement's

Figure 1.1 BASIC NATURAL HISTORY MODEL OF THE SOCIAL PROBLEMS PROCESS

Claimsmaking →	Media Coverage →	Public Reaction →	Policymaking →	Social Problems Work →	Policy Outcomes
People make claims that there is a social problem, with certain characteristics, causes, and solutions.	Media report on claimsmakers so that news of the claims reaches a broader audience.	Public opinion focuses on the social problem identified by the claimsmakers.	Lawmakers and others with the power to set policies create new ways to address the problem.	Agencies implement the new policies, including calls for further changes.	There are various responses to the new arrangements.
Example: Civil rights activists, such as Martin Luther King Jr., call for an end to racial segregation in the South, hold marches and demonstrations.	**Example:** Reporters from newspapers and television describe the conflict over the civil rights campaign.	**Example:** People become more concerned about racial segregation and more supportive of the campaign against it.	**Example:** Congress passes the Civil Rights Act of 1964 and the Voting Rights Act of 1965.	**Example:** Under the new federal laws, states and localities are forced to end formal policies of racial segregation.	**Example:** People call for additional changes to reduce racism, as well as campaigns to promote the rights of women and other groups.

SCLC, CORE, or SNCC. Lots of people want to make claims, but it is often hard to get others to pay attention. Activists must devise ways of drawing attention to their cause; civil rights demonstrators conducted sit-ins, boycotts, freedom rides, and marches as ways of attracting notice. Activists also need to recruit people to join their movement, manage the movement's operations, and maintain interest in their cause. Chapter 3 examines the role of activists as claimsmakers, as well as some of the challenges that social movements confront.

Not all claimsmakers are social movement activists. Claims also come from various sorts of **experts**, such as physicians, scientists, lawyers, and officials. These people claim to speak with special authority because they have special knowledge; for example, scientists may have done research that shows the nature or extent of a particular troubling social condition, or lawyers may argue that the law related to the condition needs to be reinterpreted. During the civil rights movement, for example, social scientists and psychiatrists claimed that segregation had harmful consequences, while lawyers devised strategies to challenge segregation in the courts. Many societies grant authority to those seen as having special, expert knowledge; Chapter 4 considers how experts can use their authority as claimsmakers.

Stage Two: Media Coverage

The second stage shown in Figure 1.1 is media coverage. Claimsmakers often seek such coverage to bring their claims to the attention of a wider audience. The nature of the media may change—from stories and photographs printed in newspapers and magazines, or reports broadcast on radio and television news programs, to the endless array of sites on the Internet—but they all offer forums that can make both the public and policymakers more aware of claims. Civil rights demonstrators depended on this reporting; traditionally it had been easy for Americans outside the South to ignore segregation, but dramatic clashes between protesters and police created major news stories that focused national attention on civil rights. The media face practical considerations that affect how they address social problems, and media coverage inevitably reshapes claims. This is the topic of Chapter 5.

Stage Three: Public Reaction

The general public, then, learns about claims either directly from claimsmakers or indirectly through media reports. The public's response to these claims forms the third stage in Figure 1.1. Usually efforts to understand the public's reactions involve public opinion polls that seek to measure people's attitudes. In some cases, claimsmaking can have dramatic effects on public opinion; during the civil rights movement, for instance, polls indicated an increase in the proportion of Americans who considered civil rights a major problem, and who disapproved of the South's segregation policies. Such shifts are considered important in a democracy because voters may elect officials who reflect their changed views. Chapter 6 looks at polling, as well as other, less traditional ways of understanding the public's reactions.

Stage Four: Policymaking

The fourth stage in Figure 1.1's natural history is **policymaking**. Social policies are the means that society adopts to address troubling conditions, and such policies can be made in various ways. Most obviously, laws can be changed, as when Congress passed and President Johnson signed the Civil Rights Act of 1964 and the Voting Rights Act of 1965—the principal federal responses to the civil rights movement (over time, state legislatures and local city councils also had to modify their laws regarding segregation). But legislation is not the only form of policymaking; all sorts of bodies set social policies: government agencies establish standards for, say, clean water; schools create dress codes for their students; and so on. Policymakers respond to claimsmakers, media coverage, and public opinion, but their own considerations also shape the policies they create. Policymaking is the focus of Chapter 7.

Stage Five: Social Problems Work

Declaring that there will be a new social policy is not the end of the matter; policies have to be implemented, carried out by police officers, social workers, teachers—whoever is responsible for enforcing the particular policy. This is **social problems work**—the fifth stage in Figure 1.1. Often claimsmakers, the media, the public, and policymakers discuss social issues in fairly abstract, theoretical terms: here's what's wrong, and this is what ought to be done. In contrast, social problems workers confront these issues as practical matters. They must deal with particular cases and address a messy real world that often seems quite complicated. For example, civil rights laws had to be translated into specific enforcement practices. It is one thing to say, for instance, that an all-white police force should be integrated, but even if everyone agrees on that principle, people may disagree about practical details regarding how officers should be selected. Chapter 8 tackles the complexities of social problems work.

Stage Six: Policy Outcomes

The sixth and final stage in Figure 1.1 is **policy outcomes**, reactions to the social problems process. Several sorts of outcomes are possible. Some relate directly to the ways in which social policies are implemented. Critics may argue that the new policies are ineffective—that they don't do enough to address the troubling condition, or that the policies actually cause new problems, even making things worse. For instance, the federal civil rights laws passed in the 1960s have been criticized for not going far enough; even though the formal system of legal segregation was dismantled, all sorts of racial inequality remained (thus, blacks continue to have lower incomes, shorter life expectancies, and so on). Other critics may argue that a policy goes too far, as with charges that the affirmative action policies that emerged from the civil rights movement themselves create unequal arrangements. There may be efforts to measure the policy's impact, to evaluate its effectiveness, but how should effectiveness be judged? Often such complaints and questions lead to new claims, and the social problems process begins anew. Such reactions to social policies are the topic of Chapter 9.

In contrast, Chapter 10 explores a broader set of outcomes that often extend over time and space. Consider the impact of the civil rights movement. The dramatic, heavily publicized campaign against segregation inspired other claimsmakers, both within the United States and around the world. Civil rights activists learned valuable practical lessons about how to organize a social movement, attract media coverage for their cause, and so on. Veterans of civil rights protests began to apply their new skills in other social movements, becoming involved in protests over the war in Vietnam or campaigns to advance women's rights, or gay and lesbian rights. Claimsmakers in other nations also tried to duplicate the success of the American civil rights movement by organizing protests over troubling conditions in their own countries. In addition to examining how claims spread, Chapter 10 considers cycles in claimsmaking—a pattern in which claims rise to attract a good deal of attention, then recede, before rising again years later.

Finally, Chapter 11 uses the discussion of Chapters 2 through 10 to revisit Figure 1.1 and develop a more elaborate natural history of the social problems process. Chapter 11 also discusses the uses and future of the constructionist approach.

ADDITIONAL THEMES

Chapters 2 through 11 are organized according to the natural history model illustrated in Figure 1.1. In general, we will discuss topics in the order in which they occur in the social problems

Figure 1.2 RESOURCES AND RHETORIC AFFECT EACH STAGE OF THE
SOCIAL PROBLEMS PROCESS

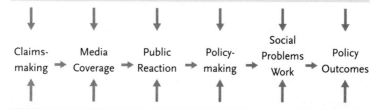

process; this is the book's central organizing principle. In addition, two other themes will run through every chapter: resources and rhetoric. As Figure 1.2 suggests, these themes influence each stage in the social problems process.

Resources

The first theme concerns the **resources** that people bring to the social problems process. A society's members are not equal; some have more money than others, or more power, more status, more education, more social contacts, and so on. These are resources that people can draw upon in the social problems process. We will discover that each stage in Figure 1.1 involves competition: claims-makers compete to attract attention to their claims, claims compete for media coverage and attention from the public and policymakers, and so on. At each stage in the social problems process, some claims succeed in moving to the next stage, while others fail to attract much notice. History is filled with claims that never attracted many adherents, and were ignored, dismissed, or discredited.

Resources affect this competition. In general, people with more money, power, and other resources find it easier to have their claims heard. The resources available to major corporate leaders give them considerable influence over social policy; they have money to spend on political contributions that allow them and their lobbyists access to policymakers. In contrast, the story of the civil rights movement is inspiring precisely because most African Americans living under segregation had such limited resources; they had relatively little in the way of money or political influence, yet they mounted a campaign that successfully changed social policy. At every stage in the social problems process, inequality—whether based on race, class, gender, or something else—means that people bring different resources to the process. It is much easier for those with ample resources to make claims and get them heard, than it is for those with fewer resources.

Rhetoric

The second theme that runs through each chapter is rhetoric. **Rhetoric** is the study of persuasion. Social problems construction is inevitably rhetorical. Whenever people make claims, they are trying to convince others that something is a problem, that it is a problem of a particular sort, and that specific action needs to be taken to deal with this problem. These arguments evolve with each stage in the social problems process; that is, every problem is constructed and reconstructed. Even people who are allied in a claimsmaking campaign may adopt different rhetoric; the claims of activists and experts often emphasize different elements. The media, when they cover claimsmaking campaigns, reshape claims to fit their needs, just as the public's awareness of social problems tends to emphasize some aspects and downplay others. Similarly, when policymakers try to devise means of addressing troubling conditions, they, too, offer their own constructions of what is at issue. And when social problems workers try to implement policies, the practical require-ments of their tasks lead them to focus on particular aspects—yet another reconstruction. Finally, at the stage of policy outcomes, there are likely to be all sorts of reinterpretations of previous claims and the policies they inspired.

Rhetoric involves appeals to emotions, as well as appeals to rea-son. Claimsmakers try to elicit emotional reactions, such as horror or sympathy, to get people to share their concerns, and of course much media coverage encourages the audience to feel outrage or compassion. Throughout the social problems process, people invoke feelings, as well as ideas, to convince others to share their views. Thus, rhetoric is a central theme in the chapters that follow because social problems claims are not static; rather they shift and morph at each stage in the larger social problems process as the rhetoric changes.

The themes of resources and rhetoric remind us that the social problems process occurs within a broader structural and cultural context. Existing social structural arrangements—resources—give some actors advantages in claimsmaking; having more money or more power makes it easier to promote particular constructions. At the same time, the larger culture makes particular claims—rhetoric—more or less compelling. At each stage in the social problems process, then, actors compete to devise claims that others will find persuasive.

Feedback

Finally, there is a third theme that both Figure 1.1 and Figure 1.2 overlook. These diagrams oversimplify the social problems pro-cess. In both, the arrows between stages of the social problems process point in only one direction; that is, claimsmaking is shown as affecting media coverage, media coverage in turn shapes public reaction, and so on. In fact, the social process is more complicated, involving a great deal of **feedback**. That is, claimsmaking does affect media coverage, but claimsmakers are also affected by that coverage (for example, if the press ignored a civil rights demonstration in the 1950s and '60s, activists knew that they needed to adjust what they were doing, in order to attract better coverage for future demonstrations). Similar feedback processes can occur at every stage in the social problems process because the actors at the various stages—the claimsmakers, people who work in the media, and so on—don't just act, but also pay attention to how others react to what they have done, and then respond to those reactions by adjusting what they're doing.

At several points in the book we will consider more elaborate diagrams that illustrate some of these feedback processes; in addition, Chapter 11 will discuss feedback processes in more detail. Remember, Figure 1.1 is designed to help us start thinking about the social problems process; it is by no means the last word.

SUMMARY

This book explores the constructionist approach to social problems. Rather than assuming that social problems are conditions that share an objectively defined characteristic, it defines social problems as a process of raising subjective concerns. This process follows a typical course, a natural history that provides a framework for the rest of the book.

The chapters that follow will focus on specific stages in the social problems process. Taken together, these chapters develop a general framework for thinking about the construction of social problems. The chapters contain many brief mentions of examples that illustrate whatever principle is being discussed. In addition, each chapter features several boxes (somewhat more detailed discussions of how a specific theme in the text is related to a particular social problem), and each chapter ends with a longer case study that explores how the ideas developed in that chapter can be applied to a particular case. Of course, all of these examples are merely illustrative. The goal of this book is to give you a better way of thinking about whatever social problems strike you as interesting.

MAKING CONNECTIONS

- *A social constructionist approach to social problems focuses on the process by which people identify social problems.*

- *As you read the upcoming chapters on claims and claimsmaking, keep in mind how claimsmakers use rhetoric to convince others that a troubling condition is a social problem.*

- *In Chapter 10 you will learn how claims about troubling conditions change depending on the time period and geographic location.*

2

■

Claims

■

Anyone who follows the news cannot help but hear claims about new social problems. Newspaper stories announce that doctors have identified a new disease, or that scientists have discovered a new environmental threat. Television commentators warn that a dangerous new drug is spreading, or that law enforcement is battling a new crime. Bloggers discuss new problems brought on by technological developments or changing lifestyles.

Often the new problem has a catchy name, such as *road rage*, *the digital divide*, *human trafficking*, or *racial profiling*. Suddenly, the brand-new term seems to be on everyone's lips. In many cases, interest in the new problem will prove to be short-lived; people will worry about it for a time, but then their attention will wander. But other terms—think of *sexism*, which first entered the language around 1970—seem to take up permanent residence in our society's vocabulary and consciousness, and the problems they identify remain topics of concern.

Constructing a new social problem involves making claims—that is, calling attention to a troubling condition. Claims are the first element in the social problems process, and they are this chapter's focus. After examining the basic structure of claims, we will consider how audiences respond to them, how they evolve, and where they fit in the larger culture.

THE RHETORIC OF CLAIMS

Every social problems claim makes a persuasive argument; it is an effort to persuade others, to convince them that a particular troubling condition ought to be recognized as a social problem, that that problem has certain characteristics, that the problem demands attention, and that it should be addressed in a specific way. When we analyze claims as arguments or statements, it matters less whether the claims are true or false than whether the people who make the claims and the audiences for those claims find the reasoning convincing.

One of the lessons of this chapter is that claims tend to take standard forms, because people who share a culture are likely to find the same sorts of arguments persuasive. Claims need to be tailored to their audiences, but of course the people who make claims usually belong to the same society as their audience, so when they devise claims that they themselves find sensible, those claims are likely to persuade their audiences. For example, members of a highly religious society may find claims based on theological reasoning compelling, whereas members of another society may be more likely to be swayed by scientific evidence. As a result, within a given society, even claims about very different problems tend to be structured in similar ways. This means that a claim you find utterly convincing will probably contain persuasive elements that resemble those in a claim you consider completely unreasonable. Keep in mind that our topic is how claims work, and understanding this does not require knowing whether the claims are, in fact, true.

The study of persuasion is called *rhetoric*, and we can analyze the rhetoric of claims. Persuasive arguments share a rhetorical structure with three fundamental components: grounds, warrants, and

Figure 2.1 THE STRUCTURE OF SOCIAL PROBLEMS CLAIMS

Grounds ⟶ Conclusions

Information and
evidence about the
troubling condition—
typifying examples,
statistics, etc. (Also
called the *diagnostic
frame.*)

Recommended
changes, new policies,
etc. to address the
problem. (Also called
the *prognostic frame.*)

Warrants

Justifications, appeals
to values—reasons why
something must be
done about the
troubling condition.
(Also called the
motivational frame.)

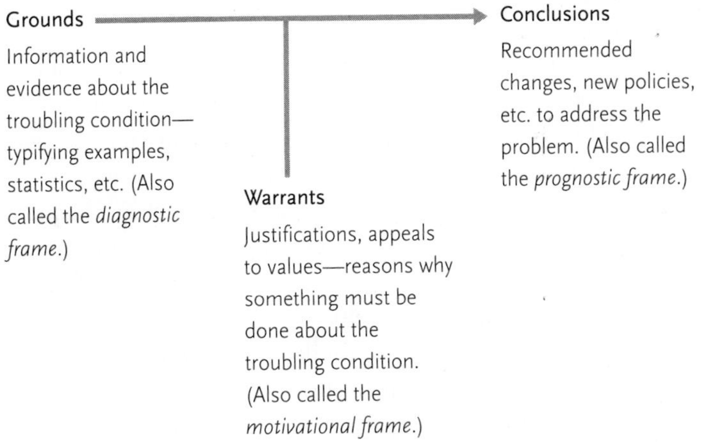

Sources: J. Best, 1990; Snow & Benford, 1988; Toulmin, 1958.

conclusions (J. Best, 1990; Toulmin, 1958). In social problems claims, *grounds* are statements about the nature of the problem, *warrants* justify taking action, and *conclusions* explain what that action should be. Figure 2.1 illustrates the connections among grounds, warrants, and conclusions. We will consider each in turn.

Grounds

Every social problems claim begins by identifying a troubling condition. Two sorts of statements are involved: those describing the condition and those explaining why it should be considered troublesome. The former are the grounds; the latter are the warrants (discussed in the next section).

The Basic Rhetorical Recipe. A claim's **grounds** usually are assertions of fact; that is, they argue that the condition exists, and offer supporting evidence. Claims in the contemporary United States often establish their grounds by following a rhetorical recipe containing three ingredients:

1. *Typifying example.* Claims often begin with a **typifying example**, a description of a particular instance of the condition. Typifying examples are, in fact, rarely typical. Usually they are chosen to illustrate the seriousness of the problem, so they tend to be especially extreme, dramatic, disturbing, memorable cases. For instance, claims about child abuse might start with an atrocity story, a description of a very young child who was beaten to death (Johnson, 1995). This would not be a typical case; most child abuse is not fatal. However, using a child's death to typify abuse is compelling rhetoric; the example characterizes the problem in melodramatic terms, in that it depicts a vulnerable, innocent youngster being menaced by a more powerful, villainous adult. This example suggests that child abuse is a very serious problem, because it can involve real, terrible harm. Because the example is so disturbing, people are likely to pay attention, to start worrying about innocent children being threatened by this evil.

2. *Name.* Next the claim **names** the problem. The fatal beating in our example will be transformed from a horrific *incident* to an *instance* of the larger problem of child abuse (J. Best, 1999). Sometimes a new name is attached to an old behavior: bad driving has long been a familiar problem, but calling it *road rage* is a relatively recent development. In other cases, both the name and the troubling condition are new; *sexting* could not exist before technology made it possible. Note that naming a problem is not the same as defining it. Many claimsmakers avoid defining a problem by instead focusing on typifying examples. In spite of all of the attention that *child abuse* and *road rage* have received in the media, it can be very difficult to find precise definitions of either term in that coverage. Rather, the people who make up the audience for these claims probably assume that they understand the nature of these problems because they are familiar with one or more typifying examples.

3. *Statistic.* A third ingredient in the basic recipe that establishes the grounds for many claims is some sort of **statistic**, a number that suggests the scope of the problem. In our child abuse example, we might be told that authorities receive nearly three million reports of suspected child abuse annually. In contemporary American culture, statistics imply accuracy and precision—that someone must have counted something. In practice, this is not necessarily true. When claimsmakers are first trying to draw attention to a social problem, they often argue that this problem has been neglected or overlooked. But if people have been ignoring a particular social condition, they probably haven't been carefully measuring its extent, which means no one has been keeping accurate statistics. As a result, early claims often feature figures that are ballpark estimates or educated guesses (J. Best, 2001a). And just as claimsmakers favor dramatic typifying examples, they usually prefer big numbers, statistics that suggest that the problem is widespread, because a big number implies there is a big problem. Particularly at the beginning of the social problems process, claims often feature big numbers that are really little more than rough estimates.

The three ingredients in the basic rhetorical recipe—a disturbing typifying example, a name, and a big number—combine to create a troubling impression. For example, a description of a small child being beaten to death, coupled with both an explanation that this death is just one instance of the larger problem of child abuse and a statement that three million cases of suspected abuse are reported each year, conveys a sense that millions of children are in danger—possibly of losing their lives. This basic recipe offers a quick, compelling case for recognizing a new social problem. It is an effective rhetorical formula, one that can be spotted in many social problems claims (see Box 2.1).

Additional Grounds. Claims often feature grounds beyond the basic recipe's three ingredients. Many different rhetorical devices

Box 2.1 THE BASIC RECIPE: GROUNDS FOR VIEWING
COLLEGE-EDUCATED WHITE MALES' JOB LOSSES
AS A SOCIAL PROBLEM

Newsweek's April 25, 2011, cover showed a gray-haired man in a soaked business suit lying facedown at the water's edge next to a headline: "The Beached White Male: He Had a Big Job, a Big Office, a Big Bonus. Now He's All Washed Up and Doesn't Have a Freakin' Prayer." The cover story, titled "Dead Suit Walking," began with two typifying examples of fiftyish, once highly successful businessmen who were having trouble finding jobs in the midst of the Great Recession.

The story suggested a name for the problem represented by these examples: "The same guys who once drove BMWs . . . have now been downsized to BWMs: Beached White Males." The paragraph following this statement began with a statistic: "Through the first quarter of 2011, nearly 600,000 college-educated men ages 35 to 64 were unemployed." Thus, the article's opening paragraphs used the standard recipe—typifying examples, problem name, statistics—to construct job losses among upper-middle-class white males as a social problem.

The story's authors went on to note that the group's unemployment rate was about 5 percent—at a time when the national unemployment rate was around 9 percent. In other words, the story drew attention to the recession's effects on a group that was relatively privileged and quite possibly the least affected by the economic downturn—an interesting choice of topic for cover-story claimsmaking.

Source: Marin & Dokoupil, 2011.

can appear as grounds in social problems claims; what follows is just a sampling.

- *Worsening situation.* Very often, claims insist that the problem is getting worse. Words like *epidemic* and *crime wave* convey a sense of urgency: the problem is spreading, and—unless something is done—it may soon spiral out of control.

- *Familiar type of problem.* Claims often categorize a problem as being of a recognizable type, such as a crime or a disease. These types are characterized by familiar patterns: we think of crime as being perpetrated by a criminal who intentionally preys on an innocent victim, and diseases as striking vulnerable individuals who should not be considered responsible for getting sick. When a claim classifies the new problem as belonging to a particular type, the claim's audience immediately has a sense of how to think about the problem.

- *Kind of people affected.* Most claims identify categories of people involved in the troubling condition, and explain how their involvement should be understood (Loseke, 2003). Among the most common person categories are *victims* (those harmed by the problem, who may be characterized as bearing no responsibility for their plight, and therefore meriting society's support and sympathy) and *villains* (those responsible for the problem, usually depicted as deserving blame and punishment). Typifying examples often illustrate the principal categories of people involved in the troubling condition (such as an innocent, abused child, and an abusive parent).

- *Range of people affected.* Another popular ground for claims is the suggestion that the problem affects a broad range of people—rich and poor, white and black, and so on. Sometimes it is argued that the problem strikes "randomly" (Best, 1999). Of course, if a problem strikes at random, then it might affect anyone, including anyone listening to the claim. Such randomness suggests that each person who hears the claim has a personal interest in doing something to deal with the problem—before it affects him or her.

- *Challenge to older interpretations.* Claims also may challenge existing or alternative interpretations of the social problem. For instance, students who don't do well in school traditionally were held responsible for their poor performance, which was attributed to their inattention, lack of discipline or effort, and so on. But recent decades have featured claims about learning disabilities arguing that many students should not be blamed, because their poor performance is due to biologically based learning disabilities that deserve accommodation (Conrad, 2007; Erchak & Rosenfeld, 1989). Such claims challenge older, more familiar constructions. These challenges may be quite explicit; claims may list—and debunk—what they describe as "myths," widely held beliefs about the problem that the claim dismisses as wrong. For example, claims that seek to reconstruct the problem of rape criticize "rape myths" for distorting people's thinking about that crime (Suarez & Gadalla, 2010).

Again, these are just a few of the many kinds of grounds statements found in claims. Taken together, a claim's grounds give a sense of the problem—its nature, scope, and future prospects. Effective grounds convince listeners that the condition is real, thereby setting the stage for the claim's warrants.

Warrants

A claim's **warrants** justify doing something about the troubling condition; they explain why something *ought* to be done. Warrants invoke values and emotions. That is, warrants argue that the condition identified in the grounds is inconsistent with what we value, and therefore we need to do something about it. Thus, claims suggest that the troubling condition violates our sense of justice, fairness, equality, or other values; in turn, we may experience anger, pity, or other emotional reactions.

Values tend to be expressed as vague principles that most—if not all—people can endorse. Most Americans can be expected to hold freedom, justice, equality, protecting the vulnerable, and humanitarianism as cherished values. But what does this mean in practice?

It is not always clear how abstract values apply in real-world situations. It is not unusual for opponents in debates over social issues to endorse the same values, even as they support opposing policies. Thus, both those who favor and those who oppose restricting access to abortion tend to invoke *rights*: pro-life abortion opponents speak of the "unborn child's right to life," while pro-choice abortion advocates speak of a "woman's right to choose." Similarly, those who favor affirmative action argue that affirmative action programs foster equality by giving advantages to those who have been disadvantaged, yet affirmative action opponents insist that the programs subvert equality because they don't treat everyone evenhandedly. Although virtually all Americans can be expected to affirm their beliefs in rights or equality, obviously they can disagree over how those abstract values should be translated into practical policies.

Warrants rise and fall in popularity. Sometimes new warrants—new ways of justifying claims—emerge, and change how social problems are characterized. For example, in recent years the rising costs of medical care have inspired a new warrant: arguments that some troubling conditions need to be addressed because they create costly health care burdens for the larger society. For instance, laws requiring motorcycle riders to wear protective helmets have been justified by the high costs of providing long-term medical care to head injury patients, just as campaigns to restrict smoking and reduce obesity have emphasized how those conditions add many millions of dollars to the nation's medical costs.

Warrants based on medical costs seem to have emerged to counter arguments that defended motorcycle riding and other risky activities using another, older warrant: personal freedom. That is, motorcycle riders, smokers, and overweight individuals have long argued that they ought to have the freedom to make their own choices, even if those choices involve risks. American culture generally considers freedom an important warrant, particularly if the person taking the risks is not harming others. Using medical costs as a warrant tries to counter this older defense based on individual liberty by arguing that helmetless motorcycle riders and other risk takers are not just endangering themselves, but are also harming everyone else, in that their risky behavior raises health care costs across the board, and society has a right to try to discourage people from taking such costly risks.

Because people can be powerfully attached to particular values, and because claims need to be compelling, claims' warrants often inspire powerful emotional reactions, such as outrage, shock, sadness, or guilt. Effective claims move people to take action. While it may be possible to assemble a claim that relies on bloodless cost-benefit reasoning to convince people that is in their best interest to respond to a social problem, it is often more effective to arouse emotional reactions, to make them feel that something must be done right away. This is why claims favor melodramatic typifying examples: it is harder to ignore the plight of innocent victims. Claims can make use of a wide range of emotional appeals (see Box 2.2).

Because claims can invoke many different values and emotions, and because those values are abstract and subject to conflicting interpretations, claims often feature multiple warrants, so different people may agree that something needs to be done about a troubling condition even though they disagree on the reasons for taking action.

Conclusions

Every claim, then, offers a justification for taking action: the grounds identify a troubling condition, and the warrants explain why something should be done about it. Thus, all claims lead to **conclusions**, statements that specify what should be done, what action should be taken to address this social problem. The nature of the conclusions is shaped by the grounds and warrants. If a claim's grounds have depicted a condition that causes terrible suffering, and the warrants speak to humanitarian concerns about the need to alleviate suffering, then the conclusions are likely to focus on ways to help the

Box 2.2. Claiming Closure

Ideas about what makes a compelling warrant change over time. In recent decades, claimsmakers have often invoked the notion of closure. Death penalty advocates argue that only execution can bring closure for the families of victims. Yet death penalty opponents insist that the prolonged legal proceedings required to determine whether an execution can proceed create prolonged uncertainty for victims' families, whereas a sentence of life imprisonment without the possibility of parole can give those families closure. Thus, the same emotion is used as a warrant by those taking opposing sides on the issue.

Claimsmakers began using closure as a common warrant only during the 1990s. The term's popularity is due, in part, to its vague definition. People think of closure in various, sometimes contradictory ways. Some people equate closure with forgetting, with getting rid of a troubling memory. Others think that closure means remembering, and may advocate establishing permanent memorials as a way to gain closure. Vendors promise that their products—everything from solemn funeral arrangements to comic decorations for a divorce party—will bring their customers closure.

Precisely because warrants tap into widely accepted, taken-for-granted values, they can be hard for us to spot. It is somewhat easier to notice closure talk, precisely because it is a relatively new warrant. But all social problems claims invoke values; warrants are an inevitable element in claimsmaking rhetoric.

Source: Berns, 2011.

afflicted. On the other hand, if the grounds emphasize the terrible nature of a particular crime, and if the warrants focus on society's need to protect its members from such evils, then the conclusions will probably advocate cracking down on this crime.

Often conclusions include both short-range and long-range goals. Within the short term, claimsmakers may be trying to arouse concern—to make others aware of the problem, to get people to join their campaign, or to encourage the media to cover the issue. Longer-range goals typically seek policy changes, by arguing that people need to pass a new law, fund a program, or otherwise deal with the troubling condition in a new, more effective way. Usually the short-range goals are seen as steps toward making these long-range changes possible.

Conclusions range from vague endorsements of change to extensive, detailed agendas for action. Early in the social problems process, when claimsmakers' primary aim is to raise awareness of the troubling condition, grounds and warrants tend to receive more emphasis. At later stages in the process, when concern about the problem has become widespread, policy choices become a more central focus, and conclusions are likely to receive greater, more detailed attention.

Summary

Grounds, warrants, and conclusions, then, are standard elements in most arguments (Toulmin, 1958). In the case of social problems claims, this rhetorical structure explains what is wrong, why it is wrong, and what should be done about it. But who hears these claims? Which audiences are these claims meant to persuade, and how do they respond?

CLAIMS, THEIR AUDIENCES, AND THE SOCIAL PROBLEMS MARKETPLACE

Every claim involves communication between at least two parties: those who make the claim (*claimants* or *claimsmakers*), and an **audience** whom the claim is meant to persuade. The audience for claims can include all of the other participants in the social problems process: people who might be enlisted in the cause, other claimsmakers, members of the media who might publicize the claims, the general public, policymakers, and so on. Audiences differ in what they find persuasive, so effective claims need to be tailored to fit their audiences' concerns. How claimsmakers understand those concerns should affect their rhetorical choices. Because there is little point in presenting claims that an audience will not find convincing, claimsmakers must devise arguments that they believe will persuade their audience.

Some claims face little resistance, quickly gaining widespread acceptance among those who hear them. For example, claims about child abuse, child pornography, and other similar threats to children tend to be well received (J. Best, 1990). American culture views children as vulnerable innocents who deserve societal protection. Therefore, claims that children are being menaced by adults can arouse widespread concern. The arguments seem so compelling that it is difficult to imagine anyone opposing such claims; how could child abuse possibly be defended? Political scientists sometimes refer to claims that inspire this sort of general agreement as **valence issues** (Nelson, 1984), although what seems as first glance to be consensus may encompass different views (see Box 2.3).

At the other extreme are claims related to entrenched controversies that probably never will lead to consensus. The debate over abortion remains intense because it features people who have taken intractable, opposing positions: some pro-life advocates argue that abortion is murder and should never be tolerated, while some pro-choice proponents insist that women must be able to control their own bodies and therefore must be free to choose to have abortions. It is very unlikely that a new pro-life claim will persuade those who hold hard-core pro-choice beliefs to change their minds, and equally unlikely that pro-choice arguments can be devised that will change the opinion of those firmly committed to a hard-core pro-life position. When addressing such contested issues, or **position issues**, claimsmakers know that they cannot persuade everyone; they can expect their claims to encounter opposition from at least some people who hear them (Nelson, 1984).

Box 2.3 Disputes within the Apparent
Agreement about Food Security

Everyone may agree that a valence issue is a problem, yet, within
that consensus, there may be competing constructions. Take food
security—ensuring that people have enough to eat. No one speaks
out against food security, but the people who make claims in its
name define the problem in very different ways:

- *Hunger.* Some claimsmakers argue that reducing hunger
  requires controlling population growth while improving
  agricultural technology; but others argue that there is already
  sufficient food produced to feed the world, that the problem
  lies a failure to distribute food to those who need it.

- *Community.* Other claimsmakers argue that groups of
  people—nations or regions—should produce enough food
  for themselves, rather than concentrating on growing a single
  crop for exporting and importing food.

- *Security.* Still others worry about protecting the food supply;
  they fear that technological solutions (such as pesticides)
  create new risks, or even that the food supply must be
  protected from terrorism.

Note that these different constructions have very different implications. Some advocates argue that the solution to food security
lies in a more efficient, globalized system of food production, while
others argue that globalization reduces communities' ability to produce sufficient food for their own populations and thereby threatens
their food security. Just because everyone agrees that food security
is important doesn't mean that they need to agree on much else.

Source: Mooney & Hunt, 2009.

The audience for claims is not an undifferentiated mass. Rather,
it can be subdivided—or **segmented**—by race, age, social class,
gender, region, and so on. Different segments of the audience tend
to have different interests and ideologies. People may respond to

a claim by recognizing that they stand to gain or lose if the claims succeed: claims probably seem more compelling to segments of the audience who perceive themselves as directly threatened by the troubling condition, while other segments may resist claims that might adversely affect them by, for example, restricting their freedom or raising their taxes.

Such perceptions of interest are often linked to ideologies or systems of beliefs; different segments of the population are likely to view the world differently, to place different emphasis on particular values, explanations, justifications, and so on. As a general rule, those who benefit from existing social arrangements are more likely to view those arrangements as just, fair, and reasonable, and they are less likely to be sympathetic to claims arguing that those arrangements need to be overturned. Thus, both their interests and their ideologies make them a tough audience, while those disadvantaged by the troubling condition are more likely to be receptive to such claims. Different segments of society, then, view the world differently, and persuasive claims need to match the various worldviews of the segments of the audience toward which they are directed.

Claimsmakers devise various methods to deal with audience segmentation. One tactic is to preach to the choir—that is, to direct claims toward those segments of the audience most likely to respond favorably. For example, abortion activists often direct their claims toward those who they believe already share their beliefs—as when they speak to sympathizers at pro-choice or pro-life rallies. Directing claims to those most likely to be supportive can be a particularly important tactic at the beginning of the social problems process, when claims are first being made: addressing a presumably sympathetic audience first can make more people aware of an issue, rally supporters to the cause, give claimsmakers a chance to hone their claims to make them as persuasive as possible, and create some momentum for carrying the claim to a broader, more diverse audience (such tactics for mobilizing supporters into a social movement are discussed further in Chapter 3).

An alternative approach is to craft claims so as to maximize their appeal to the broadest possible audience. Claims can incorporate multiple grounds, warrants, and conclusions that appeal to different people, thereby seeming to offer something for, if not everyone, at least lots of people. For instance, many advocates of vegetarianism see ethical issues as central to their cause, and they oppose meat eating as morally wrong. However, they also know that these ethical claims encounter widespread resistance; most Americans enjoy eating meat and don't consider it wrong, so moral arguments alone are unlikely to persuade a large audience (Maurer, 2002). However, other grounds and warrants are available: vegetarians can argue that eating meat is unhealthy, in that it fosters heart disease and other ailments; or they can claim that raising animals for food damages the environment. Such arguments add additional grounds and warrants to vegetarians' claims that might appeal to people who are worried about their health or the environment, even if they don't have moral qualms about eating meat. Expanding claims in this way offers vegetarians a chance to persuade people who could be expected to resist narrower ethical arguments that eating meat is wrong.

Well-crafted claims sometimes create surprising alliances among people who usually don't agree, inspiring consensus and converting potential conflict into a valence issue. For instance, political liberals and conservatives often disagree about educational policies. Yet, during the 1990s, many liberals and conservatives joined forces to promote policies requiring public school students to wear uniforms (Brunsma, 2004). Liberals argued that uniforms would make social class differences among students less visible, reduce pressure on parents to purchase expensive clothes for children, and enhance students' self-esteem; conservatives claimed that uniforms would encourage discipline and orderly behavior among students. Both sides insisted that school uniforms could reduce violence and improve learning. In this case, people who usually disagree found themselves promoting the same solution, even though they disagreed about the precise nature of the problem.

Similarly, advocates representing a wide range of ideologies support efforts to exclude troubling material from elementary and secondary school textbooks: liberals call for excluding material that might reinforce gender or racial stereotypes, fundamentalist Christians want to block content mentioning witches or other supernatural elements, and so on (Ravitch, 2003). Mandating school uniforms and regulating textbook content are just two examples of claims constructed in ways that build broad-based consensus among people who often disagree on other educational issues.

It is important to recognize that the audiences for claims are not passive. People who hear claims react, and claimsmakers must take those reactions into account, by adjusting, revising, and fine-tuning their claims to make them more effective, more persuasive. Claims should not be viewed as one-way messages, transmitted from claimsmakers/senders to their audiences/receivers. Rather, claimsmakers need to be sensitive to their audiences' reactions, to figure out which parts of their claims are working and which are not persuasive and need to be revised. In other words, claimsmakers and their audiences engage in a **dialog** in which the audience's feedback leads claimsmakers to modify their claims (Nichols, 2003).

If a particular ground or warrant fails to elicit a good reaction, claimsmakers may strike it from their claims and substitute something that they hope will evoke a more favorable response from their audience. For instance, activists campaigning to halt impending cuts in programs that had provided support to immigrants began with general claims ("immigrant rights are human rights") that proved ineffective. However, they soon found that the media and politicians responded more favorably to claims about the vulnerability of elderly, disabled immigrants, so they refocused their campaign on these more sympathetic cases (Fujiwara, 2005).

Claimsmaking is usually not a one-shot effort; it takes time to develop effective claims. Most claimsmakers have to try again and again to achieve widespread attention for their claims; they must try out claims, assess the audience's response, revise the claims, and so on, until they develop a persuasive argument. After all, claims compete within a **social problems marketplace** (J. Best, 1990; Hilgartner & Bosk, 1988). At any given moment, countless claims-makers are struggling to get their particular claims heard—far more than can hope to capture the audience's limited attention. Moreover, it is usually impossible to control either the other claims competing to attract the audience's notice or what the audience will choose to notice. Imagine a claimsmaker who had scheduled a major event— say, a combination press conference and demonstration—for September 12, 2001. Because the 9/11 terrorist attacks monopolized the nation's attention for days, no one would have paid any attention to anything the claimsmaker had to say on the twelfth. Although extreme, this example illustrates that claims do not operate in a vacuum.

The competition to capture the audience's attention helps explain some of the features of social problems rhetoric that we noted earlier. Why do claimsmakers so often begin claims with disturbing typifying examples? Why do claims usually settle for naming the problem—often with a catchy label like *road rage*—and avoid giving detailed (and therefore boring) definitions of the problem? Why do claimsmakers favor statistics that suggest the problem is surprisingly large? Why do they favor prominent targets (see Box 2.4)? Each of these rhetorical devices is arresting, eye-catching; each can draw people's attention to this claim (and away from those other claims competing for the audience's attention). The goal is to grab and hold the audience. This competition in the social problems marketplace means that claimsmakers are encouraged to devise dramatic, disturbing, easily grasped claims that will command attention over competing claims. Simpler, stronger arguments work better.

In sum, claimsmakers present what they hope will be persuasive arguments, but they must then attend to the audience's responses,

Box 2.4 Targeting Disney

Compared to other giant media conglomerates (such as Viacom, News Corporation, Time Warner, and Sony), the Walt Disney Company is a frequent target of very different claimsmaking campaigns. Conservative Christians have attacked Disney for producing R-rated movies (released, not under the Disney name, but through subsidiary firms owned by Disney) that threaten traditional social values, as well as for having various gay-friendly corporate policies. Liberal activists criticize Disney for gender-stereotyped themes in its films and for producing products in factories that are in less developed countries and that feature low wages and poor working conditions. Social scientists complain that the Disney theme parks reflect the alienation and corporate control that characterize contemporary society.

Why is Disney a target for so many claimsmakers? For decades, the corporation has sought to associate the Disney name with innocent, suitable-for-the-entire-family entertainment. To the degree that these efforts have been successful, people may think of Disney as standing for positive moral values. As a consequence, targeting Disney is rhetorically powerful: linking Disney (with its good image) to some social problem (a bad thing) is surprising—a way to capture people's attention. While the products and policies of the Walt Disney Company probably aren't that different from those of its rivals, people are less likely to have a distinct image of those other firms, and claimsmakers are less likely to choose Disney's rivals to typify social problems.

Source: J. Best & Lowney, 2009.

and those responses and their own sense of how they need to revise their rhetoric in turn may be affected by all the other claims and events that are competing for the audience's attention in the social problems marketplace.

EVOLUTION AND OPPOSITION

Social problems claims are not static; rather, they keep evolving. This process continues even after the audience becomes concerned about the problem. Once a claim has attracted recognition and acceptance, we can consider it *well established*; that is, there is widespread agreement that this troubling condition ought to be considered a social problem. Yet this is not the end of the matter; even well-established claims need to change. However compelling claims may seem when they first gain acceptance, they tend to become familiar, stale, boring (Downs, 1972). Audiences find it easier to forget about or ignore claims that can be dismissed as old news, particularly because other, newer claims are always competing for their attention. Audiences also may become frustrated by problems that aren't easily solved—where efforts to address the problem don't seem to make much progress. Each time a claim is repeated, it seems more familiar, less interesting—and less persuasive.

Therefore, claimsmakers often find it necessary to revise and repackage their claims, just to make them seem fresh and interesting. They may add additional grounds, more warrants, or fresh conclusions to give their claims a new look. For instance, instead of simply criticizing the general problem of sexism, the women's movement has been successful at calling attention to a long series of women's issues, each revealing a different aspect of sexist practices, through claims about sexual harassment, date rape, the glass ceiling (which blocks female executives from rising to the top of corporations), and so on. Constantly identifying additional forms of sexism keeps the women's movement's claims fresh.

Once a claim has gained acceptance, it is often possible to build additional claims on that foundation. One possibility is **domain expansion** (J. Best, 1990). As we have seen, initial claims often emphasize disturbing typifying examples. In the 1960s, for example, claimsmakers described the *battered child syndrome*, the problem of brutal beatings of infants or very young children. Terrible examples tend to make claims more interesting and effective; they help raise concern about an issue. In turn, once this concern has been established, it becomes possible to argue that other conditions are just as bad as—really just another form of, or the moral equivalent of—the initial problem. (Think of domain expansion as like opening an umbrella, so that more topics are covered by a social problem.)

In the case of child beating, battered child syndrome was soon renamed *child abuse*, and then the boundaries of what was considered abusive began to expand: Abuse also could affect older children and even adolescents. People began to recognize new types of abuse; beatings were now termed *physical abuse*, as distinguished from emotional abuse, sexual abuse, and so on. And advocates began applying the now widely accepted *child abuse* label to a range of other phenomena, so smoking around children, failing to strap kids into protective car seats, and circumcision, among other things, were claimed to be forms of child abuse. In other words, over time, the domain of child abuse expanded to include more and more phenomena. This sort of domain expansion can occur whenever initial claims become well established (see Box 2.5).

In a related process, claimsmakers choose to **piggyback** a new troubling condition on a well-established problem (Loseke, 2003). Again, child abuse is a good example. The popularity of the label *child abuse* inspired other claimsmakers to characterize their troubling conditions as varieties of *abuse*—so people began speaking of wife abuse, sibling abuse, elder abuse, and so on. Similarly, the successes of the civil rights movement led, in turn, to other campaigns promoting the *rights* of various groups—such as women's rights, gay rights, children's rights, prisoners' rights, and animal rights. And mid-1990s claims about road rage (typified as drivers becoming frustrated and violently attacking others) led journalists to begin identifying all sorts of other *rages*: air rage (among airline passengers), desk rage (office workers), even shopping cart rage (J. Best & Furedi, 2001). In each of these cases, a well-established

Box 2.5 Expanding Trauma's Domain

Originally, trauma was understood in individual terms, as a sort of psychological injury. However, in recent decades, the term has been adopted by a variety of claimsmakers who increasingly use the concept to refer to collective suffering. In the process, trauma's domain has expanded through society and over time.

Whereas *trauma* once referred to individuals who had experienced injuries that caused psychological damage, some contemporary claimsmakers argue that people who were not directly harmed can still be traumatized. Those who witness a traumatic event, or who know someone who was injured, or who simply belong to the larger society may be identified as potential trauma victims For instance, in the aftermath of the September 11, 2001, terrorist attacks, some claimsmakers argued that the event might prove traumatic to anyone who heard about it, that many people might experience traumatic reactions.

Similarly, trauma's reach is understood to extend across time, even across generations. Some claimsmakers explain behavior of contemporary individuals in terms of the traumatic effects of historical events such as the Holocaust or slavery in the United States. While claimsmakers do not argue that every individual who learned about 9/11 or had slave ancestors is affected by trauma, the concept is increasingly available as an explanation for behaviors that may be far removed in time and space from the events that are said to have caused the traumatic reaction.

Sources: DeGloma, 2009; Fassin & Rechtman, 2009.

social problem created opportunities to construct claims about other troubling conditions as being somehow analogous to the familiar original—in effect arguing that there was a sort of family resemblance among types of abuse, rights, or rages—that if the familiar case deserved to be considered a social problem, then so, too, did these other troubling conditions. (Claimsmakers can, in effect, borrow someone else's umbrella, using an existing term to cover an additional problem.)

Claims do not have to use the same terms—*abuse*, *rights*, *rage*, and so on—to piggyback on successful constructions. In some cases the rhetorical formula used to construct one social problem can be applied to other problems of the same general sort. There is, for example, a fairly standard recipe for identifying new drug problems: claims are made that a drug is particularly harmful, that its use is rapidly spreading, and so on (Reinarman, 1994). This familiar, well-established formula means that contemporary arguments about the dangers of Ecstasy or crystal meth do not look a great deal different from nineteenth-century warnings about opium smoking. Similarly, claims about new forms of victimization often use a well-established rhetorical formula arguing that victimization is widespread and serious yet remains hidden, so that extraordinary measures are needed to identify it, and so on (J. Best, 1999). In other words, the structure of successful claims—combinations of grounds, warrants, and conclusions that have proved effective in bringing attention to one drug problem or one form of victimization—can be copied and brought to bear on other, analogous issues.

Claims often inspire **counterclaims**, arguments in direct opposition to the original claims. Again, think of the pro-life and pro-choice movements' struggle over abortion; or the claims that global warming is a serious problem exacerbated by humans' activities, and the counterclaims that global warming may be neither as serious as has been feared nor caused primarily by people's actions. Or the disputes may be much narrower, focused on the meaning of a particular individual's life (see Box 2.6). In all of these cases, advocates with opposing views develop full-fledged arguments—each with its own set of grounds, warrants, and conclusions, and each trying to make the most persuasive case.

Such debates often revolve around confrontations over grounds or warrants. Each side may challenge the evidence—the grounds—

Box 2.6 Competing Constructions of the Lives of Homicide Victims

Claims and counterclaims may be quite narrowly focused. Consider the sorts of stories people tell about homicide victims. When individuals die violently, their family members and friends recall the victim's life; they mourn the loss and construct the death as a tragic event. Such stories of tragic loss are common whenever people die in youth or early adulthood, regardless of the cause of death, and homicide victims tend to be in their teens or twenties.

But the authorities are likely to tell rather different stories about some homicide victims. Perhaps the individual was killed by police officers, who wish to construct the death as justified. Perhaps a death occurred during a drug deal or a bar fight. In such circumstances, the authorities are likely to tell stories that suggest that the dead individual was at least partially to blame for what happened.

Such cases lead to disputes over how the individual's life should be constructed. The authorities may suggest that the individual who died represents an instance of some larger *social* problem, such as gangs or illicit drugs, and that the death should be understood in those terms. But the bereaved experience the death as a personal, *individual* problem. They resist the authorities' interpretations, and recall the dead person's life in positive terms, highlighting incidents or personality traits that cast the deceased in a positive light. Such contests reveal that social construction occurs, not just in broad, abstract discussions of issues, but also in interpreting the meaning of individual lives.

Source: Martin, 2010.

presented by its opponents, charging that those opponents have misunderstood or misrepresented the nature of the troubling condition. "Stat wars" may arise in which each side denounces its opponents' statistics and argues that its own numbers are more accurate (J. Best, 2001a). Similarly, opponents may insist that some warrants ought to be more compelling than others; in the abortion debate, for example, there are sharp disagreements about whether the rights of the fetus or those of the pregnant woman ought to be considered more important.

Many claims emerge within and are promoted as linked to particular **ideologies**—that is, more or less coherent sets of beliefs, such as libertarianism, feminism, liberalism, conservatism, or specific religious doctrines. Ideologies usually emphasize particular warrants; for example, libertarianism views liberty as a central value, and feminism opposes social arrangements that block opportunities for women. Often, too, those familiar with an ideology favor particular grounds; feminists, of course, look for evidence of sexism, and so on. In addition, ideologies often recognize competing belief systems, so liberals and conservatives anticipate disagreeing over many issues. These ideological disputes make it very easy to mount counterclaims; the news that someone associated with a rival ideology is making a claim invites counterclaims.

Claims often have to be modified in response to counterclaims. Opposition means that one's arguments will be subjected to sharper scrutiny and criticism, and those elements that prove easiest to challenge may need to be changed or reinforced. A statistic that has been debunked by one's opponents may be dropped and a more defensible number added to fill the gap, and so on. At the same time, the fact that there is opposition can be incorporated into one's claims. It may be possible to characterize one's opponents as part of the problem, turning the fact of opposition into a new ground for the claims. At least for those who share our ideology, news that the opposition is making counterclaims can reassure us that we're correct.

In sum, claims are constantly in play. They evolve, and they can inspire both other claims and opposition, so new claims are almost always shaped by those that preceded them.

CULTURAL RESOURCES

Theoretically, claimsmakers are free to assemble claims in any form they choose. In practice, however, claims have to make sense—both to the claimsmakers who choose to make them, and to the audiences whom the claimsmakers hope to persuade. This means that claims must draw upon the larger culture; they must be consistent with people's understandings of how the world works. In some societies, attributing misfortune to the acts of witches has been seen as a perfectly sensible explanation. In contemporary American society, however, claims about witchcraft are likely to be rejected out of hand by most people—although not by all. Most would-be claimsmakers recognize that this is the prevailing view, so they tend to avoid blaming witches or, more generally, constructing problems along lines that they and their audiences will find unconvincing.

Every culture, then, can be seen as a large repository of evolving, more or less familiar ideas about how the world works—and how it should work. These **cultural resources** are available to be exploited whenever claims are created. Our culture, for example, tends to idealize children as vulnerable innocents, and claims that warn about threats to children often elicit sympathetic reactions. This is such a widely shared view that we have trouble imagining people thinking any other way. However, New England's Puritans had a much darker view of children: they worried that children were born in a state of sinful willfulness, and they believed that children needed to have their wills broken to become properly God-fearing (Fischer, 1989, pp. 97–101).

Such different assumptions lead to quite different visions of, say, discipline. For some modern Americans, spanking is seen as harmful, even as a form of child abuse—one more way that adults inflict injuries on innocent children (Davis, 1994). Although the Puritans considered spanking a last resort, they used a variety of physical restraints and shaming devices, such as forcing a child who talked during church services to wear a wooden bit; such practices, which seem quite shocking to us, were standard ways of disciplining children, designed to teach them to be submissive and to understand God's wrath. It's easy to imagine that some claims about endangered children that might seem very powerful to us would have fallen on deaf ears among the Puritans.

Claims, then, draw on a society's cultural resources—the fund of words, ideas, images, and emotional reactions that most people understand to be reasonable. It is easier to arouse contemporary Americans' concern about threats to children or violence against women—two groups that are widely understood to be relatively vulnerable to victimization and therefore in need of protection—than to promote claims about endangered adult males. Nevertheless, although culture does limit the range of possible claims to some degree, it still offers a broad array of choices. For example, various segments of the U.S. population attribute different social problems to quite diverse causes—causes such as acts of God (for instance, to explain natural disasters), germs, conspiracies, belief systems (for example, particular religious or political ideologies), people's upbringing, and so on. Of course, part of being familiar with a culture is having the ability to predict which audiences will find which explanations appropriate for which problems.

Note that the fund of cultural resources is large, diverse, and not necessarily logically consistent. The point is not that all social problems have to be constructed in the same way, but that any culture offers various ideas and images that might be incorporated into successful claims. Just as American culture supports values that can sometimes conflict with one another, so, too, it encompasses other competing, conflicting notions.

This cultural diversity means that most social problems might be constructed in very different ways. For example, debates over poverty often feature dramatically different interpretations: Some commentators argue that the poor bear much of the responsibility for their plight, that they make bad choices (such as dropping out of school) that make poverty a likely outcome. Other critics insist that poverty is largely a product of a social structure that blocks too many opportunities, creating obstacles (such as a shortage of high-paying jobs) that make it hard for people to overcome poverty. Both the idea that individuals must bear responsibility for their own decisions, and the idea that a fair society should offer opportunities for advancement are familiar; both belong to the stock of cultural resources from which claims can be assembled. Such competing accounts of poverty's causes—although derived from the same culture—can reveal bitter differences within the culture. Claimsmakers may charge that rival claims are morally irresponsible because they apply inappropriate explanations, that they ignore God's laws, blame victims who should not be blamed, or err in some other way. Not everyone subscribes to every element in the larger culture—certainly not all of the time.

Moreover, the cultural context for claims is continually shifting. Ideas, values, imagery, explanations—all the elements of culture—can go in and out of fashion. In part, this fluctuation reflects people's ongoing quest for novelty: both claimsmakers and their audiences can become bored when claims seem stale—too familiar—so claims must be continually repackaged to make them appear fresh and interesting. In addition, genuinely new elements are added to the stock of cultural resources; a scientific discovery, the spread of a new disease, a new invention, or a dramatic event can have far-reaching consequences. Such novelties can reverberate through society generally, and through the social problems marketplace in particular, in complex ways.

Consider the identification of AIDS as a new disease in the early 1980s. No sociologist could have predicted all of the consequences that derived from that development: shifts in funding priorities for medical research and reforms in the methods used to test new treatments, the promotion of AIDS prevention policies (including condom distribution and needle exchange programs), all manner of art portraying aspects of the epidemic, and on and on. Or consider how the spread of cell phones has spawned new social problems claims—about the risks when drivers are distracted while talking on their phones, about the propriety of carrying on phone conversations where they can be overheard by others, about allegations of health hazards from cell phones, and so on.

Cultural shifts are reflected in social problems claims. Many social problems—for instance, gangs, cults, racism, and poverty—have been the subject of claims going back many decades, even centuries, but the particular constructions of these problems in different periods reflect current cultural developments during those periods. This means that cultural conditions during particular historical periods affect how social problems are constructed during those times. For example, the theme of expanding individual rights during the 1960s (as reflected in the civil rights movement and the sexual revolution), or the shift toward more conservative values that began in the late 1970s (as reflected in growing concerns about sex and drugs), can be seen as having influenced claims about many different social problems (Jenkins, 2006). (Chapter 10 will have more to say about the historical context of claims.)

Cultural resources, then, both constrain and enrich claims. Claims almost always use familiar language, imagery, forms of explanations, and other cultural elements. After all, the claimsmakers are themselves members of the culture, and they are almost forced to construct claims that they themselves view as sensible, claims that they also believe will receive a receptive hearing from their audiences. Thus, cultures constrain the sorts of claims that are likely to emerge. However, cultures are complex enough, multifaceted enough, that claimsmakers still have considerable leeway in choosing and shaping the arguments they present. Although we can note similarities among claims, such as cases in which new claims seem modeled on others, and we can imagine claims (about, say, witchcraft) that seem too far-fetched to succeed in our society, it is still true that claimsmakers have a lot of flexibility in devising their arguments.

Figure 2.2 DYNAMICS SHAPING CLAIMS

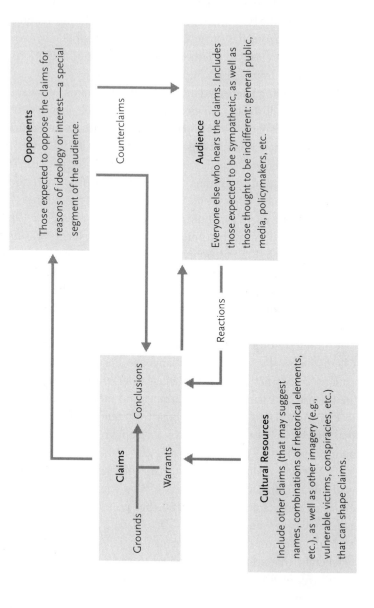

Opponents

Those expected to oppose the claims for reasons of ideology or interest—a special segment of the audience.

Counterclaims

Audience

Everyone else who hears the claims. Includes those expected to be sympathetic, as well as those thought to be indifferent: general public, media, policymakers, etc.

Claims

Grounds → Conclusions

Warrants

Reactions

Cultural Resources

Include other claims (that may suggest names, combinations of rhetorical elements, etc.), as well as other imagery (e.g., vulnerable victims, conspiracies, etc.) that can shape claims.

UNDERSTANDING CLAIMS

This chapter has explored various aspects of social problems claims. It began by considering claims as rhetorical arguments—the ways in which grounds, warrants, and conclusions structure claims. To be effective, though, claims have to persuade audiences, so claims-makers must understand who their audiences are and shape their arguments to fit those audiences' concerns. As a result, claimsmakers and audiences find themselves in a dialog as they respond to one another's ideas. Claims also are influenced by other claims. They evolve over time; claims need to be periodically revised to make them seem fresh. They are also shaped by the successes and failures of earlier claims: successful claims invite domain expansion or other efforts to piggyback on their success, just as claimsmakers try to avoid the mistakes of failed claims. And for highly contentious issues, claims face counterclaims, and opponents must respond to one another's constructions within the larger social problems marketplace. Finally, the broader culture provides a context for claims: language, imagery, and other cultural resources offer raw material from which claims can be built. Figure 2.2 illustrates all these various processes.

Of course, claims are social products; they do not exist independently of people. People assemble—construct—claims in hopes of persuading others. Although this chapter has focused on the claims themselves, the remainder of this book will concentrate on the various sorts of people who create, distribute, alter, challenge, or otherwise react to claims—the actors in the various stages of the social problems process.

MAKING CONNECTIONS

- *Claims are rhetorical arguments structured by grounds, warrants, and conclusions.*

- *The concepts of claims and claimsmakers introduced in this chapter set the stage for the next two chapters' discussion of activists as claimsmakers and experts as claimsmakers.*

- *In Chapter 5 you will learn how claimsmakers use the media to present their claims. You will also learn how the media alter the claims they present. As you read that chapter, keep in mind what you have learned in this chapter about cultural resources.*

CASE STUDY
MAKING CLAIMS ABOUT PROBLEM ANIMALS AND ANIMAL PROBLEMS

Not all social problems concern people; claimsmakers draw attention to all sorts of nonhuman troubling conditions. For example, animals are frequent subjects of claims. In some cases, the animals themselves are defined as problems. Take, for instance, pigeons in urban areas (Jerolmack, 2008). In recent decades, it has become common to characterize pigeons as "rats with wings," an expression that suggests that the birds are noxious, and perhaps a means by which disease is spread, No doubt pigeon droppings can be viewed as an undesirable aspect of urban life, but the evidence that pigeons actually are responsible for spreading diseases to humans is fairly weak. The basis for characterizing pigeons—and other creatures—as problem animals is not so much that they are dangerous as that they are out of place. Pigeons in the wild are not considered a problem, but pigeons in the city become claimsmaking targets. This reveals that animals themselves can be constructed as social problems when they are defined as interfering with people's lives, so that wild animals become claimsmakers' targets when they interfere with farming, fishing, or other human activities (Herda-Rapp & Godeke, 2005).

In other claims, it is not animals, but people's mistreatment of animals, that is defined as the social problem. Animal welfare claims find their warrant in the value that people should treat animals humanely, so that, for instance, the meat processing industry should use methods for killing animals that minimize their suffering. In contrast, animal rights claims have a very different warrant, that animals have rights analogous to human rights, so that the very idea of slaughtering animals for human consumption is deemed wrong. A major obstacle for animal rights activists is the widely shared, commonsense assumption that humans (who have rights) are different from animals (who do not). Getting people to accept animal rights claims requires devising claims that challenge this distinction (Cherry, 2010).

Most often, animal rights advocates' rhetoric seeks to blur the boundary between humans and animals. They may emphasize basic biological understandings: that humans are themselves animals; that all creatures are at least distant cousins on a great evolutionary family tree; or that humans' DNA is largely similar to that of other animals. An alternative approach is to point to lessons of history, to once taken-for-granted practices against humans that now seem barbaric, in order to challenge the commonsense assumption that humans are different from—and have a right to exploit—animals. Slavery denied millions of people basic rights (just as most people now fail to acknowledge the rights of animals); therefore, claims-makers argue, the eventual success of the antislavery movement should inspire the animal rights activists. Similarly, claimsmakers draw parallels between slaughterhouses and the Holocaust and other genocides. If, looking backward, we are horrified by the spectacle of populations turning a blind eye toward mass murder, how will more enlightened, future generations view our killing animals? An alternative strategy is for animal rights activists to symbolically cross the boundary between humans and animals, to portray themselves as being treated like animals by sitting chained in cages, or wrapping themselves in clear plastic like cuts of meat. The shock of seeing a human treated like an animal is intended to help people identify with animals' plight.

Different people define animals in very different terms: some see nothing wrong with eating meat or wearing leather, whereas others view these practices as profoundly immoral. Disputes about animals can lead to open conflict, where claims and counterclaims are exchanged in angry tones. For instance, hunters find themselves in disputes with animal rights advocates (Bronner, 2008). The hunters may see themselves as part of a long, even noble tradition, one that embodies honor, skill, self-reliance, and other virtues; in their view, hunting is one of the oldest human activities, a natural aspect of a world populated by predators and prey. In contrast, animal rights activists see hunting as an immoral activity, both cruel and unnecessary. Each side in these controversies constructs the opposition in dismissive terms. Hunters portray themselves as strong and masculine, while dismissing hunting's critics as sissified city folk. In contrast, animal rights advocates see themselves as enlightened, while suggesting that hunters may be compensating for some psychological inadequacy, even pathology (for instance, linking hunting to reports that serial killers often have histories of mistreating animals). The division between these claims is stark: hunting is good versus hunting is bad.

Such debates reflect an underlying change in people's experience with animals: in a largely rural society, many people killed animals, not just by hunting, but when they picked out a chicken for dinner; but in today's largely urban society, even the most dedicated meat eater may have no firsthand experience with the killing that produces meat. Moreover, critics can argue that killing a chicken on the farm was more humane than what happens in modern, mechanized slaughterhouses. As a consequence, the audience for claims about animal problems has changed, leading to shifts in what some people consider persuasive rhetoric.

Social problems claims about animals display tremendous variety. Animals can be constructed as a problem in society ("rats with wings"), or animals' place in society can be presented as a problem ("animal cruelty"). There is nothing inherently problematic about animals; problem animals and animal problems come into being only when people begin to make claims.

QUESTIONS

1. What are the grounds, warrants, and conclusions in some claims about animals?

2. Does it make any difference that some people are likely to actively disagree with virtually any claim related to animals?

3. Pick some other feature of the natural world (such as plants, air, or water). What are some ways it can be constructed as a social problem?

3

■

Activists as Claimsmakers

■

Claims cannot exist by themselves; people—claimsmakers—must advance them. It's tempting to equate claimsmakers with activists—people like Martin Luther King Jr.—who become passionately involved with an issue, dedicate their lives to a cause, and march and demonstrate until their claims receive attention. Indeed, this is part—but only part—of the story.

When we think of activists, we envision people who stand outside the halls of power. Because they do not hold powerful political offices or have strong ties with those who do, it is fairly difficult for these **outsider claimsmakers** to get others—the media, the general public, and particularly the officials who can make policies that might actually do something about the troubling social condition—to pay attention to their claims (J. Best, 1990). This is why activists so often resort to attention-grabbing tactics: demonstrations, sit-ins, and so on. Activists hope that these activities will lead to media coverage and that attracting publicity for their cause will bring their claims to the attention of the public, so that, in turn, both the media and the public will press policymakers to take action. That is, activists envision the claimsmaking process as shown in Figure 3.1a, where the thicker arrow between the claimsmakers

Figure 3.1 CLAIMSMAKING BY OUTSIDER AND
INSIDER CLAIMSMAKERS

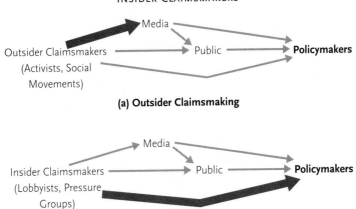

and the media identifies the media as the most important audience for outsiders' claims.

However, there is an alternative, more direct route to successful claimsmaking. Some people already have contacts with policymakers. Such people include lobbyists, major political contributors, government officials, and well-established interest groups such as the National Rifle Association (NRA), which is concerned with protecting the rights of gun owners, or the National Association for the Advancement of Colored People (NAACP), which is concerned with advancing the rights of African Americans. Those who are already well connected to policymakers form what is sometimes called the **polity** (Useem & Zald, 1982); the polity consists of those groups whose interests are routinely taken into account by policymakers, so they are often able to influence policymaking. People with such connections can act as **insider claimsmakers**; often they pursue their claims outside the glare of the media spotlight, without arousing much public attention. The activities of insider claimsmakers are depicted in Figure 3.1b, where the thicker arrow runs directly from claimsmakers to policymakers.

The activities of insider claimsmakers will be considered in Chapter 4; this chapter will focus on outsider claimsmakers—in particular, activists such as Dr. King. Activists often belong to broad **social movements**, general causes such as the civil rights movement or environmentalism. Each social movement may contain several distinct **social movement organizations** (SMOs), such as the civil rights movement's SNCC (Student Nonviolent Coordinating Committee) and CORE (Congress of Racial Equality), or the environmentalist movement's Greenpeace and Sierra Club. As we shall see, although the larger society may view a movement's SMOs as allies that share a common cause, activists frequently think of other SMOs within the same social movement as rivals.

Social movements frequently face opposition. Movements seek to promote change, and the status quo inevitably has its defenders. The most vigorous defenses usually come from those who have vested interests in the status quo; these opponents benefit from existing social arrangements in ways that would be threatened if the changes promoted by the movement were to occur. For example, some white southerners, who saw themselves as benefiting from legal segregation, opposed the civil rights movement. Moreover, it takes effort to change social arrangements, and even when people may not strongly oppose activists' claims, they may see no good reason to exert the effort that change requires; sociologists refer to such reluctance to alter existing social arrangements as **inertia** (Becker, 1995).

Chapter 2 described position issues—that is, topics that evoke controversy, inciting active disagreements about whether a particular condition should be considered troubling, or what that condition's causes might be, or what should be done to address the condition. In such position issues, claims inspire counterclaims, and **countermovements** may arise to promote these counterclaims.

Some sociologists associate the term *social movement* with liberal or progressive causes and prefer to restrict the term *countermovement* to more conservative causes. However, it makes better analytic sense to speak of social movements as calling for change, and of countermovements as resisting change. When abortion was generally illegal, there was a movement of abortion rights advocates, which was opposed by a countermovement that favored restricting abortion. Once abortion became widely legal, however, it became more reasonable to speak of a pro-life movement calling for change, and a pro-choice countermovement trying to defend the existing right to abortion. This example illustrates that countermovements are conservative in the sense that they seek to preserve the status quo; when political liberals support existing social arrangements (such as laws protecting the right to abortions), they may organize countermovements to oppose claimsmaking by political conservatives (such as the pro-life movement).

Because most social movements—and countermovements—promote claims about social problems, and because images of activists tend to come to mind when we think of claimsmakers, this chapter will focus on key aspects of social movements and the role of activists as claimsmakers. (Chapter 4 will consider other sorts of claimsmakers.) We will begin this chapter's discussion of activist claimsmakers by examining three recent approaches adopted by sociologists to study social movements: framing, resource mobilization, and opportunity structures.

FRAMING

Most social movements present claims; they identify a troubling condition and call for social changes to address the problem (Benford & Hunt, 2003). These claims can, of course, be studied in terms of their rhetoric—that is, by using the concepts developed in Chapter 2. Social movement scholars, however, often adopt a slightly different vocabulary: they speak of **framing** to describe how activists construct their claims.

Like the frame around a picture, activists' frames place a social movement within a larger context; frames locate the key issues and set them off so that they are easily understood. Like the wooden frame of a house, activists' frames provide a structure, a framework around which elaborate claims can be assembled.

The same issue might be framed in many different ways. Some frames emphasize morality, appealing to people's sense of right and wrong. Some frames elicit outrage or other powerful emotions that lead people to join and stick with a cause (Gould, 2009; Whittier, 2009) (see Box 3.1). Other frames evoke particular ideologies or political philosophies, such as Marxism or libertarianism. Still other frames emphasize political struggles between groups with competing interests. What may seem to be a single social movement—the civil rights movement, the environmental movement, and so on—can be composed of activists who frame the issue in very different ways.

Frames encourage viewing the world from a particular perspective; they give meaning to what might otherwise seem confusing, so that once someone adopts a given frame, everything seems to be clearer, to make sense. For example, the feminist movement calls attention to the various ways in which social arrangements disadvantage women; a feminist frame gives activists a particular vantage point from which they can view women's place in the world.

There are obvious parallels between constructionist scholars' examinations of claimsmaking rhetoric (as discussed in Chapter 2), and social movement analysts' discussions of frames. Frames have three components: **diagnostic frames** identify the nature of the problem (that is, *diagnostic frame* is another term for what constructionists call *grounds*); **motivational frames** explain why action needs to be taken (akin to the constructionists' *warrants*); and **prognostic frames** specify what needs to be done (similar to

Box 3.1 Framing the Grotesque

Emotion can play an important role in framing. One way to elicit powerful emotional reactions is to use grotesque images—descriptions, photographs, and such—as dramatic typifying examples that illustrate the evils of a problem, and encourage people to join the movement against it. Thus, the abolitionist movement presented graphic accounts of the brutal treatment of slaves to demonstrate that slaveholders were cruel, not the benevolent, paternalistic figures slavery's defenders liked to claim, just as the antiabortion movement's campaign against "partial-birth" (third-trimester) abortion used images of dismembered fetuses to invoke a sense of horror. Incorporating grotesque images is intended to shock people, to make the activists' frame seem more valid.

Grotesque imagery may have different effects on different audiences. Its use tends to be favored by those in a movement's more radical, outspoken wing who are convinced that their cause is morally just and that any opposition is morally wrong. Surely, they reason, people exposed to these images must accept the movement's frame. More moderate members of the movement may be leery of the grotesque: on the one hand, such imagery is emotionally powerful and may compel some people to join the cause; on the other hand, these activists worry that many people will find the grotesque images so offensive or disturbing that they may turn their backs on the movement. Framing a cause, then, involves choosing among different appeals.

Source: Halfmann & Young, 2010.

the constructionists' *conclusions*) (Snow & Benford, 1988). For our purposes, these are essentially similar classification schemes, one favored by those who think of themselves as sociologists of social problems, the other by scholars of social movements.

One reason that social movement analysts favor the language of framing is their interest in how social movements recruit new members. A key issue for most activists is enlisting supporters to their causes. Social movements need to attract new members, to convince people to share the activists' concerns and support the movement through donations and investments of time and energy. Because social movements typically promote unfamiliar ways of looking at society and its problems, they must frame issues in ways that will appeal to prospective members. In other words, activists need to align their frames with those of the people they hope to enlist in their movements.

Frame alignment refers to the ways in which social movements must address the existing frames or ways of looking at the world held by prospective members (Snow, Rochford, Worden, & Benford, 1986). Movement participants—activists—have a particular frame, with its diagnostic, motivational, and prognostic elements, but the people they might like to recruit to the movement already have their own ways of understanding the world. The goal is to bring these frames into alignment, so that others will come to adopt the activists' frame (and presumably join the movement). For example, the feminist movement seeks to introduce people to a feminist frame so that they can recognize how sexism affects their lives, and so that they will support feminist efforts to challenge sexual discrimination. Frame alignment usually takes one of four forms:

1. *Bridging*. In **frame bridging**, activists seek support from people thought to hold frames similar to their own. For example, liberal activists interested in a new issue are likely to seek supporters among those already known to be sympathetic with other liberal causes, just as conservative activists generally try to bring their new concerns to the attention of known conservatives. That is, activists seek to enlist people who have already supported other, similar causes because it should be easy to build a bridge between fundamentally similar frames.

2. *Amplification*. In **frame amplification**, activists call upon values or beliefs that they presume many people hold in order to rally others to their cause. Although the prospective supporters may not have been

active in other movements, they are presumed to hold basic assumptions that should make them sympathetic to the activists' cause. For instance, recent campaigns to register sex offenders and then restrict their rights have drawn upon popular stereotypes about the predatory nature of sex offenses, and people's sense that society ought to be protected from such predators. Frame amplification often seeks to arouse emotional reactions, such as compassion or outrage, so that people feel compelled to join the movement.

3. *Extension.* In **frame extension**, activists enlarge their frame to encompass concerns that prospective supporters are thought to have. In this case, the activists' core values or beliefs may not overlap those of their prospective supporters until they extend their frame. To return to an example raised in Chapter 2, vegetarian activists tend to be concerned with primarily ethical issues: they believe that it is morally wrong to eat meat (Maurer, 2002). However, relatively few Americans share that concern, and vegetarians have had more success gaining support by extending their frame to emphasize the health and ecological benefits of vegetarian eating—appeals that can attract supporters who worry about health or environmental issues more than the morality of eating meat.

4. *Transformation.* In **frame transformation**, activists call upon prospective supporters to reject the familiar worldview that they take for granted and adopt a new and different frame. This transformation may be limited to how one thinks about a specific troubling condition (for example, the campaign to redefine drunk driving sought to persuade people to stop thinking of it as a somewhat amusing, minor offense, and start viewing it as a serious crime that all too often leads to terrible consequences). In other cases, activists may try to convert supporters to a completely different view of the world (think of efforts to recruit adherents to unfamiliar religions).

These four forms of frame alignment pose increasingly difficult challenges to activists. Frame bridging is the most straightforward task: claims are made to prospective recruits who are thought to be ideologically predisposed to being sympathetic to the claims. Frame amplification depends on emphasizing values and beliefs that the activists already share with the audience for their claims, in order to mobilize them to action; and frame extension requires activists to modify their own frame to make it more attractive to potential recruits. Frame transformation presents the greatest challenge: recruits are asked to abandon their familiar view of the world in favor of the activists' frame.

Different SMOs within the same social movement may have distinct frames that appeal to different prospective members. Often, for instance, a movement may contain both moderate and radical SMOs, the former advocating limited reforms to the existing social system, while the latter call for more significant changes. Activists from a movement's moderate and radical wings usually frame the troubling condition and its solution differently, and they may clash in **frame disputes**, disagreements over how to think about the problem (Benford, 1993). In many cases, activists from different camps within the same social movement present their frames to different audiences: as a general rule, moderates seek to appeal to older people in the middle class (who have relatively secure places within the existing social system, and who therefore are likely to resist radical calls for dramatic social change); and radicals are more likely to seek supporters among those who are younger or poorer (who have far less invested in maintaining the status quo, and who therefore should be more open to pursuing fundamental changes).

Successful framing draws upon cultural resources; it incorporates familiar values, beliefs, imagery, and other cultural elements that prospective members find persuasive and convincing. Feminists, for instance, invoke familiar notions of fairness and equality, and argue that women have a right to equal treatment. But framing cannot be a one-way process. When activists interact with prospective members, they usually discover that some appeals are more persuasive than others in convincing people to join the movement. After all, prospective social movement members have many messages competing for their attention—television shows, news reports, advertisements, and on and on. Activists cannot simply present a frame and wait for the world to take notice; that would leave too much to chance because it would be too easy for the activists' frame to be overlooked. Rather, activists must seek out potential supporters, try to frame their message in ways that others will find interesting and convincing, and then pay close attention to what does and doesn't work. If activists find that their claims have generated counterclaims, they may need to reframe the issue to take this opposition into account. Similarly, when one version of a frame fails to elicit much response, it will need to be modified until it begins to be effective (see Box 3.2).

This need to devise frames that will attract supporters, counter opposition, and eventually influence social policy can raise issues of integrity for activists (Benford, 1993). Activists at the core of an SMO often have more ideologically coherent frames than many other movement supporters have, and they may view frame extension—altering their frame in order to make it more appealing—as a violation of their principles, as "selling out." Frame disputes within a movement often revolve around questions of compromise: should activists present what they believe to be a more correct, more principled view of the issue even if it risks rejection by many prospective supporters who will find it too difficult to understand, or even unpalatable; or should they frame the issue in weaker but more appealing terms so that prospective members will find it easier to digest? Frames inevitably reflect a combination of how activists view the world, and what they believe will be an effective message.

RESOURCE MOBILIZATION

Adopting a frame that justifies belief in a cause is not enough to make a claim successful; activists cannot trade on outrage alone. Social movements also need to deal with a variety of mundane

Box 3.2 Shifting Frames for Women's and Children's Victimization

As social movements grow, and as they endure over time, their frames are likely to become more complex. Activists within large movements may disagree about which troubling conditions are most important, or about how those issues should be framed. Over time, these debates develop histories, and early constructions of an issue may be supplanted by new thinking.

These complexities are evident in the ways the women's movement has constructed issues involving victimization, such as rape, domestic violence, and child sexual abuse. Earlier frames tended to emphasize the helplessness of victims and the need for social policies that could protect the vulnerable. Thus, women who continued to live with abusive partners were characterized as psychologically unable to break free from their abusers. But critics within the movement argued that such frames portrayed victims in unfavorable terms—as weak, even as accomplices in their own victimization. Later frames adopted the term *survivor*, suggesting that those who had experienced victimization had the strength to endure, and might become stronger yet. The solutions advocated also shifted; programs such as women's shelters were originally launched by activists, but often evolved into social service agencies staffed by professionals, who were likely to reframe the nature of the problems being confronted and the ways those problems should be addressed to fit their own therapeutic perspectives. Movements' constructions are not static, but evolve as new voices help construct a problem.

Sources: Dunn, 2010; Whittier, 2009.

problems. Organizing a successful demonstration means picking a good time and place, to maximize participation. People who might be willing to participate must be contacted and encouraged to come (demonstrations designed to attract a big crowd might require Internet postings, posters, telephone calling systems, and other ways of getting the word out); it might even be necessary to make arrangements to transport people to the event. Large demonstrations also require a lot of planning: tasks might include training people in dos and don'ts, scheduling speakers and other events, assigning monitors to supervise demonstrators, preparing first-aid stations, and possibly even arranging to post bail for people who get arrested. In addition, press releases need to be issued to inform the media that the demonstration will be taking place, and it may be a good idea to designate spokespeople to explain the demonstrators' purpose to the reporters covering the event.

In other words, one way to think about activists is in terms of the resources required by a social movement's activities. Movements need money, members, skills, and so on. These may seem like mundane considerations, especially if we think of social movements in romantic terms, consisting of plucky little guys struggling against powerful interests. But without sufficient resources, movements will have difficulty getting started, let alone enduring. Successful movements must assemble the resources they need. Sociologists refer to this gathering of resources as **resource mobilization** (McCarthy & Zald, 1977).

The resources that activists need are almost always scarce: it is hard to raise enough money, because the people who give money have lots of other ways to spend it; it is hard to get people to devote time to the movement, because there are other things they could do; and so on. The struggle to assemble resources means that SMOs—even SMOs that are theoretically allies in the same social movement—find themselves in competition with one another for the same scarce resources. They compete for members, for donations, for media coverage, and so on. If one SMO is especially effective in mobilizing resources, rival organizations are likely to find resources harder to come by.

For example, the civil rights movement—now recalled as a grand, unified movement to end segregation—was characterized by internal competition and disagreements (Haines, 1984). Different civil rights organizations had different frames that led them to favor different strategies. For many years the NAACP had pursued a legal strategy, mounting court challenges to the constitutionality of segregationist practices. Dr. King's SCLC (Southern Christian Leadership Conference) favored high-visibility protests in communities such as Birmingham and Selma, Alabama. More radical organizations, such as CORE and SNCC, adopted riskier, more confrontational tactics such as sit-ins and freedom rides. Because potential donors could choose which organizations they wanted to support, the various SMOs were rivals for those donors' dollars. The NAACP, for instance, believed that it made sense to invest in a long-term legal campaign, and it opposed spending donors' money to bail out SNCC's demonstrators who engaged in protests that were certain to lead to their arrests. SNCC, on the other hand, argued that the NAACP's approach was too slow, and tried to rally support for its riskier activities. Establishing and maintaining alliances with other movements takes work (see Box 3.3).

In contemporary America, much social movement activity revolves not around convincing individuals to dedicate their lives to activism, or even around organizing thousands of people to march in the streets, but around fundraising. Although activists do sometimes organize large demonstrations, much of their activity focuses on seeking media coverage for their cause, lobbying policymakers, and so on. These activities cost money, and activists spend considerable time soliciting contributions from people who support the movement's cause (but may not feel they have the time or energy to work directly on movement activities). Note that we can distinguish between **beneficiaries** (who stand to benefit directly if a movement is successful) and **constituents** (who support the movement) (McCarthy & Zald, 1977). Some people belong to both categories, but many movement supporters are **conscience constituents**—that is, people who contribute money or even join demonstrations because they believe in the cause, although they do not expect to

Box 3.3 Forging Alliances across Social Movements

A challenge confronting activists in a given SMO is how to deal with other activists in other SMOs, and even in other movements. While there seem to be obvious advantages in having allies, those other activists are also competitors. Successful alliances require their own framing.

A campaign to block construction of a biodefense laboratory in Roxbury (a poor, largely African American district in Boston) illustrates these challenges. Neighborhood activists defined the problem as one of environmental justice: the laboratory might be hazardous, and would not bring jobs or other benefits to Roxbury. The laboratory's other opponents tended to be white, upper-middle-class peace activists from outlying neighborhoods who defined the issue more broadly and abstractly in terms of militarism. In other words, the would-be allies were divided by race, class, neighborhood, ideology, and definition of the problem. Forging an alliance required careful framing. Thus, it became important for all the activists to acknowledge and defer to the leadership of the neighborhood groups; the Roxbury activists controlled the campaign within their neighborhood, while the allies concentrated their efforts in other areas. Those who were unwilling to abide by these restrictions were asked to leave the coalition. Over time, the allies who remained developed greater trust in and dependence upon one another. Assembling a successful alliance required agreeing on some common frames.

Source: Beamish & Luebbers, 2009.

be direct beneficiaries (think of northern whites who donated to civil rights SMOs).

The growing importance of contributions led to the emergence of sophisticated fundraising efforts using, for instance, direct-mail techniques. Mailing lists of people known to have contributed to previous fundraising campaigns were used to raise additional funds. Fundraising efforts become more sophisticated as new technologies become available; in recent years, SMOs have begun raising funds via the Internet, using websites and e-mail to solicit donations. Of course, this emphasis on bringing in money means that SMOs become dependent on the support of constituents with whom the activists have no direct contact; most of an SMO's members act only as contributors, who may never actually encounter other members face to face. This poses challenges: how to keep people emotionally committed to both the SMO and the larger cause and willing to continue their support when they have few direct connections to the movement. In response, SMOs maintain websites, send members frequent e-mail messages, and seek to convey a sense that their members constitute an electronic community (Eaton, 2010). Sending messages to current and prospective members turns into yet another occasion when troubling conditions must be reconstructed with compelling rhetoric—in this case, arguments that funds are needed urgently to respond to an important opportunity or, more often, to a looming threat. Both pro-life and pro-choice activists, for instance, raise money by warning that, unless supporters rally to their cause (by donating money to support their SMO's activities), their opponents are likely to win. Alternatively, SMOs may seek funding from other sources, such as foundations, but this support may come at a cost (see Box 3.4).

Increasingly, then, successful activism requires sophisticated skills—organizing, fundraising, media relations, lobbying, and the like. These skills tend to be portable: individuals who learn skills in one SMO can move on and apply what they've learned at another SMO, or even in another movement. Just as some veterans of the civil rights movement took what they had learned in that campaign and used their new skills to help organize antiwar protests, the women's liberation movement, and the gay liberation movement, people today pursue careers as activists, sometimes working for different causes over the course of their careers. Typically, these individuals do have ideological commitments, so they tend to move among social movements with which they are sympathetic: one individual

Box 3.4 Foundations Redirect Activism for Forest Preservation

The resources social movements require need not come from individual members. Foundations also can provide money in the form of grants to support movement activities. Of course, most foundations have been endowed by wealthy benefactors, and they tend to promote reform of existing institutions, rather than radical transformations. Foundations can shape the direction of activism by channeling funds to SMOs whose programs match the foundations' goals.

Forest certification is a program supported by foundations. A well-publicized campaign by environmental activists attacked the destruction of the rainforests and sought to organize boycotts of tropical woods. In response, the timber industry argued that it pursued environmentally responsible forest management practices, such as planting new trees to replace those that had been logged. Foundations stepped in by supplying grants to more moderate SMOs to establish and oversee forest certification programs. Corporations could apply for forest certification—designations that they engaged in sound forest management practices, and that their lumber was, in effect, part of the solution, rather than part of the problem. Certification served to divert criticism and, in the process, foundations provided support to activists willing to endorse this moderate program, rather than insisting on boycotts and other, more radical solutions to the problem of deforestation.

Source: Bartley, 2007.

may work for several liberal SMOs, while another becomes active in various conservative causes.

Resource mobilization is important because it reflects an SMO's ability to promote its claims. Organizations with more members and a bigger budget are better able to afford the services of skilled activists (who may in turn be attracted to working in campaigns that have plentiful resources and better chances of success). SMOs with money can afford further fundraising efforts, so they have better prospects for garnering future resources. Moreover, SMOs with greater resources find it easier to draw attention to their message: they are better able to gain coverage in the media; and, other things being equal, they are more likely to influence policymakers. Mobilizing resources is not glamorous, but it provides an essential base for would-be activist claimsmakers.

OPPORTUNITY STRUCTURES

Activists must worry about more than devising a persuasive frame and mobilizing necessary resources. Timing also matters. All too often, social movements face great obstacles. After all, movements seek to change existing social arrangements, and those arrangements work to the benefit of powerful people who can be expected to use their considerable resources to resist changes that might be to their disadvantage. On occasion, however, these obstacles to change are reduced, and activists must be alert for and ready to take advantage of such opportune moments. Various cultural and political circumstances can create opportunities to promote activists' claims.

Cultural Opportunities

Cultural opportunities arise when people become more willing to listen to the movement's claims (McAdam, 1994). Perhaps the most obvious cultural opportunity is the occurrence of a newsworthy event that focuses attention on a troubling condition. The September 11, 2001, terrorist attacks, for instance, suddenly moved terrorism from a peripheral concern to the central focus of national attention. Other, less dramatic events—a natural disaster, a brutal crime, and such—can have similar effects. They lead to a widespread sense that a particular troubling condition, previously neglected, must now be addressed. Activists who have been struggling to have their claims heard may suddenly find themselves in demand—reporters seek them out for interviews, legislators invite them to testify at hearings, and so on—because they are the ones who understand and have ideas for what to do about the troubling condition that is now the focus of concern.

Another sort of cultural opportunity emerges when a **master frame** becomes familiar (Snow & Benford, 1992). A master frame articulates a broad orientation that can be easily adapted for application to many issues. For instance, after the civil rights movement first drew national attention to blacks' struggle for equal rights and then succeeded in dismantling the system of institutionalized segregation in the South, the idea that demanding equal rights might be an effective way of framing social issues spread to other social movements. Within about ten years, activists were campaigning for women's rights, gay rights, children's rights, and the rights of the disabled, prisoners, and the elderly. This master frame remains influential: the abortion issue has been framed in terms of fetuses' *right to life* and women's *right to choose*; divorced men campaign for *fathers' rights*; an active *animal rights* movement has emerged; and so on. Like dramatic events, the availability of master frames creates cultural opportunities that can make it easier for activists to promote their claims.

Political Opportunities

Political opportunities to promote activists' claims arise when the distribution of power among different groups shifts, so that changes that previously would have been successfully resisted can now be implemented. Political opportunities may derive from shifting priorities, when formerly irrelevant concerns are redefined as relevant. One reason the civil rights movement gained momentum in the early 1960s was that former colonies—particularly the

African colonies of Britain and France—were gaining independence. The Cold War was at its height, and the United States wanted to minimize the Soviet Union's influence in these newly independent nations. The concern that African nations might be repelled by the treatment of African Americans in the United States created a new pressure to do something about the system of segregation found in the southern states. In this case, shifting foreign policy concerns created new opportunities for civil rights activists trying to change domestic policies.

Another form of political opportunity emerges when, for some reason, opposition to a movement becomes weaker. Those who might be expected to resist the activists' claims may be losing influence, or they may be distracted by other concerns. Perhaps more important for the social problems process is the fact that support for claimsmakers may become stronger. Successful claims lead to sympathetic media coverage, public opinion polls that reveal growing support, and political leaders' joining the cause. Support for "an idea whose time has come" can grow to the point that opponents may decide to drop their opposition. For instance, the basic principles of equal rights for African Americans and for both men and women advocated by the civil rights and the feminist movements, respectively—principles once considered quite controversial—have achieved broad acceptance.

Activists need to assess political opportunities and devise appropriate tactics for exploiting them. A tactic that is effective at one moment may be less effective at another. For instance, McAdam (1983) traces the history of tactical choices in the civil rights movement. The movement's activists devised a variety of protest tactics—sit-ins, large-scale demonstrations, and so on. Some of these tactics proved ineffective: they failed to attract media attention or to weaken the system of segregation. But others worked better, and news of these successes spread, leading activists in other communities to copy the effective tactics. Still, these successes were temporary; a tactic remained effective only for a time. News of the new tactic also inspired opposition; the movement's segregationist opponents searched for tactics of their own—responses that could minimize the movement's impact—and news of these successful opposition tactics also spread. In addition, each time civil rights activists used a particular tactic, it became more familiar and less newsworthy, so the media coverage dwindled. These processes created a cycle of tactical innovation in which a novel tactic would emerge, work for a while, then grow less effective, causing the activists to invent a new form of protest to keep the movement advancing.

Just as some circumstances can improve political opportunities, others create obstacles, occasions when claimsmaking probably can't succeed. Public attention is finite; if the media are devoting their attention to other newsworthy events, they aren't likely to cover a particular social movement's claims (see Chapter 5 for a more thorough discussion of how the media choose what they will cover). In the weeks immediately following September 11, 2001, media attention concentrated on terrorism, so there was almost no chance that claims about other issues could receive much attention. Similarly, when rival claimsmakers—activists for another social movement, or even for another SMO within the same movement—are occupying center stage and hogging the limelight, opportunities for promoting one's own claims are reduced. Rather than struggling to be heard under such adverse circumstances, it may be wiser to conserve resources and wait for a more promising opportunity.

Similarly, opportunities are unfavorable when opposition to a cause seems to be growing stronger, or when support for that cause seems to be growing weaker. Under such circumstances, activists need to consider what's wrong and make the necessary changes. Perhaps the existing frame is losing its appeal; perhaps more resources need to be assembled. At these times it is better to back off and wait for a better opportunity, rather than forcing the issue and facing certain defeat (see Box 3.5).

Box 3.5 Allies, Opportunities, and Abortion

Planned Parenthood Federation of America (PPFA) and the National Right to Life Committee (NRLC) are, respectively, the leading pro-choice and pro-life SMOs—owners of their sides in the abortion issue. Their ownership depends on being viewed as "reasonable" advocates; PPFA seeks to play down its abortion advocacy and emphasize its professionalism as a provider of reproductive health services, while NRLC is a nondenominational group intended to find common ground among pro-life groups rooted in different religious faiths. Each finds it necessary to deal with allies—groups that advocate more extreme positions than these more moderate owners want to adopt.

Political opportunities shape how PPFA and NRLC deal with their allies. When each judges the political environment to be generally favorable (when PPFA considers that the president and Congress are generally pro-choice, or when NRLC perceives them as being pro-life), it is advisable to remain silent in the face of controversy; thus PPFA does not comment when other pro-choice advocates call for unrestricted abortion on demand, and NRLC ignores other pro-life groups' endorsements of violence against abortion clinics. However, when the political environment seems threatening to their respective causes, PPFA and NRLC are forced to publicly align with their allies, and try to influence them to adopt more moderate positions. In spite of being on opposing sides of the issues, these SMOs' tactical choices are more similar than they are different.

Source: Rohlinger, 2006.

For example, Taylor (1989) traces the history of the National Women's Party (NWP), which long promoted an Equal Rights Amendment (ERA) to the Constitution that would guarantee women full equality under the law. During much of its history, and particularly during the years following World War II, the NWP confronted poor political opportunities for success. This was a period of **abeyance**; that is, the NWP maintained a modest organizational structure, continued monitoring political developments, and waited for brighter opportunities. A good opportunity arose in the late 1960s, after the civil rights movement had captured Americans' attention, making the equal rights master frame more familiar and more acceptable. In particular, new calls for women's liberation began to gain notice, and as a new wave of feminist activism began to emerge, the NWP joined the new feminists (such as the newly formed National Organization for Women, or NOW) and encouraged them to campaign for the ERA (although that particular campaign was again narrowly defeated). By tending the feminist flame during the decades of abeyance, the NWP had conserved its resources until more promising opportunities developed to use them.

Summary

Social movements can experience decades of frustration, periods when activists cannot seem to interest anyone in their cause—when they face indifference, ridicule, even repression. It helps to be patient, to wait until cultural and political opportunities develop that offer more favorable conditions for claimsmaking. For instance, the civil rights movement and the feminist movement have had long histories featuring both periods of frustration and periods of progress. These familiar examples teach other activists the importance of continuing the struggle, of hanging on until opportune moments arise.

THE ADVANTAGES OF OWNERSHIP

Activists whose efforts are particularly successful can gain **ownership** of a social problem (Gusfield, 1981). Ownership is established when particular claims or frames become generally recognized and acknowledged as the best way to understand a particular issue. It is an ambiguous status; no one receives an official certificate of owner-ship, but some claimsmakers become the recognized, go-to authori-ties on a troubling condition. If a dramatic event brings that problem back into the news, it is the owners who are asked by reporters to provide commentary and who are consulted by policymakers.

Ownership relates to framing, resource mobilization, and politi-cal opportunities. The owners' frames become influential in shaping how others approach the problem and its solution; the owners' per-spective may not be the only possible way of thinking about the trou-bling condition, but it becomes familiar, almost taken for granted by the press, the public, and policymakers. Precisely because they are well known, owners find it much easier to mobilize resources. People who want to contribute or otherwise become involved in a cause tend to know about and turn to a problem's owners, just as reporters looking for sources to comment on an issue are likely to think first of approaching the owners. And, of course, precisely because owners find it easier to garner resources, they have an easier time maintaining their ownership in the face of competing activists. As a result, owners are well placed to take advantage of opportunity structures. When, for instance, current events draw attention to a troubling condition, owners tend to be far better prepared to exploit whatever opportunities develop: they have contacts with the media and with policymakers; they are probably better placed to assess political opportunities; and they may even be integrated into the social problems process well enough to act as insider claimsmakers.

A social problem can have multiple owners. Position issues marked by intractable disagreements often feature SMOs that own the opposing sides in the debate. For example, the NRA long ago established itself as the leading SMO speaking on behalf of the rights of gun owners and in opposition to gun control. For a long time, proponents of gun control lacked a comparably influential SMO; in recent years, however, Handgun Control Inc (recently renamed the Brady Center to Prevent Gun Violence) has emerged as the most visible antigun SMO—the owner of gun control advocacy. And, as noted earlier, social movements often encompass a range of frames, from more moderate groups advocating modest reforms, to more radical SMOs pushing for more significant changes. Owners may emerge at different points along this spectrum. Within the 1960s civil rights movement, for example, the well-established NAACP favored deliberate pressure to gain favorable court decisions; while more radical SMOs, such as SNCC and CORE, became well known for organizing more confrontational activities, such as sit-ins and freedom rides. A few highly visible SMOs shared ownership of the large, broad-based civil rights movement.

Some SMOs own particular issues for extended periods. The NRA has led the fight against gun control for decades, and the NAACP has been a leading voice in the movement for African Americans' civil rights since its founding in 1909. Such owners must constantly strive to keep their issue—and their ownership—visible to the press, the public, and policymakers. Maintaining such a presence serves two purposes. First, of course, it keeps the owners' particular claims—their frame—for interpreting the issue visible and familiar, so that others find it easy to continue to think about the topic in the owners' terms. Second, it helps preserve the owners' status *as owners*. Attention—and contributions—tend to go to the most familiar advocates. Although ownership is harder to achieve in the first place than it is to maintain after being gained, it must always be nurtured.

Long-term ownership requires flexibility. Narrowly focused, single-issue movements are at a long-term disadvantage; it is too easy for public attention to drift away from an issue, and once that happens, supporters, media coverage, and access to policymakers may also dwindle. It helps to develop a broader set of interrelated concerns. The NAACP, for instance, has addressed a wide array of issues related to racial discrimination during its long history. In its early years, for example, the NAACP devoted considerable attention to its campaign against lynching. But as lynching declined and then disappeared, the NAACP turned to constructing other race relations issues, such as campaigns against discrimination in education and employment, opposition to hate crimes, and so on. As political opportunities shift, it can become easier or harder to promote particular claims, but to the degree that the NAACP maintains ownership over the full spectrum of issues related to African Americans, it can remain actively involved in the social problems process.

In contrast, narrowly focused SMOs run the risk of succeeding—and thereby losing their reason for existing. Consider the March of Dimes, a charitable organization originally launched to fight the problem of polio, a disease that left children severely disabled. Once polio vaccines were developed, the threat of polio virtually disappeared, and the organization faced a crisis. It could, of course, declare victory and disband. But why dismantle a successful fundraising apparatus? Instead, the March of Dimes redefined its purpose, declaring that it would continue to operate but would now dedicate its efforts to fighting birth defects. This was not just a new but also a broader definition of the SMO's purpose: there are many different birth defects, so although further successes might result in eliminating some of these problems, the organization would continue to be needed to address the problems that remained.

When claimsmakers begin drawing attention to a troubling, previously neglected condition, there are three ways ownership of the issue might evolve:

1. *No one assumes ownership*. This situation is most likely when a newsworthy event, such as a dramatic crime, catapults an issue into the public eye. A variety of commentators may offer their takes on this troubling condition, perhaps suggesting different ways of thinking about the issue. However, it may be that none of these claimsmakers will assume ownership of the topic, work to keep the issue visible, manage a prolonged campaign to change public policy, and so on. Under these circumstances, even topics that receive a burst of intense publicity can shift away from public attention, forgotten as soon as the next, different dramatic event commands notice. Without own-

ers to remind people of a problem's importance, issues can fade (this possibility is discussed further in Chapter 5).

2. *Activists establish a new SMO that can assume ownership*. A familiar example is the emergence of Mothers Against Drunk Driving (MADD). Although drunk driving had a long history, MADD gave the issue not just new visibility, but a new frame as a threat to children menaced by drunk drivers. MADD lobbied legislators, observed courtroom proceedings, established local chapters around the country, and generally took control over what had been an ownerless issue.

3. *Existing SMOs assume ownership of the new issue*. This is what happened when stalking emerged as a new crime problem and the battered women's movement adopted the issue as its own (Lowney & Best, 1995). Over time, SMOs can become a familiar part of the landscape and run the risk of being taken for granted. Stalking gave the battered women's movement a fresh focus—an expanded domain—so that the movement found itself back in the spotlight. In turn, the movement was able to use its resources to successfully campaign for antistalking policies. This meant that the antistalking cause benefited from more prolonged attention than it would have received if it had not been adopted by new owners, even as the new owners also benefited through their association with a hot issue.

Ownership, then, affects the prospects of both an issue and the activists who promote it. Unless someone assumes ownership, it is hard for the social problems process to proceed; it is too easy for public attention to shift away as soon as the next new issue arrives on the scene. Owners are needed to tend the topic, to remind people of its importance, to revise their claims so that the topic remains fresh and interesting. But ownership also benefits the owners: their claims seem better established; their authority seems more legitimate; and as they become familiar figures with a larger network of social contacts, they can begin to transform themselves from outsider to insider claimsmakers.

ACTIVISTS: PRINCIPLES AND PRACTICALITIES

Discussions of social movements often emphasize their principled character. That is, they depict activists as individuals committed to a particular cause, seeking to promote a higher good. But sincerity is not enough. As claimsmakers who seek to influence the social problems process, activists need to convey their message to, and influence the behavior of, the media, the public, and policymakers. That is, they need to confront the practical problems posed by social movements (see Box 3.6).

This chapter has explored four such problems (see Figure 3.2). First, activists must develop effective frames; that is, they must construct their claims so that others will find them convincing, so that people will support the activists' SMOs. Principled statements that cannot persuade others threaten to stall the social problems process before it has really begun.

Figure 3.2 Activists' Concerns in Making Effective Claims

Framing: Developing a way of looking at the world that others will adopt

Resource Mobilization: Assembling money, people, skills, etc.

Opportunity Structures: Recognizing occasions when claims are more likely to succeed

Social Movements/ Activists' Claims

Ownership: A particular frame becomes recognized as the way to think about an issue, and a particular SMO becomes acknowledged as a leader on the issue

Box 3.6 Why Isn't the Gun Control Movement Stronger?

The United States experiences far higher rates of firearms-related deaths than rates in other countries. Many claimsmakers have argued that Americans have too many guns and that it is too easy for guns to fall into the wrong hands. The issue gets a lot of media attention, particularly after highly publicized episodes of gun violence. Public opinion polls seem to show that substantial majorities favor tougher gun laws. And yet there has not been a strong, national movement for gun control. Why not?

In part, gun control advocates have had difficulty devising an effective frame. For years, they defined the issue as one of crime control (keeping criminals from gaining access to guns), but this frame implied that gun control was a police matter, not something that required citizens to take action. During the 1990s, they sought to reframe gun control as a form of child protection, depicting gun violence as an "epidemic." This attracted more public support, but declining crime rates diluted the new frame's power. As a consequence, the gun control movement has had trouble mobilizing money, members, and other resources.

In addition, of course, gun control faces a well-organized countermovement, which frames the issue in terms of liberty. Pro-gun advocates argue that gun ownership is an individual right, guaranteed by the Constitution. There are a variety of advantages to joining the National Rifle Association that lead large numbers of gun owners to become members, and the NRA is a powerful voice—the owner of the pro-gun position. All of these become obstacles to a creating an effective gun control movement.

Source: Goss, 2006.

Second, activists must mobilize sufficient resources to promote their movement's goals. Activists who prove unable to attract and manage members, money, and other necessary resources probably will not be able to keep their SMOs functioning long enough for their cause to succeed.

Third, activists need to be able to recognize and figure out ways to take advantage of opportunities. Current events and the shifting political landscape can aid—or hinder—social movements. Activists need to be careful not to miss promising opportunities, just as they should avoid expending their resources when they have no chance to advance their cause.

Finally, activists can acquire and maintain ownership over an issue. Owning a social problem allows enduring influence, a means of keeping an issue—and the activists' leadership—visible, so that the activists' frames remain familiar and widely accepted, resources are easier to mobilize, and the activists stay in position to take advantage of whatever opportunities develop.

Although they are the most obvious examples of claimsmakers, activists are not the only people who promote social problems claims. They often acquire allies—claimsmakers who, in addition to their commitment to principles, bring special knowledge or expertise to the social problems process. These expert claimsmakers are discussed in Chapter 4.

MAKING CONNECTIONS

- *Through framing, resource mobilization, and taking advantage of opportunities, activists attract attention to their claims in order to establish ownership over a problem and its proposed solutions.*

- *As you read Chapter 5 on the media, you will learn why ownership of a problem helps win attention from media organizations.*

- *To establish effective frames, activists rely on focus groups, polls, and other tools to measure public reactions. You will learn more about public reactions in the social problems process in Chapter 6.*

CASE STUDY
Mobilizing against Homophobic Bullying

The 2010–11 academic year had barely begun when news media reported that a first-year college student had committed suicide (Foderaro & Hu, 2010). The student had had a sexual encounter with another male in his dorm room, and his roommate and another student had used a hidden camera to record the sex and live stream the video online. Before killing himself, the student posted a suicide note on his Facebook page.

The online elements made this a sensational story that attracted considerable media attention, and it created a cultural opportunity for claimsmakers who might incorporate this incident into their claims as a typifying example. But it was not immediately apparent which social problem the incident typified. Was this an instance of some sort of cyberproblem, an example of the ease with which even the most personal information can find its way onto the Internet, resulting in *online humiliation* or *cyberbullying* (J. Schwartz, 2010)? Or was it an instance of the larger problem of *bullying*, or of *youth suicide*? Or was the story's key element the student's sexuality, so that this was an instance of *gay youth suicide*, or *homophobic bullying*? Initially, claimsmakers for all of these problems spoke out about the incident, but within a few weeks, activists opposed to homophobic bullying emerged as the leading claimsmakers—in effect, the owners of the issue. (On the implications of the term *homophobic*, see Box 4.1 in the next chapter.)

All of these causes had claimsmaking histories; there were activists who already had been working to draw attention to each of these issues. All could use the student's suicide as a typifying example, but the case probably had greater rhetorical value for some claimsmakers than for others. Those concerned with cyberbullying, for instance, could point to other, perhaps even more sympathetic, typifying examples involving girls or young women (such as a girl driven to suicide after the mother of a former friend used a fictitious Facebook identity to pose as a male who befriended and then dumped the girl, or a young woman who killed herself after an ex-boyfriend circulated nude pictures she had taken with her cell phone and sent to him). Given the widespread assumption that females are more vulnerable and deserving of protection, such cases were at least as useful in framing cyberbullying as a problem. Similarly, bullying advocates often use typifying examples of the harms experienced by younger children (another group understood to be vulnerable and deserving protection); they might be less likely to highlight a college student's suicide.

On the other hand, in a society where a substantial minority of people continue to view homosexuality as a moral problem, the student's suicide offered a compelling example. The student was eighteen years old—an adult. He was engaging in consensual sex in his own dorm room. His privacy was invaded. In other words, he could easily be viewed as a victim, a sympathetic figure. Like hate crimes, homophobic bullying can be constructed in melodramatic terms, so that the audience is encouraged to identify with a vulnerable victim who is being exploited by villainous figures. The student's case allowed claimsmakers to attempt a sort of frame amplification by arguing that people who value privacy and who are opposed to bullying ought to sympathize with their cause, regardless of whether these people had reservations about homosexuality.

The student's suicide also boosted resource mobilization. The syndicated columnist Dan Savage launched the It Gets Better Project (www.itgetsbetter.org). Initially designed as a website where gay and lesbian adults could communicate with youths who might be experiencing homophobic bullying, the site allowed the adults to post videos that talked both about the challenges they faced as youths and the ways things had got better for them. The videos' message was intended to help prevent suicides by encouraging young viewers to hang in there, to convince them that their own lives would indeed get better. The project soon enlisted a broad variety of prominent people—gay and straight—from politics, entertainment, and business to post messages, thereby providing a means of mobilizing broad support for the cause.

The issue also invoked powerful emotions. The suicide of any young person strikes most people as a tragic waste, and the idea that the student could have been driven to kill himself by an invasion of his personal privacy outraged many people. Not just gays and lesbians, but also straight people found the story disturbing. The student's suicide set off a wave of media coverage and created a cultural opportunity for gay and lesbian activists. Their claims steered the public's attention, not just by successfully framing the incident as an instance of the problem of homophobic bullying, but by encouraging people outside the gay community to adopt that frame. Further, they were able to mobilize some of this concern to promote actions to help address the issue.

Questions

1. What does this case reveal about the ways activists can incorporate current events in their claims?

2. How did frames, resource mobilization, and opportunities reinforce one another in constructing claims based on the student's suicide?

3. Did it make a difference that gay and lesbian activists were able to assume ownership of this problem?

4

■

Experts as Claimsmakers

■

Colonial Massachusetts was established by Puritans, and ministers were key figures in that society. They saw evidence of God's hand everywhere in the world, and their sermons sometimes commented on current events, interpreting them in religious terms. A bad harvest might be evidence of God's wrath, and problems among people were caused by sin, by individuals breaking God's commandments. Virtually any event could be interpreted within this religious framework. Ministers, then, were colonial New England's principal experts; their theological training qualified them to explain and evaluate most aspects of life. Their religious frame was seen as authoritative because it was promoted by professionals representing the society's leading institution.

The ministers' religious perspective seems less authoritative today. In at least public discussions of social problems, modern Americans rarely speak of *sin* (and when politicians or even religious leaders do invoke such language, they often come under criticism). Rather, contemporary Americans are more comfortable with a kind of medical vocabulary; when talking about social problems, we are more likely to speak of *diseases*, *syndromes*, *disorders*, or *addictions*—words that seem grounded in medical, scientific classifications. Consider how contemporary discussions of Aquinas's classical list of the seven deadly sins often redefine these behaviors as medical problems; for example, lust might be characterized as *sexual addiction*, gluttony as *food addiction* or *compulsive eating*, anger as an *anger management* problem, and sloth as *chronic fatigue syndrome*. (At the same time, modern medicine sometimes seems to promote those same deadly sins by treating their absence as medical problems that also may require treatment; consider drugs to enhance sexual performance [lust], cosmetic surgery [pride, envy], liposuction [gluttony], or concerns about workaholism and type A personalities [sloth] or low self-esteem [pride].) At least when they talk about social issues, contemporary Americans are less likely to accept the judgments of religious leaders, and more likely to defer to doctors.

The declining influence of ministers and growing clout of doctors illustrate how constructions of social problems reflect shifting patterns of institutional influence. In societies where religious authorities hold sway, social problems often are discussed in religious language; where medical authorities are more influential, social problems tend to be understood in medical terms. At different times and in different places, ideas about which people with which sorts of knowledge ought to be considered experts vary. *Experts* are presumed to possess especially authoritative knowledge, and other people—including activists, the media, and policymakers—may defer to this expertise.

In short, experts rank among the most influential claimsmakers because they are thought to have special knowledge that qualifies them to interpret social problems. Some experts are what Chapter 3 referred to as *insider claimsmakers*; their status as experts can give them easier access to policymakers, so that they are part of the polity. This chapter examines the role of experts as claimsmakers in the contemporary social problems process. It begins by exploring the central place of medical authorities in constructing social problems, then turns to other sorts of experts.

MEDICALIZATION

Sociologists who have noted the increased use of medical language to characterize social problems speak of **medicalization** (Conrad, 2007), the process of defining troubling conditions as medical problems. A century ago, it was generally recognized that some people drank too much; that is, their drinking was blamed for causing problems at work, in their homes, and so on. The common label for these people was *drunkards* (Gusfield, 1967). Being a drunkard was seen as, if not a sin, at least a moral failing; drunkards were doing something they shouldn't do, and they needed to reform (the solution to being a drunkard often involved making a pledge to practice temperance; that is, the drunkard would promise to stop drinking).

Today, the term *drunkard* has virtually disappeared from our vocabulary. Of course, there are still people who drink too much, and whose drinking is thought to cause job problems, family problems, and so on. But we call these people *alcoholics,* and we speak of the *disease* of *alcoholism.* Alcoholics may receive *treatment,* often at *clinics,* where some of the costs are reimbursed by health insurance. In short, alcoholism has been medicalized, in that we now view it as a medical problem that should be addressed through medical solutions.

Consider another example: some students do not do well in school. Traditionally, those students were blamed for their poor performance: perhaps they were of lower intelligence, or perhaps they weren't trying hard enough. Today, claims suggest that poor performance at school may be caused by medicalized conditions, that these students have *learning disabilities* or *attention deficit hyperactivity disorder* (ADHD) (Conrad 2007; Erchak & Rosenfeld, 1989). Medical language—words such as *diagnosis, symptom,* or *therapy*—increasingly frames discussions of students' difficulties, and doctors now prescribe drugs to large numbers of children to help them become more attentive.

Why is medicalization important? There are two obvious ways it makes a difference. The first is that medicalization seems to shift responsibility away from the individual. In our culture, we routinely hold individuals responsible for what we view as deliberate behavior—acts that people choose to perform. Drunkards were once seen as weak because they gave in to drink, and poor students used to be viewed as lazy; in both cases, the individuals were held responsible for their own problems. In contrast, we generally do not hold people responsible for their illnesses; we don't blame them for becoming sick. Therefore, saying that people have the disease of alcoholism or a learning disability means that they shouldn't be blamed for their problems, that they merit sympathy and support, rather than criticism.

A second consequence of medicalizing a problem is that it provides a familiar frame—sometimes called the **medical model**—for thinking about the issue. Medical problems are described as diseases, disorders, syndromes, or disabilities. The people with these problems are ill; they display symptoms. They need to become patients, who can receive treatment from medical personnel—doctors, nurses, therapists—who often work in hospitals or clinics, and who can be reimbursed through the patient's health insurance. In other words, medicalization is a claim arguing that some problem should be owned and controlled by medical experts and organizations.

Medicalization, then, frames troubling conditions in particular ways (see Box 4.1). At first glance, our culture seems to construct sins or crimes differently from illness: sinners and criminals are held responsible, blamed for their actions, and punished; people who are ill are not blamed and receive treatment instead. However, the medical model also focuses on the individual rather than the larger society. In a medicalized view, people have diseases or syndromes that lead them to drink too much, to eat too much, and so on; and they must confront and overcome these problems through healthy behavior. Medicalization shifts attention away from the ways in which larger social arrangements, such as poverty, shape these troubling conditions.

Medicalization grew markedly during the twentieth century. In part, this shift reflected dramatic changes in the practice of medi-

---

Box 4.1 Medicalizing Opposition by Using the Label *Phobia*

A phobia is an exaggerated or irrational fear. For instance, claustrophobia is a fear of enclosed spaces, so that a person affected by this condition might be distressed about being in a closet or small room with the door closed. Originally, phobias were identified and classified by psychiatrists; however, the suffix *phobia* is easily attached to new root words, making it possible for anyone to create new labels.

Consider the terms *homophobia*, *Islamophobia*, and *vegaphobia*, used to denote opposition to or criticism of, respectively, homosexuals, Muslims, and vegans. The three terms suggest medicalization, that they may have been coined by psychiatrists as diagnoses, and that they designate irrational fears. *Homophobia* does seem to have been coined by some psychiatrists and psychologists—although it was quickly adopted by gay and lesbian activists—but it is not a formal psychiatric diagnosis; *Islamophobia* became a common term in post-9/11 discussions of prejudice against Muslims; and *vegaphobia* is a term that seems to have been invented by two British sociologists.

Defining one's opponents as suffering from phobias serves to discredit their positions: theirs is not a form of reasoned opposition rooted in different values, or even a form of discrimination, a construction invoked in the labels *heterosexism* or *speciesism* (prejudice and discrimination against, respectively, homosexuals and animals). Rather, defining problems as phobias suggests that those using the terms are on the side of medical science, while the positions of those they label can be discounted as irrational.

Source: Cole & Morgan, 2011.

---

cine: doctors and hospitals became subject to tighter professional standards, so the quality of care rose; at the same time, advances in medical science led to new medications and treatments. All this meant that the chances of medical care actually helping patients rose sharply; people began to expect more of medical authorities, and the prestige and authority of physicians rose.

The rising stature of medicine encouraged the expansion of medical authority into a broader domain of social problems. In particular, psychiatrists (who were trained as physicians) began to claim that many troubling behaviors—including juvenile delinquency, unconventional sexual activity, drug addiction, and crime—should be recognized as symptoms of psychiatric problems. After World War II, the American Psychiatric Association began developing its *Diagnostic and Statistical Manual of Mental Disorders* (the so-called *DSM*), a huge catalog of all recognized mental disorders, which has continued to expand with each new edition (Kirk & Kutchins, 1992). The growing number of available diagnoses means that more and more behaviors can be understood in medical terms.

In addition to psychiatrists, whose medical training clearly placed them within medicine, practitioners in a variety of other quasi-medical professions adopted the language of *disease, symptom,* and *treatment.* Among these were clinical psychologists, licensed clinical social workers, and many others, including some with little or no professional training. Drug treatment, for instance, increasingly was provided by "professional ex-s [sic]"—recovered drug users who did not necessarily have professional credentials, but who were employed by drug treatment centers to lead therapeutic groups and who used medical language to describe what they did (J. D. Brown, 1991).

Often medicalization consists of little more than adopting a medical vocabulary. Take what is called the disease of *alcoholism*: its symptoms are drinking and getting into trouble at work, at home, and so on; there are no clear biological symptoms that distinguish alcoholics from nonalcoholic drinkers (Appleton, 1995). Similarly, treatment for alcoholism is to get people with drinking problems to choose to drink less (most often, total abstinence is recommended). The leading program for dealing with alcoholism, Alcoholics Anonymous (AA), is a resolutely amateur operation. There are no professionals; all of AA's members are people who identify themselves as recovering alcoholics. Individuals attend meetings with fellow alcoholics and discuss AA's twelve-step program for achieving sobriety.

AA insists that alcoholism is a disease, but that the cure is to stop drinking, continue attending AA meetings, and follow the Twelve Steps. Note that AA's solution for alcoholism—that is, helping the individual with a drinking problem to make a commitment to stop drinking—is not all that different from the way drunkards were expected to reform by taking a pledge of sobriety, although the language of medicine seems to impart special authority to treatment as a solution. The twelve-step model has been adapted to help people deal with a variety of troubling behaviors—including drug abuse, overeating, and gambling—that have also been characterized as addictions or diseases.

In short, various medical authorities, with very different sorts of credentials, claim ownership of many contemporary social problems. As noted in Chapter 3, ownership can bring important benefits. Experts who gain ownership of a social problem usually gain a good deal: their social visibility and prestige rises, they become more powerful, and typically they stand to benefit financially from the increased business that people afflicted with the problem bring to them. This means that experts often have a vested interest in promoting claims that depict social problems from their perspective.

In a classic constructionist case study, for example, Stephen Pfohl (1977) argued that pediatric radiologists played a leading role in bringing attention to battered child syndrome—what would later be called *child abuse*. Initially this problem was typified in terms of physical injuries to children too young to explain how they had been hurt. Pediatric radiologists—specialists in interpreting children's X-rays—argued that they could distinguish fractures caused by accidents from those caused by abuse. These claims not only promised to improve the protection of vulnerable children, but also gave pediatric radiologists—who represented a small, relatively low-prestige medical specialty—ownership of a life-threatening disease, so the specialty's status rose. Expert claimsmakers often experience such gains, and thus wind up doing well by doing good.

Experts often seek to defend their professional turf and even expand their domain of ownership. The process may be gradual. Consider the changing scope of pediatrics (Pawluch, 1996). When this medical specialty emerged in the early twentieth century, pediatricians focused their efforts on problems associated with infant feeding; the milk supply was often tainted, causing many infants to become seriously ill. However, improved techniques for managing the purity of the milk supply soon made infant feeding much safer, so the major service that pediatricians had been providing was becoming less needed. In response, pediatricians began to expand their domain to emphasize the treatment of, first, other childhood diseases, and then normal, healthy childhood development. As birth rates fell, of course, there were fewer children for pediatricians to treat, but the specialists began to extend their services to treating patients in adolescence and even early adulthood.

These efforts need not be seen as cynical and self-serving. Experts generally believe that they have valuable knowledge and offer useful services, and they are continually looking for new opportunities to apply their expertise. In periods when their services are already in high demand, they have less time to extend their domain, but when business is slack, the prospect of attacking new problems becomes much more attractive. In this way, professional domains expand and the professionals' interests are advanced.

Ideally, experts' gains can be consolidated into institutionalized ownership. For instance, rising health care costs increasingly require patients to have medical insurance. But what sorts of treatments should health insurance cover? Professionals who provide different treatments want medical insurance to cover their services, so that more patients will seek those services. Thus, the federal government's decision to define alcohol and drug problems as medical problems, and to require health insurance programs to cover some of the costs of their treatment, institutionalized these experts as owners of the alcohol problem (Weisner & Room, 1984). As Chapter 3 noted, owners have advantages in promoting their constructions of social problems; when ownership is coupled with such experts' institutionalized arrangements, experts' authority becomes entrenched.

In recent years, medicalization has taken new directions, with troubling conditions becoming subjects of **biomedicalization** (Clarke, Shim, Mamo, Fosket, & Fishman, 2003). Experts argue that biological processes are the root cause of many troubling conditions, which means that effective solutions must then address biology. For instance, the scientific revolution in genetics has led to claims that it will soon be possible to identify particular genes that cause various troubling conditions. Clearly, genetic anomalies cause some medical disorders, such as Down syndrome. But biomedical proponents argue that it will soon be possible to identify the genetic roots of all manner of behaviors, such as homosexuality or alcoholism, and research funding increasingly supports biomedical studies (see Box 4.2). This assumption that biology is at the root of many troubling conditions also fosters **pharmaceuticalization**, the process of defining prescription drugs as the solution (Abraham, 2010). Some of these claims may be borne out; others may prove false. At least for the foreseeable future, however, medicalization is likely to remain our society's leading form of expert claimsmaking.

THE ROLE OF SCIENCE

Medical authority may be seen as a subcategory of a broader form of expertise: science. As with medicine, the advances made possible by the expansion of science, particularly during the past two centuries, have given scientists considerable authority in our culture. Society has been transformed by the growth in scientific knowledge; think of the Industrial Revolution, the exploitation of new forms of

Box 4.2 The Various Meanings of Genetic Information

Genetic research can—but need not—foster medicalization. Take depression. Depression has been thoroughly medicalized; it is understood to be a disease, and its treatment is in the hands of medical professionals. Evidence that there are genetic markers linked to depression simply biomedicalizes the diagnosis. But compare the case of homosexuality. Homosexuality was once considered a psychiatric problem, but since the 1970s, it has been demedicalized, so that it is understood to be a difference, but not a disease. The fact that researchers have found evidence of genetic markers for homosexuality has not led to biomedicalization.

Or take findings that there are genetic markers for susceptibility to various chemicals. When the chemicals in question are pharmaceuticals, this is seen as a medical problem: physicians need to be concerned if a patient has a genetic marker that might make prescribing particular drugs dangerous. However, when the chemicals to which people are susceptible are environmental chemicals (such as those used in manufacturing), evidence suggesting that some people have a genetic marker for susceptibility is viewed, not as a medical problem, but as a risk to be governed by environmental policy. In other words, genetic evidence can be seen as supporting an existing medical framework (as in the case of depression or pharmaceutical sensitivity), but it is not in itself sufficient to medicalize a problem (so that evidence that there is a genetic component to homosexuality or susceptibility to environmental chemicals has not been used to justify classifying those conditions as diseases).

Source: Shostak, Conrad, & Horwitz, 2008.

energy (steam, electricity, petroleum), faster transportation, speedier communication, and so on. Increased scientific knowledge made these changes possible.

Science depends on an appreciation of evidence. A scientific theory must generate falsifiable predictions; that is, those predictions must be able to be tested, and if they are proved wrong, the theory is rejected. Scientists do research to produce evidence that can support or challenge their theories' predictions; the more supportive evidence they find, the more confidence scientists have in their theories. This system of reasoning has proved very powerful and has provided the foundation for all sorts of technological and medical advances, and in our society scientists are considered to have considerable authority when speaking about matters for which they have gathered evidence.

This is not to say that scientific evidence is infallible. Science is socially constructed; it is one of the ways people make sense of the world. To be sure, we have considerable confidence in well-established scientific findings, but it takes time for findings to become well established. Research can be flawed, and evidence can be incomplete or incorrectly interpreted. Scientists may debate issues among themselves, questioning one another's reasoning and evidence. Scientific progress can be a slow process; such debates can continue for years, even decades, until the evidence compiled becomes sufficiently compelling for a consensus to emerge among scientists.

Unfortunately, the deliberate pace of science is not well suited to news media eager to report on dramatic scientific breakthroughs. For instance, the media may publicize reports of the initial study on a particular topic, even though that research may eventually prove to have been flawed. A dramatic example was the media's reaction to a 1989 report by two researchers who said that they had observed a cold-fusion reaction in their laboratory. The implications were staggering—harnessing cold fusion would provide limitless, inexpensive energy—and the media began to speculate about the social changes this discovery would bring. Alas, other scientists soon concluded that the researchers had misinterpreted their results—that they had not found a way to produce cold fusion—and the media quickly dropped the topic.

Scientific experts' claims derive much of their rhetorical power from the understanding that scientists have special knowledge and access to particularly strong evidence, so their views deserve respect. The media's tendency to treat the results of a single piece of research as definitive leads to confusion in the case of ongoing scientific debates. Until sufficient evidence becomes available, scientists— like other experts—do not necessarily agree. Their evidence and interpretations may differ, even conflict. The press, the general public, and policymakers often find such disagreements frustrating, because they tend to look to scientists for not just authoritative, but correct, information. Apparent contradictions call scientists' authority into question.

For example, one week the media might report that a medical journal has published a research report concluding that drinking alcohol increases the risk of contracting a particular disease. The following week the media might announce that another group of researchers has concluded that moderate drinking improves one's health. What should people think? It is possible that both reports are correct—that is, that drinking raises the risk of contracting a particular disease but generally improves health. Or perhaps one of the studies is flawed (or even both are flawed). Over time, additional research is likely to lead to an eventual scientific consensus, but it is important to recognize that disagreements are normal within science and many other expert communities. Experts may disagree about which are the important questions to ask, about the best way to arrive at answers to those questions, about how to interpret the available evidence, and so on (see Box 4.3).

In general, research questions and answers are most clear-cut in the physical sciences (such as physics and chemistry), less so in the biological sciences (such as medicine), and the least so in the social sciences. The physical sciences have fewer disagreements about what constitutes compelling evidence, and debates among physical scientists often can be settled decisively; in contrast, social scientists often cannot agree about what constitutes convincing evidence. In addition, it is important to appreciate that disagreements among scientists can center around very different sorts of questions,

Box 4.3 The Path toward Scientific Consensus

Achieving scientific consensus is a process. Findings from a single study may be sufficient to produce press headlines, but they are usually insufficient to convince other scientists, who at least want to replicate the study, and may favor continuing to explore alternative theories. Researchers track citation patterns—which studies are cited by other researchers—to measure the level of consensus: when consensus is high, researchers tend to cite the same key studies; but when consensus is low, scientists in different camps may cite only various studies that support their interpretations. Over time—and the process can take decades—consensus tends to emerge, as the evidence for one interpretation comes to be generally accepted.

Topics that the public may imagine are hotly debated may in fact show high degrees of scientific consensus. The tobacco industry spent decades funding research, first to challenge claims about tobacco's carcinogenic effects and later to prove that cigarettes could be made safer; their campaign slowed—but eventually failed to prevent—the formation of a consensus among scientitsts. Similarly, in spite of news coverage that sometimes suggests that these are topics of disagreement, there is considerable consensus among scientists that the earth's climate is warming and that this change is caused at least in part by human activities, that cell phones and coffee drinking have few if any cancer-causing effects, and that vaccinations do not cause autism (see this chapter's case study). What claimsmakers and the media say about science is not necessarily what scientists themselves are saying.

Source: Shwed & Bearman, 2010.

and that the authority of science depends on the sort of question being asked.

Consider, for instance, the debate over global warming. At the most basic level is the question of whether the planet's temperature is indeed rising. Scientists have devised various ways of measuring temperatures going back through time. Although there may be some disputes about the accuracy of particular measurements, or about which methods of measuring temperature changes are most accurate, these are relatively technical matters, and there is considerable scientific consensus that cycles of global warming and global cooling have occurred in the past and that temperatures have risen about 0.74°C over the past one hundred years or so. Accurately measuring changes in temperature presents a relatively clear-cut research challenge—the sort of question that scientists are clearly qualified to answer. It is, of course, more difficult to predict what will happen in the future, although again there is fairly widespread consensus that temperatures are likely to continue to rise over the next century (but considerable disagreement about how much they are likely to rise, with estimates ranging from 1.8°C to 4.0°C).

A second issue—over which there is more debate—concerns the causes of global warming. Although some argue that the current global warming may be a natural process—just part of the long-term cycle of planetary heating and cooling—most scientists agree that at least some of the warming is due to humans' impact on the planet. Most commonly these claims focus on the role of greenhouse gases (for instance, emissions of carbon dioxide from vehicles and smokestacks) in retaining heat in the atmosphere. Note that these explanations are not mutually exclusive; perhaps the planet would be warming naturally in any case, but human activities are exacerbating the trend. At this level, the scientific issues are not as straightforward, and even experts who agree that global warming is occurring may disagree over the extent to which people's activities contribute to this process.

The debate's third level is far more contentious. Even if we assume for the moment that everyone agrees that human activity plays a substantial role in causing global warming, what should be done? Here, debates can address many different issues, including what the consequences of global warming might be, what sorts of policies might reduce global warming, what the costs of those policies might be, whether the prospective benefits justify those costs, who should bear the costs, and so on. At this stage, purely scientific issues are less central; science may offer fairly compelling evidence about the extent and causes of global warming, but scientific knowledge cannot specify the correct course of policy. Consider nuclear weapons, for example: scientists were able to design and build nuclear weapons, but the decisions to use—or not use—those weapons were made by political leaders, not scientists. Scientific knowledge ordinarily is not sufficient to set social policy.

In short, we need to understand that, when scientists participate in debates over social issues, the relevance of their expertise varies, depending on the particular questions being considered. While people—including some scientists—may like to imagine that scientific findings are sufficient to guide policy, in practice policymaking is shaped by other considerations, especially values (Pielke, 2007). In addressing a question such as how much the planet's temperature has increased during the past century, scientific expertise is likely to play the central role. However, many commentators would argue that science cannot provide authoritative answers to questions such as whether the prospective benefits of implementing a particular policy to reduce greenhouse gases will justify the policy's costs, or how the costs of controlling emissions should be distributed among richer and poorer countries. The willingness of audiences to grant authority to scientists is likely to depend on how relevant they believe the experts' knowledge to be.

Contemporary debates over scientific authority often focus on constructions of risk. The modern fascination with risk can be dated to the 1960s, when the surgeon general announced that smoking was hazardous to health, activist Ralph Nader drew attention to unsafe automobiles, and author Rachel Carson warned that pesticides were causing significant environmental damage (Gunter, 2005). These highly visible claims led to concerns about other risks, which in turn produced all manner of warnings—about the dangers of cholesterol, secondhand smoke, toxic waste, and so on.

Such claims often couple scientific evidence (suggesting, for example, that a particular chemical may be carcinogenic) with warnings that the danger is widespread and the issue urgent. Increasingly, the media cover scientists' warnings that this or that condition poses risks to individuals' health, to environmental safety, and so on. Although the evidence regarding some risks—such as the link between smoking and lung cancer—is overwhelming, scientists disagree about the extent and significance of other risks.

It can take time for scientists to agree on assessments of risk. The most compelling scientific evidence comes from experiments, but it is usually impossible to design experiments to study risk. We cannot take identical groups of infants and make sure that they have identical experiences going through life—except that we can expose the experimental group to a particular risk and keep the control group from being exposed to that risk. Such a study might produce very strong evidence, but it would be time-consuming, expensive, and unethical. In practice, researchers must settle for much weaker evidence; they might, for example, identify people exposed to a particular risk, try to match them with similar folks who have not been exposed to that risk, and then study whether the two groups have different rates of particular diseases. It is always possible to challenge the results of such studies—for instance, were the two groups matched on every relevant variable?—and it takes a great deal of evidence (such as the countless studies on smokers' health) to make a convincing case.

It is difficult for nonscientists—a category that includes most activists, members of the media, the general public, and policymakers—to assess claims about risk that refer to scientific evidence. Debates over social problems often ignore such issues as comparative risks (for instance, the number of people at risk, the number of people likely to be harmed, and so on). All kinds of activities (for example, driving to work) carry risks. Often we take these risks for granted and ignore them, even though they may be far greater than are the heavily publicized dangers of, say, exposure to secondhand smoke.

Scientific evidence—particularly calculations of risk—are not well understood, and such issues often lead to confusion in the face of what is thought to be expert claimsmaking.

EVIDENCE, INTERESTS, AND ADVOCACY

A major reason why people defer to experts is their presumption that experts command knowledge that other people don't have. Although all knowledge is socially constructed, we consider experts' knowledge to be more likely to be accurate than gossip, rumor, or other less authoritative sorts of knowledge that, we know from experience, often prove to be wrong. Thus, we tend to consider expert knowledge to be relatively correct. We defer to medical authorities because we assume that they know how to diagnose diseases, are able to understand the causes and workings of those diseases, and can recommend the best possible treatments. Similarly, we presume that scientists have done careful research and compiled evidence that offers the best available information about how the world works.

In other words, we turn to experts for sound information based on high-quality evidence, and experts' status as relatively authoritative claimsmakers depends on such understanding. Experts are commonly assumed to be impartial judges—their medical diagnoses or scientific findings grounded in facts rather than opinions. Yet experts often have an interest in promoting claims, and when they become advocates for particular positions or policies, they are not necessarily guided solely by their expert knowledge.

We have already noted that experts stand to benefit from the ownership of social problems; recall how the status of pediatric radiologists rose after they drew attention to battered child syndrome. Experts also may have social ties to parties with interests in social issues. Scientific research can be extremely expensive, and many scientists derive funding from corporations, government agencies, and so on. These funders may have an interest in the researchers' findings. For example, both medical researchers and their pharmaceutical company sponsors may have financial stakes in a new drug, and they may hope that the drug proves safe and effective, just as scientists employed by a corporation may be under pressure to affirm that the firm's waste disposal practices are safe. Other scientists may be closely associated with particular social movements, such as environmentalism.

Even though we tend to idealize scientists as objective, impartial observers, they may have allegiances that help shape their conclusions. Some legal trials feature psychiatrists hired as expert witnesses by the prosecution and the defense, who testify, respectively, that the defendant's mental state was such that the trials should or should not proceed. The point is not that social ties make science illegitimate—a very large share of scientists have such commitments—but that scientific knowledge is not produced or disseminated in a social vacuum.

In some cases, scientists' allegiances may be to the particular perspectives or approaches that characterize their disciplines. For instance, sociologists and other social scientists also act as expert claimsmakers. Just as medical authorities bring their professional training to bear when they medicalize troubling conditions by characterizing them using the language of diseases, symptoms, and other medical concepts, social scientists have their own orientations and conceptual tools. Economists, for example, argue that people can be understood as rational actors who make choices to maximize their own satisfaction. This proves to be a powerful underlying assumption, in that it can be extended to analyze all manner of choices. Thus, economists tend to see social problems as the products of particular choices, and to promote policies that will encourage people to make particular choices. For example, one way to discourage smoking is to raise tobacco taxes; if tobacco is more expensive, at least some people may choose to stop smoking.

Sociologists, too, apply their discipline's perspective to the analysis of social problems in their works (including this book).

Sociologists argue that people shape one another's actions, and that social problems are products of particular social arrangements. Thus, where a psychiatrist may approach a social problem in terms of individuals whose thinking is disordered because they suffer from a syndrome of some sort, or an economist may see it in terms of arrangements that reward some choices more than others, sociologists are more likely to point to the way culture and social structure constrain and shape people's activities. C. Wright Mills (1959) called this mode of thinking the *sociological imagination* (discussed further in Chapter 5). This book, for instance, emphasizes understanding the social problems process through which actors socially construct social problems.

In other cases, experts may have allegiances to particular ideological positions. Liberal and conservative experts can approach social problems in very different ways: they focus on different causes, and they recommend different solutions. So-called think tanks—private nonprofit organizations dedicated to policy analysis and advocacy—often have an ideology that shapes their experts' recommendations (see Box 4.4). These experts maintain connections with media outlets and politicians that share their ideological orientations, so advocates from different positions have access to expert knowledge that can be used to buttress their claims.

Although we might like to imagine that experts are completely independent, impartial authorities, without interests or ideological commitments, this perfect objectivity is, in practice, impossible to achieve. Experts are part of the larger social order. At a minimum, they believe in the value of their professions: psychiatrists consider psychiatry a valuable perspective, just as sociologists promote the value of the sociological imagination. Experts can further be expected to believe that the problems they have chosen to study are important and worthy of their attention and that the solutions they have been working on are promising. They may also have more obvious interests (such as a financial stake in the outcome of their research) or ideological preferences. Such social connections do not

Box 4.4 Think Tanks and Officials

Think tanks are organizations of experts designed to promote claims and policy responses. Typically, they represent particular ideological positions; thus, the Brookings Institution often adopts liberal stands, the American Enterprise Institute and the Heritage Foundation promote conservative positions, and the Cato Institute presents libertarian views. Think tanks often employ full-time resident scholars, and may have affiliated experts who work at universities or elsewhere. It is not uncommon for the people who work at think tanks to be former or future government officials.

Claimsmaking is a central purpose of think tanks. Their experts try to identify troubling conditions, construct them as particular sorts of social problems, and devise proposals for policies that might solve those problems. Think tanks devote considerable energy to drawing attention to their claims: they publish books, pamphlets, and magazines; their experts try to place pieces in leading newspapers or make appearances on television programs; and major think tanks operate websites and send out daily e-mail summaries of their activities. In addition, think tank experts operate as insider claimsmakers, trying to bring their concerns to the attention of legislators and officials in government agencies, so as to directly influence the policy process. Many of these experts benefit from being well connected to both the press and policymakers, so that their views are often taken into account, although their ideological opponents may dismiss their recommendations as being predictable and driven by ideology.

Source: Weidenbaum, 2009.

necessarily mean that the experts are wrong, but they do suggest that experts may be less than perfectly objective, and may think less critically when they confront ideas that fit their prejudices, so their claims should not be automatically accepted.

Expert knowledge is imperfect because it is produced by scientists, physicians, and other experts who are themselves actors in the larger society. It should be no surprise that experts' ideas evolve as new information becomes available. But it takes time for novel ideas to emerge and gain acceptance. As evidence accumulates, consensus is likely to develop, but this process cannot occur overnight. This is why expert knowledge is best understood as a special type of claim, part of the larger social problems process.

OFFICIALS AS EXPERT CLAIMSMAKERS

Another important category of expert claimsmakers consists of officials, particularly those employed by government agencies, such as the Centers for Disease Control and Prevention (CDC) or the Environmental Protection Agency (EPA). Such agencies have various responsibilities: they may compile information (collecting data to measure the crime rate, the unemployment rate, and so on); they may administer regulations (regarding workplace safety, pollution, or other issues); they may fund research through grants to experts outside the government; they may disseminate information to the citizenry; and so on. The work of many agencies bears upon one or more social problems. Because the federal government spends billions on the budgets of its various agencies, these officials can draw upon substantial resources. Usually they are able to compile more and better information about troubling conditions than unofficial claimsmakers can, giving officials' claims special authority in many social problems debates. Official agencies often achieve a level of ownership for social problems (see Box 4.5).

Agencies compete with one another for budget allocations and other scarce resources. Often multiple agencies have an interest in the same social problem. For instance, alcohol issues are the concern of several federal agencies: the Bureau of Alcohol, Tobacco, Firearms and Explosives (ATF); the National Institute on Alcohol Abuse and Alcoholism (NIAAA); the National Highway Traffic Safety Administration (NHTSA), which is concerned with alcohol-related

Box 4.5 Officials, Hedgehogs, and Foxes

Philosophers sometimes distinguish between two ways of think-ing, characterized by the metaphorical categories *hedgehogs* and *foxes*. Hedgehogs know one big thing—that is, they are guided by some particular idea. Think of Marxists or free market capitalists, or Freudians, fundamentalists, or feminists; each has a relatively complex ideology that can be applied to identify the causes of all sorts of social problems, and to derive solutions that address those problems. Experts tend to be hedgehogs; for instance, economists or psychiatrists can bring their professional ideologies to bear on all sorts of topics. In contrast, foxes are said to know many little things. That is, foxes have less allegiance to any single idea; they are more flexible, borrowing as convenient from different sources. Calling officials *pragmatic* implies that they are foxes—more inter-ested in finding workable solutions than in maintaining a logically consistent stance. We can think of hedgehogs and foxes as adopting two very different styles for constructing social policies.

Officials must devise all sorts of policies to address all sorts of problems. What's the best way to reduce crime, or boost the economy? In practice, none of these choices is likely to work per-fectly, although some may work better than others. Although officials sometimes promote particular interpretations with hedgehoglike intensity, the evidence suggests that, in many cases, the fox's flex-ibility is better able to accommodate the complexity of social issues.

Source: Tetlock, 2005.

traffic fatalities; and on and on. Imagine how many federal agencies must be concerned with any particular aspect of racial inequality. Just as social movement organizations find themselves competing with one another, officials—at least some of the time—view other agencies as competitors, both for resources and for ownership of particular social issues.

Protecting and, if possible, expanding an agency's turf becomes a central concern for officials, and claimsmaking provides one weapon for bureaucratic infighting. That is, drawing attention to a particular troubling condition, devising a program to deal with the problem, and then administering that program can serve two ends. On the one hand, it is easy to imagine that most officials are sincere, that they have joined an agency because they believe that it does important, valuable work. Like other claimsmakers, officials probably believe their own rhetoric and adopt the frames they promote. At the same time, officials have instrumental reasons to promote claims: successful claimsmaking is likely to serve the agency's interests, to increase its power, influence, and budget. Whatever their convictions, officials often have an interest in the claims they promote. For example, officials of the U.S. Bureau of Narcotics undoubtedly saw marijuana as a dangerous drug when they first called for a federal law against it in the 1930s, but that law also helped protect the bureau from further budget cuts (Dickson, 1968).

Officials may recognize that their agencies could address certain additional troubling conditions if they could help launch the social problems process. Happily, agencies often control significant, flexible resources that can be used to jump-start the claimsmaking process. In the 1960s, for instance, the U.S. Children's Bureau (CB) was under fire from critics and losing control of some programs that were being shifted to other agencies (Nelson, 1984). At the same time, CB officials had long been in contact with the American Humane Association, an organization that had historically been concerned with the physical abuse of children. The CB began funding the research that drew national attention to what was initially called *battered child syndrome*, soon to be renamed *child abuse* (Pfohl, 1977). Child abuse became a visible, dramatic subject of considerable public concern, and in the process helped restore the CB as an important agency of the federal government. As an owner of the child abuse problem, the CB could extend its programs—funding further research, helping develop legislation requiring doctors and other professionals to report child abuse, and so on.

Although the expert claimsmakers in these examples were federal officials, analogous processes can occur in state or local governments, wherever officials become involved in drawing attention to troubling conditions. In some cases, national attention on a problem may lead local officials to call for action in their communities; in other locales, officials may be slower to acknowledge that the problem exists in—and requires action in—their jurisdictions. The policies of different cities toward homelessness, for instance, depend on how local officials respond to the issue (Bogard, 2003). In other cases, claimsmaking by officials may focus on purely local issues—such as whether an old building should be demolished to permit new development, or be preserved as part of the community's historical heritage (Lofland, 2003).

Officials working in government agencies usually have special knowledge or expertise that justifies their participation in claimsmaking. They are insiders, and their activities often occur behind the scenes, out of the public view. In sharp contrast are the claimsmaking activities of elected officials—presidents, senators, and the like—who may seize upon an issue and become active claimsmakers. These officials may lack special expertise, but their visible positions make it much easier for them to attract media attention and help publicize a cause.

EXPERT CLAIMSMAKERS IN THE SOCIAL PROBLEMS PROCESS

Chapter 3 explored the role of activists and social movements in claimsmaking; this chapter has concentrated on the claimsmaking of experts—particularly medical authorities, scientists, and public officials. In many cases, claimsmaking campaigns feature alliances between activists and experts. Activists often contribute enthusiasm,

Box 4.6 Are Experts Enough?

Think tanks are what sociologists call *nonmembership advocacy organizations* (NMAOs). Whereas social movements can argue that they represent the views of their members, NMAOs' influence is based on their expertise. Some critics have worried that NMAOs discourage citizen involvement in social issues, making debates and the policymaking process less democratic, as experts push ordinary people aside.

In practice, NMAOs and membership-based SMOs coexist and complement one another; when a social movement is growing, it tends to add both more SMOs and more NMAOs. Effective claims-making campaigns can benefit from both. The media are more likely to cover a cause that seems to have both popular support and the backing of experts. Policymakers understand that most issues are complex, and they depend upon experts' knowledge to help them shape policies. Whereas SMOs suggest that a cause has moral legitimacy (that is, that many people want policymakers to do something to address the troubling condition), NMAOs can provide expert understandings regarding the nature of a problem, its causes, and the likely effects of different courses of action.

Effective claimsmaking campaigns, then, tend to result in alliances among activists who can mobilize broad support, experts who can provide convincing evidence, media that can draw public attention to the issue, and policymakers who can promote particular solutions.

Source: Walker, McCarthy, & Baumgartner, 2011.

passion, and whatever organizational resources their movements may control, whereas experts provide authoritative knowledge (see Box 4.6). (This is obviously an oversimplification: many activists become quite knowledgeable, and experts can become highly dedicated to claimsmaking campaigns.)

Knowledge is an important commodity in claimsmaking. Remember that social problems claims begin with grounds statements—that is, statements about the facts concerning the troubling condition. When claimsmakers are trying to draw attention to a neglected condition—one that hasn't attracted much attention—often they discover that little information is available and no experts are studying the problem yet. One solution is for activists to begin to collect their own information. For instance, it was only after gay and lesbian activists in some cities tried to gather reports of homosexuals who had been assaulted that official efforts to collect hate crime statistics started (Jenness & Grattet, 2001). Similarly, residents living near toxic waste sites may begin to collect their own evidence of health problems as a way of arousing concern about the risks they face (P. Brown, 1992). In such cases, amateurs try to generate the sort of knowledge that experts have failed to collect, in order to fill what would otherwise be a gap in their claims. Figure 4.1 illustrates

Figure 4.1 Experts' Role in the Social Problems Process

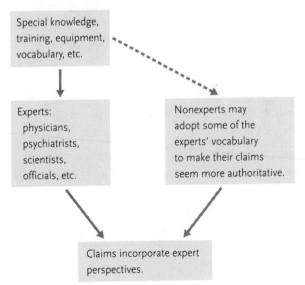

how both trained professionals and those without formal training as experts can make use of professional knowledge when making claims.

Just as activist claimsmakers must be alert to the responses of others—particularly the media, the public, and policymakers—so, too, must experts be concerned with feedback from other actors in the social problems process. Because experts are likely to consider the knowledge that they contribute to the social problems process especially valuable, they may be disappointed that their statements are not more influential. Audiences may have trouble interpreting what experts have to say, particularly when the experts present their findings using a professional, technical vocabulary. To bridge the gap, experts may discover that they need to popularize their work, to translate their findings into lay language.

Another problem is that audiences may have impossibly high expectations for experts' contributions; as we have suggested, experts may add to our understanding of a troubling social condition, but their knowledge usually is not sufficient to identify policies that can make the problem disappear. Ultimately, whether experts' claims— or, for that matter, the claims of activists—are widely understood depends on the treatment they receive in the media.

Making Connections

- *The role of experts in the policymaking process is discussed further in Chapter 7.*

- *The media rely on experts to make claims about social problems. In the next chapter you will learn how experts and the media collaborate in the social problems process.*

- *In Chapter 9, the role of experts in evaluating the outcomes of social problems and making new claims about problems will be discussed.*

CASE STUDY
THE AUTISM EPIDEMIC AND DISPUTES
OVER EXPERTISE

In recent decades, a rapidly growing proportion of young children has been diagnosed with autism, a cognitive disorder that affects a person's ability to interact and communicate with others. These diagnoses begin to be made around the child's first birthday because it is difficult to assess cognitive functioning much earlier. The news that autism diagnoses have become much more common has led many people to search for the cause of the increase, and the fact that childhood vaccinations are often given around the first birthday made some suspect that vaccines might be causing autism (Offit, 2008).

Suspicion of vaccines has a long history, and every vaccine produces a small percentage of adverse reactions among those vaccinated (Heller, 2008). In addition, there have been popular movements by patients, their relatives, and others campaigning to draw attention to particular diseases and their causes (e.g., ACT UP members working on HIV/AIDS, participants in the pink ribbon campaign against breast cancer, or the neighborhood activists who drew attention to the health hazards at the Love Canal). Sociologists noted the rise of "popular epidemiology"—activists' efforts to document health risks (P. Brown, 1992). These conditions made it relatively easy to mount and maintain a campaign against vaccines as a cause of autism (Kitta, 2011).

The movement received a boost in 1998 when the *Lancet*—a prominent British medical journal—published a research study that examined eight autistic children and claimed to have found evidence that autism might be caused by an adverse reaction to the MMR (measles-mumps-rubella) vaccine. Antiautism activists seized on this apparent proof that medical research confirmed their suspicions; they demanded an end to MMR vaccinations and sought to sue vaccine manufacturers for damages.

However, other scientific evidence did not support the MMR-autism link. Several large-scale studies comparing children who had and had not had the MMR vaccine found no differences in their rates of autism diagnoses. In addition, critics argued that the report in the *Lancet* was, at best, badly flawed and possibly an instance of scientific fraud. The journal retracted the paper in 2010, and its author lost his license to practice medicine in Great Britain. As consensus emerged that the MMR vaccine was not the cause of autism, new claimsmakers proposed that thimerosal (a preservative found in some vaccines) might be to blame, but that finding also failed to gain scientific support (because autism diagnoses continued to rise after thimerosal was removed from vaccines). Undeterred, antiautism activists suggested that perhaps no one vaccine was to blame, that it could be the total number of vaccines given to infants and small children that had caused the increase in autism.

Although most of the medical-scientific literature has challenged claims that vaccines cause autism, the parents' movement remains active (Perez, 2010). Its members have dismissed much of the research that challenged their claims as bad science, part of a cover-up that involves an alliance between the government (especially the CDC [Centers for Disease Control and Prevention]), the vaccine manufacturers, and researchers (who, the activists argue, depend on the government and manufacturers for research funding). In contrast, the researcher whose now discredited study showed the link between the MMR vaccine and autism continues to be hailed by some activists as a brave individual willing to speak the truth.

But if vaccines aren't at fault, what has caused the "epidemic"—the increase in autism diagnoses (Liu, King, & Bearman, 2010)? At least four factors have made it much easier to diagnose autism:

- The definition of autism was expanded. Originally, in order to be diagnosed as autistic, a child needed to display all of several defining symptoms; later, a child who had some of a longer list of symptoms could qualify as autistic, and advocates began speaking of the "autism spectrum" in order to suggest that there were degrees of severity of autism, that some individuals might be "high-functioning" people with autism. It is almost inevitable that a broader definition will encompass more cases, so that the number of cases reported in an earlier period (when the definition was narrow) will be lower than the number reported later (once the definition has broadened).

- In addition, increased attention to autism meant that more physicians were aware of the diagnosis, regularly screening their patients for autism's symptoms, and choosing to apply the diagnosis to more children. In particular, this meant that, while in the past children with cognitive disabilities tended to be lumped together within the category of mental retardation, some of these children were now labeled autistic.

- When autism was first coming to public attention, it was constructed as a psychiatric disorder caused, in particular, by "refrigerator mothers" who were cold and distant from their infants. Parents with an autistic child became stigmatized— their bad parenting had supposedly harmed their child. Under these circumstances, parents resisted the label of autism, and physicians were reluctant to apply it. As autism came to be biomedicalized, the stigma associated with the diagnosis— and the reluctance to apply the label—diminished, enabling some parents to redefine themselves as heroic claimsmakers championing their children's cause (Sousa, 2011).

- Children with cognitive disabilities need special social services. In earlier periods, when there were few services available for autistic children and relatively more for those with retardation, an autism diagnosis might prevent a child from receiving needed help. Improved services for autistic children have made physicians more willing to apply, and parents more willing to accept, the autism label. In fact, living near another child who has already been diagnosed as autistic increases a child's chances of receiving a diagnosis, which suggests that news of supportive services spreads by word of mouth.

In other words, the "epidemic" of autism coincided with a set of developments that made it much easier to label a child as autistic.

This explains why, during the same years that autism diagnoses have been increasing, diagnoses for mental retardation have been falling. Some data show that the total rate of diagnoses for both autism and mental retardation has remained quite stable, suggesting that the "epidemic" largely reflects shifts in the ways medical professionals construct children's problems.

However, these arguments have not convinced many autism activists. The contentious debate over autism illustrates not just the importance of expert claimsmakers in giving shape to social problems, but also the sorts of disputes that can emerge over whose expertise ought to be recognized as authoritative.

QUESTIONS

1. What explains the debate over autism's causes?

2. What role does scientific evidence play in claims and counterclaims about autism?

3. How are physicians' decisions to diagnose autism shaped by social factors?

5

■

The Media and Claims

■

Analyses of the mass media's role in the social problems process often focus on the issue of **bias**. Conservative critics charge that the media systematically present a liberal point of view:

> The argument over whether the national press is dominated by liberals is over. Since 1962, there have been 11 surveys of the media that sought the political views of hundreds of journalists. . . . And the proportion of liberals to conservatives in the press, either 3-to-1 or 4-to-1, has stayed the same. That liberals are dominant is now beyond dispute. (Barnes, 2004)

Meanwhile, liberals counter that the media have a conservative bias:

> Even the genuine liberal media . . . [are] no match—either in size, ferocity, or commitment—for the massive conservative media structure that, more than ever, determines the shape and scope of our political agenda. (Alterman, 2003, p. 11)

These critiques address the news media that report information (such as newspapers, newsmagazines, and radio and television news broadcasts), but also the entertainment media (such as television dramas, novels, or movies) and so-called infotainment that uses entertaining formats to discuss social issues (such as television talk shows, or "reality" shows that depict police at work).

All forms of **media coverage** tend to alter how social problems are constructed, although not necessarily in the ways that critics of media bias imagine. The social problems process typically begins with claimsmaking that precedes the media's involvement; usually activists or experts present the initial, or **primary, claims** (J. Best, 1990). Unless these claimsmakers are insiders who have ready access to policymakers (see Chapters 3 and 4), they probably hope that the media will cover their claims, thereby bringing those claims before a larger audience than the claimsmakers could hope to reach on their own. Newspaper stories, talk show episodes, or movies with plots involving troubling conditions can bring claims to the attention of millions of people in the general public, as well as policymakers. However, media coverage almost inevitably alters the claims that it presents.

Media workers face their own constraints: they work under deadlines, so they rarely have time to become thoroughly familiar with the claims they cover; their presentations are usually constricted (for example, newspapers can print only so many inches of news per day [journalists call this the *newshole*], and television news programs have only so many broadcast minutes available); and they need to make their coverage interesting enough that the audience won't stop reading or watching. The media, then, translate and transform claimsmakers' messages into what we will call **secondary claims**, typically by making them shorter, more dramatic, and less ideological than the original primary claims.

Because there are many claimsmakers and the media can cover only a limited number of stories, claimsmakers find themselves competing for media attention. Savvy claimsmakers realize that they need to package their claims so as to interest the media in covering them. The media prefer to cover new, seemingly fresh material, so it is important to present claims in novel ways (the first sit-in or peace march may get a lot of coverage, but each additional sit-in or march is likely to get less, unless it offers an interesting new angle). The media like to be able to plan their coverage in advance, so it helps to issue press releases and schedule press conferences so that reporters know when and where they can find someone willing to talk with them. The media favor claims presented by interesting people, so claimsmakers need to find spokespersons who seem engaging (note how often claimsmaking campaigns use either celebrities—interesting in their own right—or highly dramatic figures, such as parents who have suffered the loss of a child, to present their claims). Television seeks visually interesting material that can accompany a story, so claimsmakers favor marches, demonstrations, and other easy-to-film ways of presenting their claims. In the competition for media attention, claimsmakers who take the media's needs into account have an advantage (Sobieraj, 2011).

Hilgartner and Bosk (1988) suggest that the marketplace for social problems can be understood as composed of multiple **arenas**. Each arena is a venue where social problems claims can be presented; the pages of a newsmagazine, a TV talk show, or the hearings of a congressional subcommittee are all arenas. Each arena has a limited **carrying capacity** for presenting claims: magazines have only so many pages per issue, talk shows schedule a set number of episodes per season, subcommittees hold only a limited number of hearings, and so on. In Chapters 3 and 4, we considered the perspective of claimsmakers, who understand that they are competing for attention in various arenas. In this chapter we will adopt the perspective of those who work in the media. We can think of them as managing different arenas and having the job of sorting through all the competing claims and choosing which ones will receive attention in their arena.

In general, sociologists who have observed how news reporters and editors decide which stories to cover and how to cover them conclude that bias—in the sense of an underlying political ideology—is less important in shaping how the news is covered than the nature of the work that reporters and editors do. This chapter begins by considering the nature of those jobs—and the parallel considerations that shape how social problems are treated in entertainment media—before examining the forms that secondary claims tend to take. The chapter ends with a caution against exaggerating the media's influence.

WHAT'S THE NEWS?

The term **news work** draws our attention to the fact that reporters and editors have the job of locating and presenting news to the larger public. Like all other occupations, news work has constraints (Gans, 1979; Schudson, 2003; Tuchman, 1978). Some constraints are economic: it costs money to collect and produce news, and news workers operate within budgets, so newspapers and television news operations can afford only so many employees; the newshole (that is, the number of available column inches or broadcast minutes) can contain only so many stories; and so on. Other constraints are cultural. News workers have their own understanding of what they should do; that is, their sense of professionalism also shapes their coverage.

News workers operate under pressure. They have schedules and deadlines; newspapers and magazines need to reach the printer on schedule, just as radio and television programs need to be ready in time for their broadcasts. News workers cannot simply sit back and wait for news to happen and come to their attention; rather, they must try to plan ahead, to anticipate what might be and ought to be covered. Many news organizations assign reporters to beats—types of news that are expected to generate suitable stories; for example, a reporter on the police beat covers stories about crimes. News workers also are drawn to predictable events; a scheduled demonstration or even a press conference can be attractive precisely because reporters and editors have some sense in advance of what sorts of stories those events might generate.

Box 5.1 Turning Events into News

News reporting is a way of socially constructing reality. News workers do not simply "report what happens"; they must choose which events merit their attention, and how they will present those events. This process often goes unnoticed, because many news stories present familiar topics in familiar ways. Many stories fall into routine patterns—a politician holds a press conference, the stock markets goes up or down, and so on—and both news workers and their audiences have a pretty good idea of what ought to be reported.

In contrast, the terrorist attacks on September 11, 2001, illustrate the construction of news amid confusion. The airliners struck the World Trade Center towers in the city where several major television news networks had their headquarters, so reporters were able to reach the scene quickly. Within minutes of the first attack, the networks had replaced their regular programing with live news coverage, but the nature of the story was still unclear. The on-air commentators wondered whether there had been an explosion, a terrible accident, or perhaps a terrorist attack. After the second plane struck, of course, there was consensus that this had been terrorism—further confirmed when the third plane struck the Pentagon. Over the next few hours, confusion and uncertainty were replaced by a single interpretation—there had been a terrorist attack, probably mounted by Al Qaeda, and that this constituted an act of war, analogous to the attack on Pearl Harbor. Within hours, terrorism vaulted to the top of Americans' list of social problems.

Source: Monahan, 2010.

News workers also judge some stories as being more deserving of coverage than others. Most obviously, they consider some stories to be more important, or, as they say, more newsworthy. Important stories involve consequential events, things about which people need to know (see Box 5.1). But importance depends on the news workers' audience. Imagine a passenger jet crashing and killing, say, 150 people. How much attention should a newspaper give that story? If the crash occurred in the city where the newspaper is published, we can imagine this dramatic local story consuming most of the front page. If it occurred, say, in a city a thousand miles away, and if there were other compelling stories competing for the paper's attention, the crash story might well be pushed off the front page. If the crash occurred in a foreign country (and especially if no Americans were killed), it is likely to receive no more than a paragraph or two, somewhere well inside the paper. In other words, it is not just the death toll that makes a story seem important, but also the story's perceived relevance to the paper's readers.

In addition to being of varying importance, stories strike news workers as being more or less interesting to their audience. Television news, for example, favors stories that can be accompanied by videotaped footage showing something happening. The earliest television news broadcasts featured newscasters facing the camera and reading stories to the audience. Television workers soon realized, however, that theirs was a visual medium, and that audiences found these "talking heads" boring. There is, then, a strong preference for having some sort of videotaped action to illustrate the story, even if the activity shown is mundane; this explains why stories about ongoing trials—where cameras are often forbidden in the courtroom—routinely feature footage of trial participants walking into the courthouse, so that viewers have something to watch, to accompany the sound of a reporter describing what happened in court that day.

There are, of course, other ways of making stories interesting. Like claims generally, news stories often begin with typifying examples. For example, a story on homelessness might begin by describing the experiences of one or two particular homeless individuals; such an introduction puts a human face on the story and gives the problem "human interest." Stories that seem less interesting can easily lose out in the competition for media attention; news workers will favor covering stories that can be presented in an interesting manner.

Another quality of an attractive story is novelty. Notice the very word *news*—that is, "what's new." In general, news workers prefer stories that are current (especially "breaking news") and that seem different. "Fresh" news is preferred to stories that seem too familiar, that have grown "stale." After all, if there isn't something new to report, why should news workers expect the audience to pay any attention? This means that familiar, troubling conditions that affect many people—such as world hunger—may not attract nearly as much media attention as the latest sex scandal or lurid murder.

In assembling the stories they report, news workers apply other professional standards as well. For example, when the story's subject is clearly an issue about which people disagree, many news workers consider themselves obliged to *balance* their coverage by reporting the views of "both sides." This expression reveals an assumption that most issues have only two sides—pro and con, liberal and conservative, or whatever. The news media often resist reporting complex stories in which there are more than two competing positions; they prefer to construct the issue as a straightforward, two-party disagreement. Note, too, that news workers do not feel the need to balance coverage when they perceive a general unanimity of opinion (concerning what Chapter 2 called *valence issues*). If there is general, widespread agreement that, say, child pornography is bad, then reporters will not consider themselves obliged to balance their coverage by reporting the views of child pornographers.

Because most news workers keep track of coverage by rival news organizations, they often feel obliged to *follow one another's lead*. The very fact that another newspaper or newscast is covering a story suggests that that story must be newsworthy. When several news organizations rush to follow the same lead, the result can be a wave of news coverage. This often happens with social problems coverage, which is why criminologists have long understood that crime waves are not so much waves in criminal activity as waves in news coverage (Vasterman, 2005).

Considerations such as importance, interest, novelty, balance, and what other news organizations are covering shape how news workers construct the news. These are inevitably matters of judgment, with editors making choices—deciding which stories deserve more attention, which deserve less, and which can be ignored. In some cases, news workers may act as primary claimsmakers; that is, they might originate the claimsmaking through their coverage.

For social problems claimsmakers, the challenge is to construct claims that will strike news workers as sufficiently important and interesting to merit news coverage. Sophisticated claimsmakers learn to take the news workers' concerns into account: they make it easy to cover their claims by, for example, staging demonstrations and other events that will seem interesting and therefore newsworthy; they schedule these events and press conferences in advance so that news workers will know when and where to go to get their stories; they designate articulate spokespersons who can present the claims, answer reporters' questions, and help them identify suitable typifying examples; they devise novel, visually interesting ways of presenting their claims—new forms of demonstrations, new evidence, and such—so that their message seems fresh and the story well suited for television; and so on. For instance, a small San Francisco prostitutes' rights movement managed to attract a great deal of media attention by organizing the "First Annual Hookers' Ball" (Jenness, 1993). Understanding the news media's concerns allows claimsmakers to package their claims in ways that will appeal to news workers, and thereby makes it more likely that those claims will, in fact, become the subjects of news coverage (see Box 5.2).

News workers are not naive; they understand that experienced claimsmakers tailor their campaigns to attract news coverage. On the one hand, news workers may be wary of being manipulated; they particularly want to avoid wasting time covering a story that will strike them and their audiences as familiar and boring. They want to be convinced that the information they're being given is fresh, accurate, and interesting; they have no interest in attending

Box 5.2 When Do Reporters Find Activists Newsworthy?

A study of press coverage of social activism at Republican and Democratic presidential nominating conventions illustrates the challenges of gaining media coverage. Realizing that many reporters cover these conventions, activists hold demonstrations designed to attract attention to their causes. They hope to get media notice for their claims, but most are disappointed by the press coverage they receive.

The press favor stories about disorderly demonstrations: scenes of police trying to restrain demonstrators who threaten to break through barricades or angry exchanges between activists who take opposing sides on some issue can be turned into dramatic news coverage. However, activists may discover that, while they've made the news, such coverage doesn't say much about their claims. Many social movements try to engineer more favorable coverage: they designate spokespeople who can articulate their groups' positions, who can summarize their claims. Yet reporters can be wary of relying on such prepackaged information; instead, they may search for "authentic" sources, preferring to quote ordinary demonstrators who express outrage or other dramatic emotions. Similarly, reporters favor narrowly focused causes; activists promoting broad, ideological critiques find that their claims are considered too abstract, too far outside the political mainstream, to warrant coverage. As a consequence, reporting on protests tends to favor particular kinds of stories, and even media-savvy activists may have trouble shaping media coverage.

Source: Sobieraj, 2011.

yet another press conference where the same speakers make the same old claims. Still, depending on what rival stories are under consideration, it may be easier to cover a well-packaged story. There are, after all, "slow news days" when there seems to be a shortage of newsworthy stories, just as summer has long been known among journalists as the "dog days" or the "silly season"—months when the federal government and other news-generating institutions are less active, so that competition for coverage is less intense and it is easier for offbeat stories to attract news coverage. A well-assembled claim can become very attractive to news workers if there aren't strong alternative stories competing for attention.

Geography also plays a role in this process. News workers are not evenly distributed across the country; rather, they are concentrated in larger cities (J. Best, 1999). In particular, three cities have exceptionally large concentrations of news workers: New York is the nation's largest city, and it remains the traditional base for such important news media as the *New York Times*, the *Wall Street Journal*, and the three major television network news broadcasts; Los Angeles is the second-largest city, and as the center of the entertainment industry, it has its own concentration of news media; and Washington, D.C., is, of course, the center of the federal government and attracts a vast army of news workers devoted to covering the government's actions. Events that occur near such concentrations of news workers are more likely to attract coverage.

Such geographic concentrations of news workers are important because where there are more reporters, there are more opportunities for claimsmakers to get their claims covered. There is nothing to keep people from making claims in a small town in a remote rural location, but it is more difficult to get news workers to travel there to cover the story. It is far easier for a claim to gain widespread attention if the claimsmakers bring their case to a major media center, to a location where many news workers will have convenient access to the story. Thus, even claimsmakers who begin in distant places tend to migrate to larger media centers.

All of this is to say that the news is a social construction, produced by news workers operating under various constraints that force them to make choices—to prefer stories that can be covered in ways that fit their sense of what good news ought to be. Claimsmakers who ignore these considerations do so at their own peril.

CHANGING NEWS MEDIA

Note that the news media's forms shift over time. During television's first thirty years, the great majority of Americans relied on broadcast signals; even those living in fairly large urban centers might receive signals from only half a dozen stations. The three major networks (ABC, CBS, and NBC) originally ran fifteen-minute news broadcasts on weekdays, which were expanded to thirty minutes in the early 1960s, then later to six days per week; in addition, local stations offered their own news broadcasts a couple times a day.

Today, most households receive either cable or satellite television signals offering access to dozens, if not hundreds, of channels. Several channels offer round-the-clock news coverage. This shift has had all manner of consequences: the audience for the networks' evening news broadcasts has grown smaller as viewers turn to all-news channels at more convenient times; the audience for print journalism—both newspapers and weekly newsmagazines—has also declined as more people rely on electronic media for their news; and some cable networks have begun to adopt overt editorial stances (as the emergence of FOX News as an unabashedly conservative network illustrates).

For claimsmakers, one important consequence of these changes in the media is that competing twenty-four-hour news channels have a colossal appetite for fresh stories. In television's early years, when the networks broadcast five fifteen-minute shows per week, it was far tougher to get an issue covered on national television than it is today. Television's carrying capacity for news has increased vastly. (On the other hand, as their advertising has declined, newspapers and newsmagazines have been shrinking in size, so their carrying capacity has grown smaller.)

As television channels have increased in number, they have increasingly aimed at targeted audiences. Theorists once worried about the "mass media" that would turn society into an undifferentiated mass receiving the same media messages (Turow, 1997).

In practice, the media find it more profitable to practice **audience segmentation**, to aim at particular demographic groups; because people fitting a particular demographic profile (defined by age, sex, income, and so on) are more likely to watch programs aimed directly at their interests, the audience for those programs will be relatively homogeneous, and advertisers who believe that their customers will be concentrated in that segment of the larger audience will prefer—and even pay a premium—to place their ads on those programs. Thus, there are cable channels aimed at women, Spanish speakers, people in particular age groups, and so on, just as websites are aimed at people with distinctive interests or concerns. (A similar process changed magazine publishing: general-interest magazines such as *Life* that once sought to appeal to huge mass audiences have folded, yet a visit to a newsstand reveals hundreds of titles aimed at people with particular interests.)

Audience segmentation affects the media's role in the social problems process. Because different television channels or magazines seek to appeal to demographically distinct audiences, their coverage of claimsmaking will reflect their sense of which issues will strike their viewers or readers as interesting and relevant. Because advertisers often favor more affluent customers who can afford their products, the news media are less likely to target poorer audiences, which means that social problems coverage tends to downplay claims of greater concern to the poor and the powerless. Newspapers' economic reporting, for instance, tends to devote far more attention to the concerns of corporations than to those of workers or the unemployed (Kollmeyer, 2004). The consequence of audience segmentation for social problems claimsmaking is that, although it is becoming easier to gain media coverage for claims, that coverage often is tailored for the particular audience that follows the television programs or magazines that choose to cover the claims.

The obvious example of changing media is the emergence of the Internet. The Internet is a boon to claimsmakers in that Web sites, discussion groups, and blogs can be established quite easily, and at minimal cost. Claims of all sorts can be posted and made accessible to anyone who knows how to use a search engine; in effect, the Internet has an unlimited carrying capacity. Because there is little in the way of filtering, the Internet offers a forum for even the most controversial claims, and sites can be *cloaked* so as to conceal the posters' identity (Daniels, 2009). However, it becomes difficult for news workers to evaluate the various claims that wind up posted in cyberspace. (In contrast, those working in print and broadcast journalism routinely sort through prospective stories and have standards for rejecting some claims.) Moreover, posting a claim does not guarantee that it will gain a large audience; bloggers have learned to encourage traffic to their sites by providing mutual links to other sites. Still, it seems likely that the Internet will have a long-term effect on claimsmaking. In some instances already, websites or bloggers have forced more established news media to cover particular issues by breaking stories about those issues (see Box 5.3).

Thus, the news media's structure is changing: Some media, such as newspapers and magazines, are losing part of their audience, shrinking their coverage, and becoming less influential. Others, such as television news, are expanding their coverage and shifting forms (by, for example, becoming more openly ideological). At the same time, new, Internet-based forms, such as blogs, websites, and electronic discussion groups, are emerging. Thus far, these changes seem to make it easier to gain some sort of media coverage of claims, although, because the target audiences for different media tend to be smaller and more homogeneous, it is not necessarily easier to bring claims to the attention of a broad, general audience.

PACKAGING SOCIAL PROBLEMS IN THE NEWS

In short, the nature of news work and the structure of the news industry shape which stories are covered and the form that coverage takes. In particular, news about claimsmaking tends to display some fairly clear patterns.

Box 5.3 How New Are New Media?

The Internet has plenty of enthusiastic promoters who argue that it has—or will—transform society. For sociologists who study social problems, the Internet seems to be an arena with an infinite carrying capacity. The costs of posting a claim on the Internet are low, so that anyone can become a claimsmaker, and all claims are available to anyone with an Internet connection via search engines. Take blogs, for example: in early 2011, there were well over 150 million blogs. That's a lot of potential claimsmakers.

Obviously, no individual can hope to follow more than a tiny proportion of all the available blogs. The vast majority of blogs have very few readers; the blogger may make claims, but there aren't many folks paying attention. In order to gain an audience, blogs rely on hyperlinks to other blogs (so that someone reading Blog A can move directly to Blog B without searching). There are a few elite blogs that attract millions of different individual viewers each month; the most successful are actually sites within which several bloggers post their work (this means that, while a lots of people may visit a site, the number that read any particular posting is likely to be vastly smaller). Just as a major urban daily newspaper is more likely to draw attention to a news story than is a small-town weekly, the few elite blogs can advance claims far more easily than the great mass of their infrequently read counterparts.

There are important social problems claims that have originated in blogs, but, at least so far, blogs' influence derives from having their claims picked up by traditional media—such as newpapers or television news—which reach audiences larger than those of the largest blog.

Source: Maratea, 2008.

The Advantages of Issue Ownership

First, remember that particular claimsmakers sometimes assume ownership of their social problems. That is, they become widely recognized as *the* authorities on the problem, as especially knowledgeable. One of the principal benefits of such ownership is that, when news workers find themselves covering a story related to a certain social problem, they routinely turn to the problem's owners for comments. This status is self-reinforcing; once the media have used particular activists or experts as sources for one story, they are more likely to seek out the same sources for future, related stories.

Of course, achieving ownership is easier for some people than for others. The news media frequently turn to government officials as sources for their stories, and other experts have credentials that make their comments seem particularly authoritative. The news media also favor covering people who are already well known; thus, when movie stars or other celebrities enlist in claimsmaking campaigns, they often draw press attention. (Another way to claim ownership and control the media message is for corporations or other interest groups to run advertising that presents their claims [Silver & Boyle, 2010].) In short, the news media prefer to collect their information from those who already have high status.

The flip side of ownership arises when the media define some claimsmakers as lacking the legitimacy to deserve coverage. We might call these *dispossessed* claimsmakers (that is, they are the opposite of owners). News workers may view people who are poorer—who lack power, wealth, or high status—as less news-worthy, and claimsmakers representing these people find it hard to get their claims covered. Similarly, those with views considered too far outside the mainstream—too unpopular or too radical—find it much harder to gain media coverage for their claims. Remember, the media often try to balance their coverage by presenting "both sides" of an issue—typically understood to mean liberals and con-servatives, or Democrats and Republicans. Those who adopt other, very different positions—who are too radical or too reactionary, who hold unpopular beliefs or values—usually find it difficult to break into the news media that have the largest audiences. As a result, claimsmakers whose rhetoric strikes news workers as too far out-side the mainstream—think of vegans, hate groups, or unfamiliar new religions—may find themselves ignored by the major media. Those newspapers, newsmagazines, and television networks with the largest audiences tend to concentrate their coverage on less controversial claims.

Dispossession also reflects the news media's efforts to appeal to their target audiences. Although we might imagine that newspapers or television news broadcasts want to gain the largest possible audience, audience segmentation leads them, in practice, to be more concerned with reaching some people than others (Hamilton, 2004). Advertisers are more likely to place their ads in media that reach particular types of consumers, and editors may favor stories that will appeal to their target audience. To the degree that social problems claims address troubling conditions thought to be of concern to that target audience, it is easier to get coverage; however, claims that may be of more concern to people outside the target audience have a tougher time getting covered. Again, advertisers—and therefore the news media—tend to be especially interested in reaching more affluent audience members, and less interested in attracting poorer readers and viewers; therefore, claims about problems that face the poor may have a harder time gaining news coverage (see Box 5.4).

Not all social problems come to have owners, because claims-makers must themselves choose which issues are most important (J. Best, 1999). Consider the media coverage of school shootings that began in 1998; there were several heavily publicized incidents (most notably, of course, at Columbine High School in 1999). Various claimsmakers sought to explain these episodes, but the cacophony of explanations was remarkable. School shootings were blamed on insufficient gun control laws, violent video games, the Goth subculture, bullying, theaters admitting those under seventeen into R-rated movies, the gun culture, and so on.

This is a common pattern: reports of novel sorts of violent crime often lead to all sorts of commentators offering competing explanations and solutions. In the case of school shootings, none

Box 5.4 Covering Conditions, Rather Than Problems

A series of murders of homeless men in Denver, Colorado, became the subject of local newspaper coverage. Although homelessness was a central element in these stories, they did not all construct homelessness as a *social* problem. That is, many stories did not portray homelessness as a social pattern caused by the high cost of housing, a lack of jobs, low wages, or other structural conditions in society; rather, some stories argued that individuals were homeless because they had personal problems, such as mental or physical health problems, troubled family relationships, or drug or alcohol problems. Further, many stories did not imply that there should be some public policy—a social solution—to address homelessness. Stories were more likely to emphasize the role of social causes and solutions when they were written to cover claims made by activists or experts, rather than when they reported on events (such as the murders).

Whereas the study of Denver press coverage restricted the term *social problem* to those claims that identified social causes and solutions, this book has argued that the social problems process can involve claims about all sorts of causes and solutions, including those with biological or psychological causes. Still, these findings are important, because they illustrate how news coverage is shaped, both by the subject of the story (is the reporter trying to understand a series of murders, or to cover a demonstration by activists, or even to explain the causes of homelessness?). Which claims find their way into news stories will depend on what reporters and editors define as relevant information—what they think their readers will need to know in order to make sense of the news.

Source: R. Best, 2010.

of these explanations emerged as dominant; that is, no single set of claimsmakers assumed ownership. Why not? Probably because school shootings were not central to the causes of any of the commentators who spoke out on the issue. Gun control activists, for example, saw school shootings as just one small part of the larger gun problem; they wanted to continue to draw attention to all of the aspects of that problem, rather than to focus on school shootings. The emergence of ownership requires claimsmakers who are motivated to continue promoting an issue, as well as news workers who treat those claimsmakers as authoritative.

The Dominance of Landmark Narratives

Second, particular typifying examples—what are called **landmark narratives**—often come to dominate news coverage of a topic (Nichols, 1997). That is, a particular case may become the central focus of media coverage of a social problem—the subject of more newspaper and magazine articles than other, similar cases, or represented in more of the video clips that accompany numerous TV news stories on the topic. Just as the typifying examples chosen by claimsmakers are often quite atypical—more serious, dramatic, or troubling than most cases—so news workers choose landmark or iconic narratives not because they accurately reflect the larger problem, but because they are the stuff of compelling news (see Box 5.5). These cases serve as landmarks in two senses: they guide news workers' thinking about the nature of the problem and how it should be covered, and they shape the terms by which the news audience understands the problem.

Constructing Packages

Third, landmark cases often belong to larger constructions called **packages** (Beckett, 1996; Gamson, 1992; Gamson & Modigliani, 1989). A package is a familiar, more or less coherent view of a social issue, including its causes and what ought to be done about it. A package has a core idea, or frame; for example, arguments that global warming is substantially caused by humans' activities, that it poses a serious threat, and that steps need to be taken to minimize

Box 5.5 Crimes Become Iconic

Sensational news stories—such as terrible crimes involving children killing children—can become the focus for dramatic media coverage, with hundreds of stories appearing over months. In such cases, initial reports of the crime lead to additional stories about the backgrounds of the victim and the perpetrator, about the crime's impact on community residents, about the trial, and so on. These cases explore many aspects of the story, including trying to understand the actors' motives, and the many factors that may have led them to act as they did. In such cases, the story becomes more than a typifying example for claimsmakers pushing a particular construction of a problem; rather, it becomes an *iconic narrative* that symbolizes all the ways that people can understand what's wrong.

Intense media attention favors novelty; keeping a story alive requires uncovering new aspects that can justify further coverage. Some involve new developments—once the arrest follows the crime, it is in turn followed by the trial. But other stories can explore new angles: the perpetrator's medical or mental health issues, problems in school, earlier troubles with the law, family dynamics, and on and on. In this way, a problem such as "youth violence" can be linked to multiple, even contradictory constructions; audience members can draw very different lessons about what caused the crime, and what steps need to be taken to solve the problem. As a consequence, iconic narratives can become touchstones invoked by competing claimsmakers.

Source: Spencer, 2011.

the problem are at the core of one familiar package. Similarly, arguments that global warming is not necessarily caused by humans' activities and may not constitute a serious threat are the frame for a rival package. Within a package, there is room for disagreement: people may accept the same basic frame yet disagree about specifics, such as the exact processes causing the problem or what needs to be done. Not everyone who shares the basic concern about global warming has to agree on every aspect of the package.

In addition, packages offer **condensing symbols**, shorthand elements—landmark narratives, typifying examples, slogans, visual images, and so on—that evoke the package. Editorial cartoons in newspapers depend on the fact that readers will understand such symbols; a figure in a Klansman's robe and hood denotes racism, a smokestack belching smoke symbolizes pollution, and so on. Similarly, a bumper sticker's slogan—"When Guns Are Outlawed, Only Outlaws Will Have Guns"—can encapsulate a larger package of ideas about guns and gun control. Condensing signals remind people of the larger package, which presents claims that define the nature of the problem, its causes, and a vision of what ought to be done about it.

Note that packages draw upon the larger stock of cultural resources. Like primary claimsmakers designing their claims, news workers want to assemble coverage that seems sensible to them, and that also will seem sensible to their audiences. Their stories, then, incorporate the culture that they take for granted—values, symbols, worldviews, and so on. These underlying assumptions are invisible to those who share them, although they may seem quite glaring to others. Consider Americans' shock when they discovered that, during the hostage crisis of 1979–80 (perhaps the first time serious tensions with the Muslim world became apparent), Iranian media had described the United States as the "Great Satan." In most cases, however, the way news coverage draws upon cultural resources that are taken for granted goes unnoticed.

Media packages help organize people's thinking about social problems. News workers sort through many, if not all, of the available claims, select some as worthy of coverage, and give that coverage shape. The packages they choose may change over time. News workers' choices are influenced by the nature of the claims they encounter, but also by other considerations, including the need to produce news under the pressures of news work, the range of available stories competing for coverage, the desirability of tailoring coverage to the target audience, and so on. Social problems packages are one outcome of this process; they give the news media's secondary claims a sense of coherence: among all the things that might be said about race or crime or anything else, these become the most visible positions. It is relatively easy for the public to become familiar with the packages presented by the news media, and considerably harder for people to learn other ways to think about social problems.

Packages help make the media coverage of social problems seem more coherent; they turn a lot of information into a *story*—a word that is significant, because it reminds us that news is often presented as narratives (Nichols, Nolan, & Colyer, 2008). In the process, some elements are highlighted, while others are pushed to one side. This helps explain why analyses of media content regularly find that the depictions of people or events mirror popular images of problems, and are a less accurate reflection of official measures of a problem's dimensions. Our notions of who is likely to be victimized by a hate crime or what it is like to be poor not only derive from images presented in the media, but also shape the imagery the media choose to present.

It is possible to exaggerate the media's role in packaging social problems; they do not have a completely free hand. News workers have to derive and present packages that they believe will make sense to their audiences. American culture, for example, places great weight on the idea of individual responsibility; this idea runs through much commonsense thinking about life. We tend to hold individuals responsible for their circumstances; people who are poor, overweight, or addicted to drugs bear, most Americans agree, at least part of the blame for their troubles. It is, then, relatively easy to devise frames and packages in which individual responsibility plays a key role, but much harder, for instance, to present explanations that argue that individuals' actions are largely determined by social forces.

IS IT JUST ENTERTAINMENT?

We assume that the news media will cover social problems; after all, it is their job to report on serious matters. But social problems claims are also picked up by a wide range of entertainment media and are portrayed in what is called **popular culture**. Television talk shows, for instance, often present episodes focused on particular sorts of relationship problems, addictions, and the like. But even fictional genres, such as mystery novels, adopt topics from the news: when missing children became a national concern, fictional detective heroes tried to find missing kids; once stalking attracted notice, some of those same heroes confronted stalkers; and so on. And just as the demands of news work shape how the news media cover social problems, entertainment media are constrained by conventions that affect how they construct social problems.

Consider the format for a typical TV talk show: the host moderates a discussion among several guests, a group typically including several "ordinary people" who have firsthand experience with the problem at issue. For instance, a show on compulsive gambling might feature two or three gamblers who can tell tales of being unable to control their gambling, as well as a couple of spouses or other relatives who can describe the frustration and despair of dealing with a compulsive gambler. Toward the end of the show, the host often turns to an expert, perhaps a psychologist who medicalizes the problem by explaining that gambling is a disease, and that the solution lies in the twelve-step program of Gamblers Anonymous. This formula resembles a religious revival, in which sinners confess, repent, and are shown the path to salvation (Lowney, 1999).

Every popular-culture genre has its own conventions and constraints—a formula that it follows. Television situation comedies need joke-filled scripts that will last about twenty-three minutes (thirty minutes less time for the commercials and the opening and closing credits), in romance novels the main characters fall in love, and comic book superheroes confront and defeat supervillains. The people who produce popular culture follow these formulas because they are known to work; that is, they appeal to each genre's respective audience. Romance authors, editors, and publishers, for instance, doubt that their readers want stories about people who can't find love.

These formulas shape how entertainment media deal with social problems claims. Although popular culture often reflects current social problems claims, with stories "ripped from the headlines," its depictions of those claims must conform to the different formulas' requirements (Gitlin, 1983). For example, to be dramatic, a confrontation requires an uncertain outcome; this means that the hero must face a villain who seems capable of winning. For instance, detective heroes—whether on television or in mystery novels—must be matched with powerful lawbreakers. As a result, fictional criminals tend to be far more powerful than their real-world counterparts: fictional child molesters belong to organized rings of wealthy abusers, drug dealers are millionaire industrialists, or gang leaders command hundreds of highly trained, well-armed followers. In comparison, real-life offenders, often people with very limited resources, offer poor material for entertaining plots.

Sociologists often complain that popular culture's conventions focus on individuals rather than on social forces. Novels, movies, and television series tend to match good people with heroic virtues against bad people with villainous vices, instead of exploring how social problems emerge from social arrangements. Thus, when racism appears in popular culture, it is often treated as a sort of personality defect: villains and other unsympathetic characters express racist sentiments, thereby affirming their poor character. Where sociologists view racism as a widespread problem with roots in social arrangements and consequences for the larger society, popular culture often treats racism as a personal characteristic of flawed individuals, because the formula requires a hero triumphing over a particular villain. Similarly, talk shows and other genres that mix elements of news and entertainment feature the same emphasis on flawed individuals. They present problem gambling as a psychological compulsion that affects some individuals, rather than emphasizing how social institutions, such as government and the gaming industry, exacerbate the problem by promoting gambling.

In other words, the formulas used in entertainment media highlight stories about individuals (Berns, 2004). This individual focus is found in both fictional popular-culture genres (such as mystery novels) and the quasi news of infotainment (such as talk shows). Entertainment media may address social problems claims, but regardless of whether primary claimsmakers view a problem as widespread and systemic (think of claims about racism, environmental degradation, or global warming), entertainment tends to translate those claims into stories about the struggles and successes of particular people. This focus on telling compelling stories about individuals is central to the formulas for many entertainment genres, and the people who work as creators and producers within the media understand the need to focus on typifying individuals (see Box 5.6).

This means that entertainment media have an especially difficult time adopting what C. Wright Mills (1959) called a **sociological imagination**—that is, viewing the world in terms of social arrangements and social forces. Mills noted that, in everyday life, people focus on their private troubles, such as not having a job. Adopting a sociological imagination requires seeing those private troubles in terms of larger public issues; for example, whereas an individual may have trouble finding a job, the larger society confronts the more general problem of unemployment. Sociologists, then, tend to downplay the experiences of individuals and focus on larger, social patterns. (To use concepts from Chapters 3 and 4, the sociological imagination can be understood as the frame that sociologists as experts use to construct social problems.) No wonder sociologists— as well as many primary claimsmakers—often criticize the entertainment media's portrayal of social problems; by translating claims

Box 5.6 Infotainment and Shame

The term *reality television* is continually redefined to describe various formulas, such as those for *Cops* (videos of police on patrol) and *America's Most Wanted* (best known for reenacting crimes and calling on viewers to help locate the offenders). From 2004 to 2007, *Dateline NBC: To Catch a Predator* campaigned against sexual predators. The show's formula involved a collaboration with Perverted Justice (a group of individuals who posed as underage children in computer chatrooms in order to strike up conversations with men trolling for child sexual partners). Once the show's producers had rented a house and set up cameras, the "child" would invite the man to the house, where he would be confronted, shamed, and humiliated on camera, after which he would be arrested by local police when he tried to leave.

To Catch a Predator constructed the problem of child sexual abuse as a form of stranger-danger, of predators prowling cyberspace, whereas social scientific findings consistently show that most cases involve family members or others known to the children. It valorized the tricksters at Perverted Justice who lured the men into the trap, the program's role in bringing people to justice, and the local police who—once the would-be offenders were delivered into their hands—could arrest the men. Its formula featured an emotional payoff: confronting the would-be offender, and denouncing and publicly humiliating him. Although produced by NBC News, *To Catch a Predator* reshaped reality to fit the demands of a dramatic popular-cultural formula.

Source: Kohm, 2009.

into dramatic tales about individual suffering and redemption, the media favor constructions that run counter to more sociological interpretations.

Critics worry that media constructions—whether in news or entertainment genres—are important because they are influential.

That is, it seems obvious that people who follow the news or consume entertainment must be affected by how these media portray social problems. But is this true?

THE MEDIA'S IMPACT

Commentators often assume that the media are extremely powerful and influential, that members of the audience are regularly affected by media messages. To be sure, most of us would deny that we, personally, are easily manipulated by the media. We are made of stronger stuff; we take an attitude of healthy skepticism toward the messages in news, entertainment, and especially advertising. But others, we worry, must be easily bamboozled by the media and may require protection.

The media's powerful influence may seem obvious, but it turns out to be fairly difficult to document. Consider claims that televised violence leads to violent behavior. Television is nearly universal in our society (which makes it difficult to construct experimental studies of its effects, since there is no natural control group lacking exposure to television), yet most people do not engage in violent acts. Similarly, most people who view commercials do not rush out to purchase the advertised products. Although claimsmakers often insist that media exposure has damaging effects, it is hard to observe and measure these consequences. Clearly, the media don't have the same effects on everyone.

If we are to understand the media's role in the social problems process, we need to specify what forms its influence might take. One thing we might mean is that the media can bring a social problem to public attention. As we have already noted, this is a central goal of many claimsmakers. When claimsmakers are calling attention to a new problem—that is, to a troubling condition that has been generally neglected or ignored, one that is unfamiliar to many people—getting media coverage can bring the topic out in the open. Media attention can make the public aware that the issue exists or encourage the public to think that something ought to be done to remedy the problem. This is sometimes called **agenda setting** (McCombs, 2004).

Just as a meeting may be guided by an agenda—a list of topics to be addressed, usually in order of importance—we can envision a society's members as needing to prioritize their concerns. All people have countless topics competing for their attention. Many of these concern the individuals' personal lives—routine errands, conversations with friends and relatives, and on and on. The media—particularly the news media—provide some sense of what's occurring in the larger world, suggesting what else deserves people's notice. Media coverage, then, can make people aware of a social problem—get it on society's agenda. Agenda setting can affect both public awareness (as will be discussed in Chapter 6) and policymakers' sense of what deserves their attention (a topic covered in Chapter 7).

Note that the media do not have a free hand in agenda setting. They are constrained. First, some events—say, a major disaster—may demand media coverage. Second, the media can be influenced to cover particular topics—by claimsmakers who convince the media that a problem deserves their attention, by officials who herald a particular new policy, even by other media outlets whose coverage suggests that a topic must be worthy of coverage. Third, as we have already noted, people working in the news and entertainment media are limited by the resources available to them, by their sense of the sort of coverage they ought to produce, and so on.

Nevertheless, in one sense the media make choices that are consequential. We have already noted that the media translate and transform social problems claims. In the case of contentious issues, topics (such as abortion) about which claimsmakers may advance contradictory claims, media coverage can structure the debate by assembling a small set of claimsmaking packages. Although the media cannot force people to adopt particular ideas, they make some constructions readily available, so it is easier to come to understand social problems in particular ways. In some cases, media coverage may give individuals a new perspective on their personal lives, to help them redefine their personal troubles as part of larger social problems.

The public and policymakers pay attention to what the media cover for a couple of reasons. First, they use the media as a source of information: media coverage may be how the public and policymakers first learn about particular social problems. Second, policymakers may begin to hear from members of the general public who, having learned about the problem via the media, may call for action. Although the media are by no means all-powerful, they do help shape the social problems process.

THE MEDIA IN THE SOCIAL PROBLEMS PROCESS

Part of the reason why commentators exaggerate the media's power is that the media play an especially visible role in the social problems process. Outsider claimsmakers view media coverage as almost essential for making the public and policymakers aware of their claims. More powerful people use press conferences and other public relations techniques to attract and shape coverage for their activities. Meanwhile, much lobbying and other insider claimsmaking is hidden from the public (unless an enterprising reporter draws attention to it). Media coverage remains the easiest way for most people to learn about social problems.

This chapter has argued that the media must also be understood in terms of their social arrangements. Figure 5.1 illustrates some of the key features of these arrangements. First, note the distinction between news and entertainment media; the figure portrays news coverage as occurring first and often shaping the entertainment media's coverage of social problems. Second, the figure draws atten-

Figure 5.1 THE MEDIA'S ROLE IN THE SOCIAL PROBLEMS PROCESS

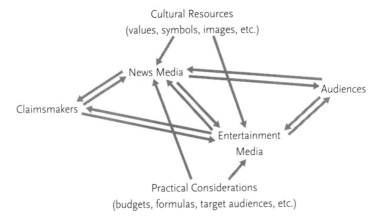

tion to the role of cultural resources. News workers' sense of what is newsworthy, as well as how news stories should be assembled and reported, depends in part on their understanding of how the larger culture will make sense of claims; a parallel set of considerations will shape what will be considered entertaining. Finally, note that both news and entertainment media have their own organizational constraints—operating budgets, production schedules, established conventions and formulas, and so on—that also influence what the media produce.

In addition, the media constantly receive feedback. Most obviously they worry about the reactions of their audiences: Are people interested in the news or entertainment they produce? If not, the media are likely to modify what they're doing. But also the media may hear from claimsmakers who offer congratulations or complaints about coverage, from segments of the general public who are not in their target audiences (and who often have their own criticisms), and from policymakers who may endorse or challenge what the media have done. The people who work in the media, then, should not be seen as all-powerful, as able to dictate what others think. Rather, they are connected to—and influenced by—the other actors in the social problems process. And just as the media transform and translate primary claims into the secondary claims presented in news coverage or entertainment, the media's audience—the public—reworks those messages for its own purposes.

MAKING CONNECTIONS

- *The media are eager for new claims and fresh ways of framing problems. Chapters 3 and 4 explain how activists and experts frame their claims to attract the most media attention.*

- *Claimsmakers use the news media to encourage recognition of a problem. In Chapter 7 you will learn about the essential role that the media play in introducing a social problem into the policymaking process.*

- *In the next chapter you will learn how the public responds to media coverage of social problems.*

CASE STUDY
REPORTING ABOUT RISK

Sociologists characterize ours as a **risk society** (Beck, 1992). Their point is not that our lives are especially risky—they obviously are not. Compared with people living at other times and in other places, we have long life expectancies; we have reduced all sorts of risks— everything from smallpox to tiger attacks. Rather, a risk society is one that is conscious of and organized to control risks. The media play a key role in a risk society by reporting about risks.

Most media coverage of risks relays the social problems claims of activists or experts. The term *risk* carries connotations of science and medicine, of someone having measured relative danger. Thus, it is common to encounter a news story about research reporting that something (such as using a cell phone, drinking diet soda, or whatever) increases the risk of some negative outcome (such as getting some disease or dropping out of school). These can be interesting news stories, particularly if the risky activity is widespread, so that it involves many people in the news audience, and if the outcome seems dire, so that a story reporting on risk can seem quite compelling ("Good grief! I'm in danger!").

Moreover, news stories about risk take a familiar form. Such stories have been commonplace for decades, which means that claimsmakers can draw upon ideas about risk as a cultural resource in assembling claims that the media are likely to find newsworthy, and they can borrow rhetoric from earlier, successful campaigns to raise concern about some risk, just as news workers have a good sense of how to rework those claims into news stories. Moreover, it isn't necessary to ground antirisk claims in research. The language of risk can be applied to all sorts of topics; claimsmakers and news workers use the expression *at risk* freely, to speak of children at risk, and so on. Such claims draw attention to the need to take precautions: if we don't act to protect them, some people at risk may be harmed. The implication of this rhetoric is that risks are not just bad but unacceptable, and that they ought to be prevented.

Media critics note that there are problems with reporting about risk. For one thing, the fact that a risk is measurable does not mean that it is especially important. To be sure, some risks are a big deal. Take smokers' risks of getting lung cancer. There are a lot of smokers, lung cancer is relatively common (more that a quarter of cancer deaths involve lung cancer), and smokers are about twenty times more likely than nonsmokers to be diagnosed with lung cancer. We can imagine that, if no one smoked, there would be a substantial drop in lung cancer deaths, so covering smokers' lung cancer risks seems newsworthy. But suppose that researchers conducted a careful study and found that people who, say, eat cookies had a 20 percent greater chance of coming down with a rare, fatal disease. If the disease afflicts five people per million among people who don't eat cookies, then the rate among cookie eaters is six per million (6 is 20 percent greater than 5). In other words, for every million people who eat cookies, one additional person will get the disease and die. Is the researchers' study newsworthy? Does it warrant launching an anticookie campaign?

Claimsmakers may argue that even very small—one in a million—risks should be prevented. But avoiding risks may have costs. Some people like to eat cookies—but then, people like to smoke, too. Weighing the costs and benefits of risk avoidance is not a simple matter, but media coverage rarely gives these issues much consideration. Note that any large engineering project entails risks. Building bridges and skyscrapers is dangerous work; even when people take precautions, there will be accidents, even fatal ones. Should the risks of fatal accident preclude building bridges and buildings? Similarly, we know that while society as a whole benefits when people receive vaccinations (which lead to reduced numbers of people getting sick), a few people will have serious, adverse reactions to being vaccinated. Does it make sense to refuse a vaccination (and eliminate the small risk of an adverse reaction), if it means that one faces a higher risk of becoming sick? Should people stop smoking? Stop eating cookies? Should there be social policies to reduce these risks? Not everyone will agree about these issues, but media coverage, which often seems to imply that there is a simple choice between a bad risk and some no-cost alternative, often has difficulty covering these debates.

There is another issue: correlation is not proof of causation. The fact that research shows an association between two phenomena (such as cookie eating and a disease) is not proof that one causes the other. It is important to offer a theory, an explanation why there might be a causal relationship. It is easy is understand how smoke particles might irritate lung tissues, but why should eating cookies cause the disease? There is also the danger that a single piece of research may be mistaken. Science requires replication. (The reason we are confident that smoking causes lung cancer is that we have many, many studies that support that conclusion.) But media coverage is more likely to favor a dramatic story about scientific "discovery" ("This just in! Cookies may raise your risks!") than a report explaining why the preponderance of the research evidence favors a particular conclusion.

Risks also figure in entertainment media. Films and novels turn risk into melodrama, with heroes (such as idealistic lawyers) struggling to expose the risks being caused by powerful villains (such as polluting corporations). There is little room for ambiguity about the nature of risk in these portrayals.

In a risk society, claims about risk are commonplace. However, the practices of media workers tend to emphasize particular aspects of these claims. It is much easier to construct risks as simple, straightforward dangers than to present a thoughtful, coherent assessment of risks and their alternatives.

QUESTIONS

1. How do the needs of claimsmakers and the media combine to shape coverage of risks?

2. What are the advantages and disadvantages of reporting on a study that finds a new risk?

3. Why do claims regarding technological innovations and natural disasters often focus on risks?

6

▪

Public Reaction

▪

Discussions of the social problems process usually assume that, at some point, claims reach and influence members of the general public. Sometimes there's a direct connection between the primary claimsmakers and the public, as when people hear a claimsmaker give a speech, or find themselves listening to a claim during a conversation. More often, of course, claims reach the public via the media; people encounter secondary claims on television or radio, or through reading newspapers, magazines, web pages, or books. All this simply reflects the media's ability to reach very large audiences; claimsmakers who receive media coverage can be exposed to a far larger segment of the general public than they can hope to reach through face-to-face contacts.

As part of the audience for claims, members of the public are not completely passive; they can react in various ways. They may be energized and moved to action by some claims, deciding to contribute to a social movement organization, participate in a demonstration, write their legislators, or relay the claims to others they know. Some may treat a claim as interesting information—something to talk over with friends and acquaintances. Others may be indifferent, apathetic; they may find the claim boring and ignore it. Still others may react negatively, disagreeing with the claim and opposing its conclusions. Probably all claims elicit all of these possible reactions in different people.

Because the public is both large and diverse, because people can respond to claims in different ways, and because many of those responses are relatively private (in that people may keep their opinions to themselves or share them only with others they know well), interpreting the public's role in the social problems process poses special problems. Nonetheless, the other actors in the process want to understand the public's reactions. Claimsmakers use the feedback they receive from the public to modify their claims, in hopes of making them more persuasive; the media also attend to feedback from the public, in order to better devise news and entertainment that will capture the audience's attention; and policymakers may respond to public pressure to do something about a particular social problem. Thus, many people want to learn what the public is thinking, in spite of the difficulties in doing so.

This chapter will focus on the methods that claimsmakers, the media, and others involved in the social problems process—as well as sociologists—use to assess public reactions. It will consider several of these, beginning with the most familiar method—public opinion polls or surveys.

MEASURING PUBLIC OPINION

Public opinion polls have become a part of our political landscape that we take for granted. We are used to hearing news reports that polls show one candidate favored to win the upcoming election, that the president's approval rating has risen higher or fallen lower, that the public is more or less concerned about particular issues, and so on. Before considering how public opinion figures into the social problems process, we need to consider how the very methods of polling can affect a survey's results.

The Impact of Polling Methods

Efforts to measure public opinion through polling came of age during the early twentieth century. Usually this research involves conducting a **sample survey**. Because it would be prohibitively expensive to contact, say, all voters or all citizens (what statisticians call the **population**), the poll approaches a **sample** of people within that population and asks them questions. The responses to the poll can be tallied to reveal, for instance, the proportion of sampled voters favoring Candidate A in an election; in turn, the sample's results provide a basis for generalizing about the population by projecting the likely outcome of the election.

Many people are suspicious of sample surveys because the samples seem too small to promise accurate results. National surveys often use samples of 1,000 to 1,500 respondents. How, critics ask, can such a small number of people accurately represent the huge U.S. population (over 300 million)? However reasonable this question might seem, it emphasizes the wrong issue. A relatively small sample—say, 1,000 people—can produce fairly accurate results, as long as it is a **representative sample**—that is, as long as the sample is not selected in ways that make it more likely that some sorts of people will be chosen than others. (Statisticians calculate that, for a population of 300 million, a poll with a representative sample of 1,000 will produce results accurate within about 3 percent, 95 percent of the time. Thus, if a survey shows that 54 percent of voters favor Candidate A, there is a 95 percent probability that between 51 and 57 percent of the population favors A's candidacy. Moreover, larger samples aren't that much more accurate: a 10,000-person sample—for which collecting the data would cost about ten times as much—will produce only slightly more accurate results: accuracy within 1 percent, 95 percent of the time [de Vaus, 1986].)

However, statistical theory's assumptions about representative samples often have to give way to the realities of survey research. It is both difficult and expensive to design perfectly representative samples, and unrepresentative samples can lead to inaccurate results. Consider some sampling problems that affect today's pollsters: an increasing number of households screen calls using answering machines or caller ID, and some of those people may choose not to answer the pollsters' calls; in addition, a growing proportion of the population has only cell phones (which the law requires must be hand dialed, making them more expensive to contact) (Link, Battaglia, Frankel, Osborn, & Mokdad, 2007). Can we assume that people who refuse to answer—or who can't be reached via landlines—have the same distribution of opinions as those who pick up the phone, or should we suspect that those who don't respond or can't be reached may have somewhat different opinions from those of the respondents? Refusal to take the pollsters' calls or having only a cell phone—like any other factor that may make the sample less representative—can damage the accuracy of a survey's results.

In addition, survey results are sensitive to many other influences. Pollsters know that the wording of a question can affect the results. Polling is expensive, and often the costs are covered by claimsmakers who hope to use the results to support their campaigns. As a result, many polls ask questions worded in ways that encourage people to produce the answers that the poll's sponsors favor (see Box 6.1). Of course, when the claimsmakers or sponsors release the poll results to the press, they tend to ignore the questions' wording, while emphasizing the favorable results.

Another important problem is that surveys usually try to distill people's thoughts about complex, multifaceted issues into one or two questions. The result is inevitably crude and oversimplified. For example, many discussions of abortion attitudes imply that people can be classified as either pro-life (opposed to abortion under any circumstances) or pro-choice (in favor of women having complete freedom to choose whether to have abortions) (J. Best, 2001a). But the largest proportion of Americans' attitudes fall somewhere between those extremes: these people favor permitting abortion for

Box 6.1 Wording Survey Questions about Climate Change/Global Warming

Responses to surveys can be affected by how the questions are worded. Terms that some people might assume to mean the same thing can produce very different results. For example, one survey asked half its respondents whether they thought global warming had been happening; the other half were asked whether they thought climate change had been occurring. Overall, 74 percent of the respondents reported believing in climate change, but only 68 percent said they believed in global warming. The wording made no real difference to respondents who said they were Democrats, of whom 87 percent reported believing in global warming, while 86 percent believed in climate change (for independents, the percentages were 70 and 74 percent, respectively). But word choice made a dramatic difference for Republicans: 60 percent acknowledged the reality of climate change, versus only 44 percent who accepted the idea of global warming. This presumably reflects how political leaders in the two parties have addressed the issue, and particularly the efforts of some Republican politicians to discredit claims about global warming.

This is not the only case in which the words used to characterize a social issue have made a difference in survey responses; people are, for instance, much more likely to favor "assistance to the poor" than they are "welfare." Interpreting the results of public opinion requires thinking critically about the questions that were asked.

Sources: Bishop, 2005; Schuldt, Konrath, & Schwarz, 2011.

"good" reasons (such as pregnancies resulting from rape or incest, or cases in which continuing the pregnancy might endanger the woman's life), but they have reservations about allowing abortions for less compelling reasons. A simple question asking whether the respondent favors or opposes abortion cannot hope to accurately measure these complicated attitudes.

We should also remember that answering a survey is a social situation. That is, respondents who are interacting with a pollster usually want to make a good impression, to be a good respondent. This means that some respondents may try to say whatever they believe the pollster might think they ought to say. For example, if a pollster asks whether X should be considered a serious problem, the very fact that the question is being asked suggests that at least some people consider X a problem, and some respondents may feel that they ought to agree that, yes, X should be considered a serious problem. But responding in that way to a question does not mean that the respondent actually spends much time thinking about—let alone worrying about—X.

In short, a variety of methodological issues—who is polled, how the questions are phrased, and so on—can affect the results of survey research. Every survey's results have been shaped by the choices that the people conducting the surveys have made, and those people may have designed their poll to produce particular results. This doesn't mean that all survey results are meaningless, but they need to be viewed with some caution. After all, media coverage of poll results is fairly common, and this measure of public opinion often becomes a factor in the social problems process.

Constructing the Meaning of Public Opinion

Typically, discussions of the role of public opinion in the social problems process have two distinct themes. First, analysts argue that public opinion is a product of claimsmaking and media coverage of social problems, that effective claims can make the public aware of and concerned about some social problem. Second, policymakers are assumed to be responsive to public opinion; that is, it is assumed that high public concern about a social problem will in turn lead policymakers to try to do something about that problem.

Factors Affecting Public Opinion. Some evidence suggests that public opinion can be affected by media coverage. However, it

Box 6.2 How Citizens Make Sense of News

People do not passively accept the messages they receive from the media; rather, consuming the news is an active process. Interviews with ordinary citizens about how they respond to the news reveal a set of complex attitudes. Most people get their news from multiple places; they aren't receiving all of their information from a single source. They are also fairly critical of the news, which they interpret as being shaped by a variety of factors, including the influence of advertisers, upon whom both print and electronic journalists depend; the policies of the companies that own the media; the media's need to attract an audience by supplying people with the sort of coverage they will find appealing; the various deadlines and other time pressures that impinge upon news workers; and the ideological biases of those producing the news. Interestingly, most people are satisfied that they personally consume enough news to have a pretty good understanding about what is happening in the world, even as they suspect that many of their fellow citizens are not well informed.

In other words, ordinary individuals play active roles in constructing their own ideas about the world. They do not simply and uncritically accept information that they get from others. They have ideas about where that information comes from and how and why it might have been shaped by other actors. Public reactions to claims involve further reconstructions of social problems as people decide what they should think about media coverage.

Source: Ostertag, 2010.

is important not to exaggerate the media's influence; people are not passive recipients of media messages who automatically must accept whatever the media tells them (see Box 6.2). The media are probably more effective at agenda setting than at communicating particular messages. That is, they may be better able to influence what topics people are thinking about than what exactly people think about those topics.

For example, one study (Beckett, 1994) found that the proportion of people who expressed concern about crime in polls did not correlate well with official crime rates—concern for crime might rise even when the crime rate was falling; similarly, public concern about illegal drug use did not correlate closely with official measures of drug use. In other words, the shifts in public concern about crime and drug use revealed in surveys do not seem to have been responses to changes in the actual levels of those conditions. However, public opinion did correspond fairly closely with media coverage of crime and drug use, and particularly with officials' announcements about anticrime and antidrug policies (which were, of course, covered by the press). The media coverage tended to rise first, with public opinion following somewhat later; that is, opinions lagged behind media coverage. Thus, increased media coverage of crime and drug problems led to higher proportions of poll respondents expressing concerns about crime and drugs.

This example suggests that the public can be influenced to at least pay attention to heavily publicized social problems. And naturally the perception that this is true affects the behavior of claimsmakers, who work hard to promote their constructions of social problems by gaining media coverage, in hopes of arousing public concern. Of course, concern is not spread evenly throughout the population. On most issues, opinions vary with the respondents' characteristics: differences in race, social class (as measured by education or income), age, gender, and region often influence people's opinions. The media cannot affect everyone equally, but they can sometimes arouse fairly broad public concern about a particular troubling condition.

The Impact of Public Opinion. Survey results contribute to the social problems process in two major ways. First, polls offer feedback at earlier stages in the process. Claimsmakers use polls to determine whether their claims are effective or ineffective, hoping that their efforts—particularly if they have received a reasonable amount of media coverage—will cause public opinion to shift in the direction the claimsmakers favor. For instance, imagine that gun control advocates mount a campaign to promote a new law restricting guns. They may organize demonstrations, testify before legislators, appear on talk shows, and so on, in an effort to make the public aware of the issue. If polls taken following this effort suggest that a growing portion of the public is aware of and favors the proposed gun control law, the claimsmakers will view this result as evidence that their campaign has been effective. But, of course, if the poll results do not reveal a substantial shift in public opinion in support of their position, the advocates may look for ways to alter their claims, in hopes of making them more effective. Polls, then, provide feedback to claimsmakers.

The second major way polls affect the social problems process is that policymakers often follow poll results. In particular, elected officials may view evidence of widespread concern about a troubling condition as an indication that they need to take action, to develop a new policy to address the problem. This is not an automatic response. Poll results are one of the considerations that may influence officials, but they are by no means the only one. Still, it is possible to track poll results as "the voice of the people," and to justify policymaking as a response to what the public wants. Polls become one element in the construction of policymaking—a topic that will receive further attention in Chapter 7.

FOCUS GROUPS AND OTHER INTERVIEWS

Survey questionnaires are limited by the questions asked. Sampling does allow analysts to measure the relative distribution of opinions in large populations, but each respondent's views tend to be reduced to relatively simplistic responses to particular questions; moreover, as we have noted, those responses can be affected by precisely how the questions are worded, the order in which questions are asked, and so on.

Sometimes researchers try to circumvent these problems by organizing **focus groups**. Focus groups are sets of people to which a moderator poses questions that stimulate discussion on a particular topic. Group members may be chosen so that the group has a particular racial composition, level of education, and so on. Sometimes the members are acquaintances, who presumably will feel comfortable talking with one another about controversial social issues. Focus groups have several advantages over surveys. Individuals have more freedom to express their ideas about the topic, to qualify their remarks and explain what they really mean. In addition, the group is a social setting in which people can respond to one another's comments.

Focus groups often reveal that the public's views about social problems are more complex than the simple pro/con disagreements revealed by many surveys. Analysts tend to imagine that the public's views are internally consistent, and that they reflect the sorts of ideological consistency that claimsmakers often bring to the social problems process. Compared with these expectations, the views of members of the public often seem confused, ambivalent, or uncertain. These apparent inconsistencies can become evident in focus group discussions. Focus groups also allow individuals to express emotional reactions to issues.

Studies of focus groups reveal that individuals tend to draw upon at least three sorts of information when discussing social problems (Gamson, 1992; Sasson, 1995b): First, they use popular wisdom—"commonsense" understandings about how the world works as expressed in aphorisms, stereotypes, and so on. Second, people refer to personal experiences—things that have happened to them or others they know. Third, they may adopt various information and ideas derived from media messages about the larger world, including not just news reports, but also the various forms of infotainment and popular culture that depict the workings of the world beyond our personal experience. Popular wisdom, personal experiences, and media discourse are resources that can be used to construct public definitions of social problems, and focus group conversations reveal how people weave these elements together (see Box 6.3). In general, groups that are able to integrate all three sorts of information—to combine their personal beliefs and experiences with information about the larger world—are more confident that their constructions are correct and more willing to defend their views.

Given the importance of experiential knowledge in focus groups, it should be no surprise that people with different backgrounds construct issues differently. Such background characteristics as race, social class, gender, age, and education affect how people think about social problems. For example, among groups given the task of discussing crime, references to racism in the criminal justice system were relatively common in all-black groups, but relatively rare in all-white groups (Sasson, 1995b). In some cases, African American group members presented conspiracy theories, arguing that powerful whites supplied guns and drugs to poor black neighborhoods as a means of keeping them disadvantaged (Sasson, 1995a). Such findings illustrate a strength of focus groups; survey researchers might not even think to ask questions that could reveal whether their respondents hold such views.

The results of focus groups can, in turn, influence claimsmakers. Like political consultants trying to understand voters' views during election campaigns and firms seeking to market their products to consumers, activists sometimes use focus groups to better understand what the public is thinking. Identification of the frames that emerge within focus groups can be used to revise claims so that they are tailored to influence the public more effectively. For example, when opponents of abortion successfully campaigned against public funding for abortions during the 1980s, abortion rights advocates organized focus groups that revealed that people who opposed such

---

Box 6.3 Telling Stories about 9/11

Focus groups need not involve face-to-face encoutners. After the 2001 terrorist attacks, an online forum was established where people could discuss future plans for the World Trade Center site (such as what sort of memorial would be appropriate, or whether the site ought to be used for low-income housing). While some participants simply presented their reasons, others told stories about their own experiences or those of other people.

Storytelling might seem to be an indirect way of talking about social problems, but that's the point. Those who told stories tended to be in the minority on the issue being discussed. Rather than confronting the majority directly, they used stories to suggest why they disagreed, to illuminate issues that the majority might be overlooking, and thereby to try to redirect the discussion. It was a tool favored by the weak; those who believed that most others agreed with them could simply give reasons, but those who sensed that most people disagreed with them found it useful to tell stories, to make their point without direct confrontation.

Similarly, participants in focus groups often draw upon their personal experiences, as well as popular wisdom and information gleaned from the media, to support their views. Claims of first-hand experience are difficult to discredit; others may be reluctant to directly challenge a story, although they may of course draw conclusions different from those of the storyteller.

Source: Polletta & Lee, 2006; Sasson, 1995b.

---

funding also objected to government intrusion in their lives (Saletan, 2003). Abortion rights advocates used this knowledge to craft a new argument—that the right to have an abortion was tied to a broader right to privacy; in this view, restrictions against abortion became another form of government interference in people's private lives. This new pro-choice campaign proved relatively effective.

As a source of information about public reactions, focus groups obviously have limitations. They are relatively costly in terms of time and money, and it is impossible to know how representative particular groups may be. Much depends on the moderator's skill in directing the conversation, making sure that the various participants have their say, and so on. Still, focus groups can be an important way of discovering what ordinary people think about social problems.

LEGENDS, JOKES, AND OTHER FOLKLORE

Public opinion polls and even focus groups involve somewhat artificial, formalized situations in which people know that their opinions are being solicited for analysis, and this knowledge may affect what the people who participate are willing to say. But talk about social problems also is the stuff of everyday conversations. It would be nice to know how members of the public construct social problems when they are not self-conscious about being observed. Studying folklore offers one way of examining such everyday constructions.

The term *folklore* refers to information that is disseminated informally, among the *folk*—that is, among ordinary people. Traditionally folklore was transmitted orally, rather than through writing: people told one another folktales, or taught each other folk songs, folk dancing, or folk crafts. You may have a mental image of a folklorist seeking out old folks living in remote corners of society, hoping to capture traditional folk wisdom that is in danger of disappearing as the last generation to have this knowledge fades. This common image equates folklore with an elderly person perched in a rocking chair on a rickety, unpainted front porch, talking about the old days.

This is a mistaken image because it is far too narrow. *All* people have folklore—young people, people living in cities, everyone. Contemporary folklore spreads in new ways—in photocopied bits of humor posted in offices (Dundes & Pagter, 2000) or through faxes ("faxlore") and e-mail messages—as well as by the traditional means of word of mouth. And some of the time, this folklore expresses ordinary people's reactions to social problems claims. Let's consider two common folklore genres: contemporary legends and joke cycles.

Contemporary Legends

Sometimes called *urban legends*, **contemporary legends** are stories that people tell one another (Ellis, 2001; Fine, 1992). In general, contemporary legends lack supernatural elements; they are far more likely to feature criminals than, say, ghosts. Typically the teller claims—and the listener believes—that the story is true, that the events in the story really happened. Often the teller offers evidence of the story's truth, such as identifying the place where it happened (perhaps a nearby shopping mall), or explaining the teller's connection to a person who witnessed or experienced the events: "This really happened to my roommate's cousin's neighbor." Folklorists refer to this sort of attribution as a *FOAF* (for *Friend Of A Friend*). Efforts to trace the story back to the FOAF inevitably fail; the roommate's cousin's neighbor may agree that the story is true but explain that "it actually happened to my mother-in-law's brother's friend."

As legends spread, the details tend to shift. A story about a horrible crime at a shopping mall may be revised so that it is relocated at the local mall; the shocking thing that someone said on a TV talk show may be said to have occurred on several different programs, and so on. Folklorists call the differing versions of the same tale **variants**. Variants often make the story more interesting to the audience; for example, the story is better if, instead of having happened at an unknown mall somewhere, the events are described as having actually occurred at a nearby mall.

Contemporary legends must be good stories—good enough for people to remember them and want to repeat them—in order to spread. Thus, effective legends tend to evoke strong emotional reactions, such as fear or disgust (Heath, Bell, & Sternberg, 2001). People are more likely to recall—and repeat—stories that pack a punch. Often legends warn that the world is far more dangerous than we might imagine: that gang members lurk beneath our parked cars or in our backseats, that terrible crimes occur in the mall where we shop, that having a drink with an attractive stranger may lead to having a kidney stolen, and so on.

What is the difference between a rumor and a legend? The distinction is somewhat blurry. Basically, *rumors* tend to be specific, confined to a particular time and place. They spread in conditions of uncertainty; they report "improvised news" when more authoritative information is not available, and they tend to be short-lived, one-of-a-kind stories (Fine, Campion-Vincent, & Heath, 2005; Shibutani, 1966). Rumors tend to have local relevance: they refer to a case of corruption by a local official, a local business in trouble, and so on.

In contrast, *legends* can survive over decades—they may lie dormant for a time, only to be revived. A story may pass through a city, disappear for years, but then reappear. Though a legend may include local references ("It happened at our mall"), the same story may be told as having occurred in many places. Legends often invoke familiar **motifs**; that is, the same elements recur in many legends. For example, many contemporary legends involve maniacs with sharp objects—the escaped killer with a hook replacing his missing hand, the man (disguised as an old lady) with a hatchet, Halloween apples laced with razor blades, and such—just as a surprising number of contemporary legends involve terrible crimes at shopping malls (see Box 6.4). Legends can supply raw material for rumors; that is, familiar legendary elements, such as villainous conspiracies, can easily be reworked to become the stuff of a new rumor.

What do rumors and contemporary legends have to do with social problems? They often reflect contemporary claimsmaking: when the media report on the dangers of drugs, stories circulate

Box 6.4 Don't Take a Card, Any Card

A colleague forwarded the following e-mail message to me (I have edited it a bit—the original message specified the location of the gas station in Delaware and supposedly originated with a Wilmington police officer):

A female was approached by a man in a pickup truck at the gas station on [location]. A man got out of the truck and passed out his business card while the other man stayed in the driver's seat of the truck. The card advertised a yard work/maintenance company. There was an e-mail address but no telephone number to contact.

She said no, but accepted his card out of courtesy and got in her car. As the lady left the service station, she saw the men following her out of the station at the same time. Almost immediately, she started to feel dizzy and could not catch her breath. She tried to open the window and realized that the odor she had been smelling was on her hand; the same hand which accepted the card from the gentleman at the gas station. She then noticed the men were immediately behind her and she felt she needed to do something at that moment.

She drove into the first driveway and began to honk her horn repeatedly to ask for help. The men drove away but the lady still felt pretty bad for several minutes after she could finally catch her breath. Apparently, there was a substance on the card that could have seriously injured her.

This drug is called 'BURUNDANGA' and it is used by people who wish to incapacitate a victim in order to steal from or take advantage of them. This drug is four times more dangerous than the date rape drug and is transferable on simple cards. So take heed and make sure you don't accept cards at any given time you are alone or from someone on the streets. This applies to those making house calls and slipping you a card when they offer their services.

I received this version in 2011, but the story has been in circulation since at least 2008. It has been debunked on several websites devoted to hoaxes and contemporary legends.

This tale incorporates several motifs that appear in other contemporary legends: the gas station as a public place where one may encounter dangerous strangers, the menace of a powerful drug that can incapacitate the unwary, and a lone woman who cleverly outwits the villains who intend to harm her. Passed along as a warning, this story constructs the social world as a threatening place, where individuals can be victimized by social problems.

about drug dealers giving small children LSD-laced lick-on tattoos; when gangs become a hot news story, tales of vicious gang initiation rites circulate; and so on. Many contemporary legends respond to current claims, but they also reconstruct those claims to fit the constraints of legend. Their need to be memorable means that legends tend to be melodramatic; these stories feature innocent, vulnerable victims preyed upon by villains whose evil nature explains their crimes. Why would drug dealers distribute LSD to preschoolers? That's just the sort of bad thing those bad people do. Just as news and entertainment media reshape primary claims to fit the demands of their respective genres, legends rework the topics of the media's secondary claims to make them disturbing, dramatic, and memorable—the qualities of successful legends.

Rumors and legends often revolve around social conflicts. Many tales, for example, center around racial or ethnic conflict (Fine & Turner, 2001). Typically, these stories circulate within one ethnic group and describe the nefarious activities of people of another ethnicity. In the United States, for instance, there is a long history of both whites spreading tales about blacks, and blacks telling stories about whites. Sometimes these stories are mirror images of one another—the same story, only with the races reversed. A major race riot in Detroit in 1943 featuring open conflict between blacks and whites, for example, was inspired by rumors that a woman and her baby had been thrown off a local bridge (Langlois, 1983). But the story whites told one another featured a white woman and baby thrown off the bridge by blacks, while blacks shared a story of a black woman and baby thrown off the bridge by whites. In either case, the incident was apparently imaginary; there was no evidence that anyone had been thrown off a bridge.

Stories based on ethnic tensions do not necessarily have such precise counterparts. Several stories circulating among African Americans, for instance, warn that particular companies have connections to racist groups (for example, that a fried-chicken franchise is owned by the Ku Klux Klan); or report that a popular clothing designer appeared on a TV talk show and stated that he (or she—the story is told about different designers) did not want black people wearing the designer's clothes, so he (or she) deliberately designed clothing lines that would not fit blacks (Fine & Turner, 2001). Such stories share an underlying theme that African Americans have a subordinate place in a largely white-controlled economy. Not surprisingly, whites do not have many such tales about black-controlled firms (although they have circulated warnings that some businesses are controlled by other conspiratorial elements, such as satanists).

Other contemporary legends explore gender conflict. For example, women pass along warnings about methods that gang members, rapists, and other criminals use to prey on women, just as men share stories about seductive women who intend to harm males. Any social fault line—between ethnic groups, the sexes, bosses and employees, students and professors, and so on—can inspire rumors or legends (see the case study at the end of the chapter for a discussion of legends about immigration).

Other social changes also inspire contemporary legends. For instance, numerous legends warn about the risks of AIDS, including the widespread story of a person who awakens after a sexual encounter to discover the message "Welcome to the World of AIDS" written on the bathroom mirror, and warnings that AIDS-infected

IV-drug users leave used needles in the coin return slots of pay phones (Goldstein, 2004). Similarly, stories of organ thefts—that is, of stolen eyes, kidneys, and other human organs—have global popularity (Campion-Vincent, 2005). In less developed countries, these stories warn about westerners who only pretend to adopt children but actually harvest their organs to be used for transplants in the United States; Americans and Europeans tell one another about people awakening after sexual encounters only to discover that a kidney has been removed. The morals of these stories—warnings about imperialistic exploitation or the risks of casual sex—reflect issues that are themselves the subject of claimsmaking (see Box 6.5).

As these examples illustrate, the larger significance of rumors and contemporary legends is that they are, in a sense, ripped from the headlines. They translate topics of claimsmakers' concern—racial and ethnic tensions, the impact of immigration, the spread of AIDS, and so on—into melodramatic, disturbing stories, however unlikely, that people tell one another, assuring their listeners that the tales are really true, that the events happened nearby, to someone who knows someone they know. To be sure, many of those who pass along these stories do not think of themselves as participating in the social problems process. Rather, they consider these merely memorable stories, troubling and worth repeating. They probably don't view themselves as claimsmakers, or these stories about social problems as claims.

Note, however, that many rumors and contemporary legends do share a worldview. They generally warn that the world is a dangerous place, bedeviled by dangerous villains, and that one can't be too careful. Ordinary activities, such as driving in a car, visiting the shopping mall, and striking up a conversation with a stranger turn out to be portals into a world of violence and victimization. Thus, there is a sort of conservatism underlying most contemporary legends, a worldview characterized by the suspicion that change is dangerous and needs to be approached with great caution.

Box 6.5 Worrying about Spiked Drinks

Warnings that would-be rapists slip drugs into the drinks of young women are widespread; concern about this threat is especially pervasive on college campuses. Students are encouraged to take elaborate precautions to prevent anyone from spiking their drinks; many report that they know someone who had a drink spiked, and some even insist it has happened to their own drinks.

Perhaps surprisingly, law enforcement officials discount these fears. Chemical tests of suspected spiked drinks routinely fail to reveal any evidence of drugs. Some police have dismissed drink spiking as an urban legend.

What accounts for students' insistence on a threat that police consider imaginary? Contemporary female students drink more than their counterparts did in earlier years; there is an expectation that young women—no less than young males—should be able to manage the effects of alcohol. Moreover, weight-conscious students may eat relatively little while they are drinking. The effects of drinking on an empty stomach may include dizziness, even loss of consciousness, yet the expectations that women can handle their drinking means they must search for some other explanation. Therefore, someone who gets woozy after drinking must have been the victim of a drink spiker. In this way, a contemporary legend offers a framework for interpreting everyday experiences, for explaining a difficult drinking experience, not as a personal lapse in control, but as evidence of a larger social problem.

Source: Burgess, Donovan, & Moore, 2009.

Joke Cycles

A second form of contemporary folklore that builds on social problems claimsmaking is the **joke cycle**. Joke cycles are sets of jokes that share a form ("knock knock" jokes) or a topic (jokes about blondes); a cycle often becomes quite popular for a time, before losing favor. Some folklorists seek to explain the emergence of particular joke cycles as reactions to awareness of social problems; Dundes (1987) argued that the popularity of elephant jokes in the 1960s reflected public attitudes toward the civil rights movement, and the dead-baby joke cycle of the 1970s was a reaction to concern about abortion and contraception.

At first glance, these interpretations may seem peculiar, but Dundes noted that elephant jokes (for instance, "Why do elephants paint their toenails red? To hide in cherry trees") often ridicule the elephant's efforts to fit into a particular setting, and they often portray elephants as sexually dangerous. The timing of this joke cycle—it emerged in the 1960s, when the civil rights movement was at its height—suggests that this may have been an indirect means of expressing resistance to the cause of integration.

Similarly, the dead-baby joke cycle (for example, "What's red and sits in a corner? A baby chewing razor blades") presented various disturbing images and emerged during the early 1970s, shortly after the contraceptive pill became widespread and around the time that abortion was being legalized. It is not impossibly far-fetched to view joking about dead babies as linked to ambivalence about these changes. Although not everyone finds them convincing, such interpretations suggest that even the silliest-seeming joke cycles may be part of the social problems process.

Many joke cycles pose much less difficult interpretive problems. There is a long tradition of joke cycles that play on and reinforce racial, religious, or ethnic stereotypes (Dundes, 1987). Similarly, other joke cycles are grounded in stereotypes regarding gender or sexual orientation. Various joke cycles depict different target groups as being lazy, stupid, dirty, sexually promiscuous, or having other undesirable qualities. Repeating such jokes can be seen as a sort of claim about different sorts of people, although of course it is always possible for those telling the jokes to deny this, to insist that they're just joking.

The links between joking and claimsmaking are especially apparent with joke cycles inspired by dramatic current events—such as the explosion of the space shuttle *Challenger* in 1986; the deaths at the Branch Davidian compound in Waco, Texas, in 1993; or the terrorist attacks on the World Trade Center on September 11, 2001 (Ellis, 2003; Lowney & Best, 1996; Oring, 1987). One important quality of such **topical joke cycles** is that we know the date they started spreading. Obviously there were no *Challenger* jokes before January 28, 1986 (the day the explosion occurred).

Studies of topical joke cycles reveal that such jokes spread widely and very rapidly through informal channels. Media commentators, for instance, noted the existence of jokes about the *Challenger* within a few days following the catastrophe, although the jokes themselves were not circulated by the media (which viewed the jokes as in very bad taste and therefore unrepeatable). In these cases, both the number of jokes told and the number of people who reported having heard them increased rapidly in the days and weeks following the event that inspired the jokes (Ellis, 1991; Lowney & Best, 1996). Of course, after a few weeks people stopped telling these jokes, presumably because those who might have enjoyed them had, by that time, already heard them, but also because the subject no longer seemed topical.

Topical jokes tend to spread where they have relevance. Local scandals may become the subject of local joke cycles, but they are unlikely to spread beyond that locality. For example, the on-camera suicide of Pennsylvania's state treasurer in 1987 inspired a joke cycle in that state, but those jokes did not spread widely beyond the area where he was a familiar figure (Bronner, 1988). In much the same way, the 1986 Chernobyl nuclear reactor disaster—which released radiation—did not become the subject of extensive joking in the United States (which seemed geographically far removed from the danger), but it did become the subject of a substantial joke cycle in Europe (where people worried about their exposure to radioactive contamination) (Kurti, 1988).

Why do people tell jokes about disasters? It is easy to argue that there is nothing funny about these events, and that such jokes are

---

Box 6.6 Joking about Disasters

In March 2011, a major earthquake off the coast of Japan caused a destructive tsunami wave that killed many thousands of people and triggered a series of accidents at nuclear power plants. This terrible disaster commanded the attention of the news media, but it also inspired jokes, most of which were posted on Internet sites. These jokes, in turn, attracted outraged criticism that there was nothing funny about the tragedy; a couple of celebrities who had tweeted jokes were denounced and forced to issue public apologies.

Jokes cycles following disasters are actually fairly common; the explosion of the space shuttle *Challenger*, the accident at the Chernobyl nuclear power plant, and the devastation of New Orleans following Hurricane Katrina all became subjects of joke cycles. Some jokes imply a point of view, such as criticism of the authorities, but others seem to be nothing but silly puns. Often the jokes themselves become subjects of claimsmaking; they are criticized for being tasteless, inhumane, or expressing racist or sexist sentiments.

Public opinion is not uniform; opinions—including opinions about what is funny, and what are appropriate subjects for joking—vary. But many jokes are topical, and they offer one way that ordinary people can participate in the social problems process. While we cannot assume that everyone who tells a joke endorses a particular point of view, jokes at least let people express views that they might be reluctant to voice in a more serious manner.

---

inappropriate. The most popular explanations are psychological—either that such jokes are symptoms of a "sick" society, or that telling jokes is cathartic and eases people's psychological strain. Sociologists might argue, however, that topical jokes, like contemporary legends that address subjects of current claimsmaking, offer an indirect way of expressing public attitudes toward troubling social conditions. Jokes often reveal skepticism: the vast majority of jokes about the Branch Davidians characterized them as deviant, and jokes about other disasters often seem to question the authorities' wisdom (see Box 6.6).

Here it is worth noting one other form of folk humor: the pho-
tocopies of jokes, cartoons, mock memos, and such that are posted
in offices and other workplaces (Dundes & Pagter, 2000). This
"office folklore" has become much easier to reproduce and disseminate, thanks to improved technologies, such as photocopiers,
fax machines, e-mail, and computer software, which allow people
to create, modify, store, and transmit photos and other graphics
very easily (Ellis, 2003). Often these bits of folklore suggest considerable skepticism about the workings of bureaucracies and the
abilities of their leaders. Like legends and joke cycles, such office
humor often addresses ethnicity, class, gender, and other familiar
bases for social conflict. The fact that they are widespread suggests
that their subversive reconstructions of different social problems
are relatively popular, although—as is the case with all other types
of folklore—it is always possible to shrug off objections by insisting that these postings aren't serious commentary, that they are
just in fun. Still, such folklore remains one way in which ordinary
people can express their thoughts and respond to more visible
claimsmakers.

THE PUBLIC'S ROLE IN THE
SOCIAL PROBLEMS PROCESS

Although opinion polls, focus groups, and contemporary folklore
all offer ways of understanding something about how the general public responds to constructions of social problems made by
claimsmakers and the media, none of these methods can hope to
tell the whole story. After all, the general public is very large and
very diverse. It includes people who virtually ignore social problems
claims, but also people who follow claimsmaking with enthusiasm.
It includes people from a wide range of social groupings—different
occupations, different ethnicities, different social classes, different
genders and sexual orientations, different political ideologies, and

on and on. These various groups have, if not different values, at least different interpretations of which values are most important and how they ought to be realized. There are, then, all sorts of differences that can affect how people in the general public will respond to particular social problems claims.

Moreover, even people who seem to respond in the same way—who, for example, give the same response to a survey question—may, in fact, be quite different. Some people may be energized by particular claims—they may become committed, inspired to join the cause, to devote their time, money, and energy to bringing about change. Others may become interested enough to follow the issue, to read books and articles on the topic, watch TV coverage, and become well informed, although they may never actually enlist in the cause. Still others may be only dimly aware of the claims, knowing enough to tell a pollster that they think the problem is serious, but not moved to do anything more. In other words, what people mean when they respond to a survey question indicating their concern is not at all clear.

Similarly, people who hear and repeat contemporary legends or jokes may understand this folklore in very different ways. Some may indeed view themselves as participating in the social problems process, as expressing particular beliefs or attitudes; for example, probably many people who tell ethnic jokes understand that, in so doing, they are promoting particular stereotypes. But others may insist that this is just innocent fun, that it has no larger meaning.

Earlier chapters noted that claimsmakers often hope to affect public opinion, to make people aware of and concerned about a troubling condition, and that the media justify their own activities by referring to the importance of an informed public. Similarly, policy-makers (discussed in Chapter 7) often argue that they are responsive to the "will of the people." Other actors in the social problems process, then, argue that public reactions play an important role. Claimsmakers, the media, and policymakers want to reach—and influence—the public, but those actors also pay attention to the

Figure 6.1 THE PUBLIC'S ROLE IN THE SOCIAL PROBLEMS PROCESS

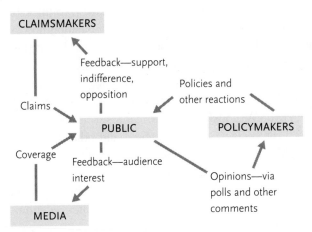

public's reactions and try to adjust their own behavior in response (see Figure 6.1).

This book has emphasized the competitive nature of the social problems process: there are countless claims being promoted, and nearly as many media reports about troubling conditions. With all these bids for the public's attention, some claims inevitably must fail to attract the public's notice. This is why rhetoric—the way claims and media coverage are packaged—becomes important; the public is likely to ignore many claims and focus only on those that it finds particularly compelling.

This chapter has argued that all the ways in which social scientists measure public reactions, including public opinion surveys, focus groups, and folklore, offer indirect, imprecise ways of interpreting what the public is thinking. We might wonder, then, whether we can hope to fully understand this stage in the social problems process.

However, there is other evidence of public reactions. Over time, we can also witness changes in people's behavior that reveal responses to claimsmaking. For instance, motorists have become more likely to use seat belts; some of this change is doubtless due to laws that subject people who fail to buckle up to fines, but it is also true that a growing proportion of the population now buckles up automatically, as a matter of habit. Over time, the proportion of the adult population that smokes has fallen—again, partly because of higher taxes and restrictions on where smoking is permitted, but also partly because a growing proportion of people sees smoking as risky behavior. Although our ways of measuring these changes are imperfect, the incidence of child abuse and other family violence has probably fallen, people's willingness to express racist sentiments in surveys has dropped, and so on.

We can, in short, find evidence of actual changes in people's behavior motivated, at least in part, by the public's redefining what is wise, prudent, or appropriate. Although we cannot measure the public's reactions with precision, we can still recognize that the public is responsive to—and an active part of—the larger social problems process.

MAKING CONNECTIONS

- *Claimsmakers study public reactions and reframe their claims on the basis of the feedback they receive from the public. See Chapters 2, 3, and 4 for more about the claimsmaking process.*

- *Public opinion polls that measure the reaction to claims about a social problem also help determine which issues garner attention from policymakers. In the next chapter, you will learn more about the policymaking process.*

- *Public reactions to social problems change over time. Chapter 10 discusses how reactions to social problems have evolved throughout history.*

CASE STUDY
Public Reactions to Immigration

Public reactions to social issues can be complicated, particularly regarding valence issues that feature competing claims and counterclaims. While news reports often depict public opinion in simplistic, straightforward terms, attitudes often vary in complex ways.

Americans have a long history of worrying about immigration; the current concern is neither a recent development nor especially intense. Survey research shows that opinions about immigration are divided (Segovia & Defever, 2010). For instance, the Gallup Poll regularly asks whether immigration should be kept at its present level, increased, or decreased (Gallup, 2011). Between 2005 and 2010 about 45 percent of Americans favored decreasing immigration, but about 35 percent favored maintaining the current level. This actually represents more favorable attitudes than in the not-too-distant past: in 1995, more than 60 percent favored decreasing immigration, while less than 30 percent approved of present levels. On many questions, large proportions of people express concern about or disapproval of immigration; for instance, about 40 percent say they worry a great deal about immigration, and another quarter say they worry a fair amount.

Still, the public also has some positive things to say about immigrants: about 45 percent believe that immigrants work harder than native-born Americans, while another 40 percent say they work just as hard; and about twice as many agree that immigrants generally contribute to America as argue that immigrants generally cause problems—although somewhat more respondents say that immigrants mostly hurt the economy than say they mostly help. Nor do Americans agree about what should be done about immigration: a 2011 poll found that 43 percent favored, but 55 percent opposed, a law "to give some illegal immigrants living in the U.S. a path to legal status"; but only 44 percent favored taking steps "to deny automatic citizenship to children born in the U.S. whose parents are illegal immigrants" (Gallup, 2011). Although they can't agree about what should be done about immigration, solid majorities report they are dissatisfied with current policies.

Studies of survey attitudes toward immigration in the United States parallel the findings of research conducted in European countries, which also find concern about immigration levels and dissatisfaction with immigration policies (Ceobanu & Escandell, 2010). In general, researchers find that opposition to immigration is unevenly distributed: the more education survey respondents have, the less likely they are to express anti-immigration attitudes; and people who are employed or have jobs that pay well are less opposed to immigration than those whose economic position is less secure (and therefore are more likely to view immigrants as competing for jobs they might like to have).

Public concern with immigration is also evident in a variety of folklore (Fine & Ellis, 2010). Some of this involves overt claims about immigrant groups, as when rumors circulated in several cities in the aftermath of the September 11, 2001, terrorist attacks claiming that Arab Americans had been seen publicly celebrating the destruction of the World Trade Center towers (Langlois, 2005). But other contemporary legends are more oblique. For instance, take the tale about an American couple who vacation in Mexico and discover an adorable little dog that they decide to smuggle back home; when they take their new pet to the veterinarian to get its shots, they are told that it is not a dog, but a "Mexican sewer rat." Similarly, another young couple supposedly bought a Mexican yucca plant as a decoration; when they brought it home, it proved to be infested with poisonous spiders. Or someone buys something—a rug, a jacket, whatever—imported from Asia that turns out to contain a poisonous snake. At first glance, none of these stories seem to be about immigration, but they all share a common theme—a danger coming from something imported from abroad. Moreover, these foreign imports come from Mexico or Asia, the places considered to be the leading sources for illegal immigration. What makes the interpretation that these are stories about immigration especially compelling is that parallel versions of these stories (the plant filled with poisonous-spider eggs and so on) are told in European countries, but in those stories, the foreign elements are imported from North Africa—a major source of illegal immigration into Europe. In other words, there is very good reason to view these tales as expressions of public concern about immigrants and immigration.

Immigration is also a frequent topic for joke cycles. Ethnic jokes often promote stereotypical views—people of this ethnicity are sexually promiscuous, stupid, lazy, dirty, and so on (Dundes, 1987). Often the groups being targeted are current or recent immigrants; probably every ethnic group newly arrived in the United States has faced such joke cycles, often considered deeply offensive by the members of the ethnicity depicted in the jokes. While jokes targeting religious, racial, or ethnic groups have themselves been constructed as a social problem, as tasteless and even harmful, and are perhaps less likely to be shared openly than in the past, even professional entertainers sometimes make immigration a subject for humor (Santa Ana, 2009). The pointed, often hostile criticism that runs through many of these jokes reveals considerable public resistance to immigration.

Issues about which people disagree, such as immigration, reveal the complexity of public reactions in opinion polls, rumors and contemporary legends, and even joke cycles, as people rework primary and secondary claims to express their own concerns.

Questions

1. Why is it important to examine the responses to more than survey questions in trying to assess public reactions to immigration?

2. What role do rumors and legends play in expressing public attitudes toward immigration?

3. What can be learned from examining jokes about a new immigrant group?

7

■

Policymaking

■

Most claimsmakers hope to do more than simply draw attention to a troubling condition; they also want to change things, to improve social arrangements so that the problem can be, if not eliminated, at least made better. Toward this end, claimsmakers seek to change social policies, to alter how the society deals with the troubling condition; and this means that their claims must reach those who have the power to make policy changes—the **policymakers**.

The most obvious way to change policy is through the law. Laws define what is and is not legitimate within a particular jurisdiction; they specify what is required, what is permissible, and what is forbidden. So the study of policymaking turns first to the study of legislative bodies—Congress, state legislatures, city councils, and so on—that not only pass laws but also allocate funds and issue guidelines to the various official agencies that administer those laws.

We are used to seeing media coverage about legislative debates over proposed new laws; such debates can be a high-visibility arena for policymaking. Votes on controversial legislation—to fund or cancel a program, to criminalize or decriminalize a behavior, and so on—are dramatic, visible policymaking moments. But much policymaking is less visible. Many new laws attract little attention, and once passed by legislators, those laws must be implemented, which creates further opportunities for behind-the-scenes policymaking. All manner of government agencies enforce and implement laws. Though our thoughts may turn first to law enforcement agencies (such as the FBI or local police forces), we must recognize that all sorts of administrative agencies oversee how particular laws are applied (for example, the Environmental Protection Agency is charged with administering many federal environmental policies). Even local governments have specialized officials responsible for enforcing health ordinances and other local laws. And because laws usually cannot spell out how they should be applied in every possible circumstance, much of the work of interpreting how the law should be applied falls to such agencies, which therefore find themselves making policy.

In addition, in the United States, court rulings have the power to shape the law. Appellate courts, for example, can rule that legislators have exceeded their authority by passing laws that are unconstitutional, or they can rule that the way a particular law is being applied or enforced is not legal. In dramatic cases (such as the *Roe v. Wade* ruling, which dictated that states could not restrict a woman's access to abortion during the first trimester of pregnancy), Supreme Court rulings can shift fundamental perceptions of what is considered legal. Thus, sometimes government agencies and courts also act as policymakers.

However, we should not equate policy with law. A wide range of organized nongovernmental bodies—think of corporations, churches, professions, charities, and so on—set their own rules or policies. When a homeless shelter announces rules regarding who is qualified to seek admission or how people must behave if they are to be allowed to remain in the shelter, this, too, is a form of policymaking. Although this chapter will tend to concentrate on how legislatures and other government bodies establish laws, we should not forget that policymaking occurs in many different settings.

POLICY DOMAINS

One way sociologists think about how legislators and other policymakers organize policymaking revolves around the concept of
policy domains (Burstein, 1991). A policy domain is that part of
the political system that focuses on a particular social issue, such as
family problems, criminal justice, or health policy. A given domain
includes many people who are especially concerned with the issue
addressed by that domain, including legislators, other officials, and
people outside the government. For example, Congress has committees that deal with health issues; various federal agencies, such
as the Centers for Disease Control and the National Institutes of
Health, address those issues; and outside the government, there
are interest groups, think tanks, medical professionals, and other
experts especially concerned with health policy. In general, health
policy is likely to be formulated by those who belong to that policy
domain; after all, these are the people most knowledgeable about—
and most willing to devote time and energy to—health policy issues.
Although Congress as a whole must vote on health-related legislation, the legislation itself is shaped within the health policy domain.

The concept of a policy domain is akin to but not the same
as the concept of an arena (see Chapter 5). An *arena* is a setting
where claims can be presented (a congressional committee's hearings might be an example). A *policy domain* is a network of people
who share an interest in a particular policy issue; those people
may oversee several arenas in which claims about that issue can
be presented (such as different committees' hearings, specialized
newsletters, and so on).

We can begin thinking about policy domains by considering
the social circumstances of legislators. Although analysts usually
focus on the federal Congress, we can assume that similar considerations affect state and local legislative bodies. Imagine a social
problems claim that has been attracting attention: the media have
been covering the story, public opinion polls may indicate that

people are expressing concern about this troubling condition, and claimsmakers and constituents may contact legislators and ask them to take action. These circumstances might lead to a new law—to policymaking—but then again, they might not.

A new policy is by no means an automatic outcome. After all, there are lots of people who want legislators to do lots of different things, and legislators cannot possibly respond to all of these demands, because there are simply too many calls for action, it would cost too much to implement them all, and many of them call for legislators to take contradictory actions. Moreover, legislators may have their own ideas about what ought to be done (see Box 7.1). Although some claims about valence issues enjoy nearly unanimous agreement (see Chapter 2), people disagree about many position issues, so there may be both people who favor and people who oppose passing a particular law. How can legislators sort out all of these demands?

Recall that Chapter 5 spoke of the media's role in agenda setting. It helps to think of legislators as having an agenda—a prioritized list of things they want to address. The list of demands they face is impossibly long; legislators don't have enough time or enough money to do everything that they are asked to do, so they need to establish priorities, to decide which things really need to be addressed now.

Once again, we see the competitive nature of claimsmaking. Just as claimsmakers must compete for media coverage and public attention, they also must compete for places on legislators' agendas. During this process, claimsmakers may wait years until they finally get legislators to address their concerns. Because laws touch on virtually all aspects of social life, there is terrific competition for legislators' attention among people calling for new laws or changes in existing laws. One result is the establishment of lobbyists, professionals responsible for knowing the ins and outs of the legislative process, who maintain networks of contacts with legislators and their staff members, and who understand how to

Box 7.1 Legislators' Understandings of Sex Crimes

In recent decades, many states have passed tougher laws to control sex offenders, such as laws requiring sex offenders to be registered, restricting where they can live, and even allowing for civil commitments (continuing to hold violent offenders after their sentences have been completed). When legislators vote for tougher laws, what are they thinking?

Interviews with Illinois legislators revealed that they understood sex offenders as a particular type of person—males who were "sick." There was less agreement about the causes of this illness; most thought sex offenders were a product of psychological abnormalities, some blamed biological defects, and a few thought pornography was to blame. Many assumed that, without intervention, sex offenders would eventually attack and even murder children. Moreover, regardless of what they thought might cause sex offending, none of the legislators believed a cure was possible; hence they believed extreme measures were needed and justified.

As it turned out, legislators' ideas about sex offending came from their sense that their constituents were outraged by sex offenses and wanted something done about the problem, and also from the legislators' exposure to media coverage of sex offenses. Experts who had studied or treated sex offenders had relatively little influence on the legislators' thinking.

Given how the legislators constructed the problem of sex offenses—and given the intense publicity that terrible cases receive from the media and the resulting public outrage—it is not difficult to understand why severe policies toward sexual offenders become law.

Source: Sample & Kadleck, 2008.

effectively package claims so as to attract legislators' interest and support. Most industries, professions, and other well-established interest groups maintain permanent lobbying operations to try to influence lawmaking.

Recall the discussion of ownership in Chapter 3—how some claimsmakers become the established authorities on an issue, and how other people turn to those claimsmakers when questions arise regarding their issues. One way to maintain ownership of an issue is to establish a lobbying operation, so that someone is always ready to convey your views to those assembling legislation.

Attempting to influence policymaking can require patience. The political scientist John W. Kingdon (1984) offers one model for understanding how particular policies arrive at the top of Congress's legislative agenda. He describes three streams: (1) the problem recognition stream, (2) the policy proposal stream, and (3) the political stream. Each stream is constantly flowing, but the three streams often have minimal contact with one another. On occasion, however, they seem to converge, and when they do, Congress is more likely to act. While Kingdon's focus was Congress, his three-stream model has implications for other policymakers.

The Problem Recognition Stream

What Kingdon calls the **problem recognition stream** is already familiar; it has been the focus of the preceding chapters. In the process of problem recognition, claimsmakers identify troubling conditions, name those conditions, devise compelling rhetoric to persuade others to become concerned about those conditions, and campaign to bring those conditions to the notice of the press, the public, and policymakers. These claimsmakers' efforts can receive a boost from current events—an attention-grabbing news story about a terrible crime or a natural disaster can catapult an issue into prominence. But most claimsmakers who hope to influence policy need to work to keep their constructions visible, interesting, fresh, and compelling so that they can maintain continual pressure for policymakers to act; thus the claimsmakers' particular views are readily accessible, should the policymakers' attention begin to turn toward their issues.

The Policy Proposal Stream

Kingdon's second stream—the **policy proposal stream**—consists of more specialized constructions, those that offer specific proposals for new legislation. Such proposals may be fairly general, in that they sketch broad ideological approaches toward a new policy; for example, at any given time, there are probably advocates calling for the government to create new programs to help the poor, as well as other advocates arguing that existing antipoverty programs are misguided and ought to be cut back. Other policy proposals may be quite elaborate and specific; advocates may design detailed plans for action or even draft suggested legislation for consideration.

All sorts of people work at devising policy proposals: in addition to the various experts, think tanks, and officials discussed in Chapter 4 who may develop proposals as part of their claimsmaking, there are lobbyists, as well as legislators and their staff members. Whereas outsider claimsmakers tend to concentrate their activities in the problem recognition stream, the policy proposal stream features far more insiders, those members of the polity who populate particular policy domains. Just as claims compete for public recognition, policy proposals compete for policymakers' attention. Again, patience is required: policy advocates must continually test the waters, constantly revise and repackage their proposals, and wait for a moment when those proposals can get a hearing (see Box 7.2).

The Political Stream

Finally, what Kingdon calls the **political stream** refers to what we might think of as the current political situation. Who has been elected, what ideologies do they hold, and what interests do they tend to represent? A new president or a new Congress may favor particular approaches to government (such as being relatively sympathetic or unsympathetic toward government regulation). Any legislature's activities reflect its composition: Does one party have a

---

Box 7.2 Waiting for the Next Policy Wave

The political scientist John W. Kingdon (1984) quotes an analyst for a Washington interest group:

> When you lobby for something, what you have to do is put together your coalition, you have to gear up, you have to get your political forces in line, and then you sit there and wait for the fortuitous event. For example, people who were trying to do something about regulation of railroads tried to ride the environment for a while, but that wave didn't wash them in to shore. So they grabbed their surfboards and they tried to ride something else, but that didn't do the job. The Penn Central collapse was the big wave that brought them in. As I see it, people who are trying to advocate change are like surfers waiting for the big wave. You get out there, you have to be ready to go, you have to be ready to paddle. If you're not ready to paddle when the big wave comes along, you're not going to ride it in. (p. 173)

The competition for space on policymakers' agendas is intense, and not all claims can succeed. This quote suggests that advocates need to be persistent, prepared, and flexible enough to take advantage of shifts in the policymaking environment. There may be various ways to frame an issue in order to advance the desired policies.

---

dominant majority? Do the legislature and the chief executive come from the same party? What other issues are competing for the politicians' attention? Is the economy fairly robust, or are budgets tight? Such factors shape the degree to which legislators believe they have a free hand. Politicians also track public opinion, and they may respond to perceived shifts in what the public favors. The political situation is constantly evolving, affecting what legislation might receive consideration—let alone pass—at any given time.

The Policy Stream Model:
Convergence of the Three Streams

Kingdon's policy stream model (Figure 7.1) illustrates how these three streams come together and assumes that, at any given moment, people are actively promoting the recognition of different problems, the adoption of different policies, and assorted political opportunities. All of these people are competing for attention and influence over the policymaking process. This intense competition ensures that most of these efforts will fail; it is just too hard to gain a place near the top of the agenda. However, sometimes the streams converge, with each reinforcing the others' influences. Sometimes a particular construction of a troubling condition complements a particular policy proposal that, in turn, coincides with the current political alignments. In those cases, proposals for new policies stand a much better chance of being enacted.

The competitive world of policymaking, with its cacophony of diverse claims demanding attention, helps explain why policy domains are so important. Policymakers cannot hope to master all of the issues, to stay on top of every topic. Instead, people specialize; they become familiar with one or two domains. Legislatures, for example, assign their members to committees (and often those committees are divided into more specialized subcommittees) charged with overseeing particular sorts of legislative proposals, and many committees can be seen as belonging to particular policy domains. These committees are much smaller than the larger legislative body, and they offer individual legislators opportunities to become relatively familiar with the issues within a specific policy domain. Policy domains bring knowledgeable people together: lobbyists, officials from related agencies, and legislative staff members often specialize in particular policy domains, and they focus their attention on the committees most concerned with that domain. This greater familiarity with a domain's issues translates into influence; committees' recommendations often influence the larger legislative body. After

Figure 7.1 KINGDON'S POLICY STREAM MODEL

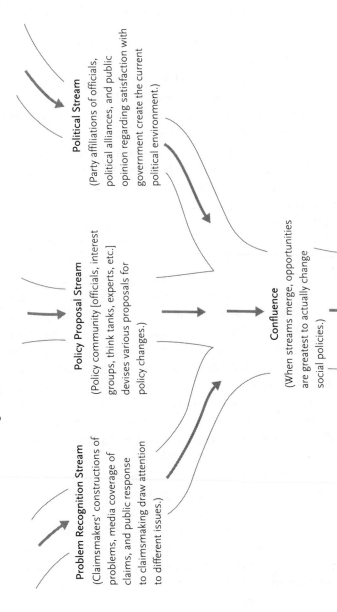

Problem Recognition Stream

(Claimsmakers' constructions of problems, media coverage of claims, and public response to claimsmaking draw attention to different issues.)

Policy Proposal Stream

(Policy community [officials, interest groups, think tanks, experts, etc.] devises various proposals for policy changes.)

Political Stream

(Party affiliations of officials, political alliances, and public opinion regarding satisfaction with government create the current political environment.)

Confluence

(When streams merge, opportunities are greatest to actually change social policies.)

Source: Kingdon, 1984, pp. 92–94.

all, these committee members are the people most knowledgeable about the issue.

In advancing policies, legislators can draw upon a repertoire of tactics. Once they decide to emphasize particular issues (rather than any of the multitude of other possible issues they might promote) and choose to endorse specific policy proposals (among the broad array of available choices), legislators can adopt a public posture to promote their chosen policies: they can make speeches, publish their thoughts, appear on television programs, and generally seek to draw attention to their proposals. Others work backstage. Whether their efforts are public or relatively private, legislators must try to muster allies among their colleagues; they must find others who share their concerns and are willing to join the cause.

Legislators' committee positions serve as an important resource; legislators can use their committee positions to hold hearings to draw attention to the issue they're promoting. They can invite people to testify at these hearings, to present their views. Note that the power to control these invitations, to decide who will speak at these hearings, allows legislators to ensure that the hearings will highlight particular positions or proposals. Again, hearings vary in the degree to which they seek publicity. Sometimes witnesses are chosen for their ability to draw media coverage; hearings featuring show business celebrities, sympathetic victims who can recount their sufferings, or figures who have been implicated in scandalous events are more likely to become subjects of media reporting. Well-orchestrated hearings—that is, those that attract heavy media coverage and involve dramatic presentations by witnesses—can help increase an issue's visibility and can give a cause the momentum needed to get legislation passed.

Sometimes this process results in what seems to be a significant, sudden policy change: the passage of a pathbreaking law. However, when we step back from the legislature's final vote and examine the streams leading up to the shift, we may recognize that the legislators' change of heart was preceded by social changes, particularly in problem recognition—in how claimsmakers, the media, and the public constructed the troubling conditions. There also may have been a long series of policy proposals appearing to be headed nowhere, before someone devised what proved to be a winning package. And often the political situation will have changed as well, making available the necessary votes. In other words, dramatic new legislation tends to emerge only when the three policy streams converge. For example, although earlier laws treated adolescent runaways as delinquents, subject to incarceration in juvenile facilities, by the 1970s Congress had shifted to a new policy affirming that running away was not a criminal matter and funding shelters to protect—but not detain or return—runaways (Staller, 2006).

More often, however, legislative reform is incremental, rather than sudden. A first bill may create a tentative, exploratory program, with advocates settling for a modest, compromise measure that can be implemented. They hope this new policy will be a foot in the door—that once they have gained this initial level of acceptance, it will be possible to press for further policy measures. Passage of a first, relatively minor law may be followed by a series of additional laws over the next few years that expand and further institutionalize the policy shift. For example, the initial federal hate crime law was the Hate Crimes Statistics Act (1990), which merely required that the FBI begin keeping records of reported hate crimes (Jenness & Grattet, 2001). The Hate Crimes Sentencing Enhancement Act, which followed in 1994, allowed federal judges to impose harsher sentences on those convicted of some hate crimes. In the meantime, most state legislatures passed their own hate crime statutes, and in many cases they passed additional laws that expanded the definition of hate crimes or increased the penalties for those convicted. Over time, then, the domain of hate crime policy expanded.

Although policymaking is obviously a key stage in the social problems process, it has largely been taken for granted by sociologists (political scientists have tended to be the social scientists most interested in policy formation). The remainder of this chapter will try to suggest some sociological dimensions for analyzing the policymaking process; it will look at social organization and the pressures on policymakers before turning to policies as social constructions, to the rhetoric of policymaking.

PRESSURES ON POLICYMAKERS

We have already noted that policymakers operate under constraints. Lots of people insist that they take action, yet policymakers have limited resources at their disposal. Hence, they must set priorities and establish an agenda. But the effect of these constraints varies among policymakers—and among the issues they are asked to resolve.

We tend to think first of the most visible, most contentious policy issues. For example, consider abortion: this issue can be easily understood by most people; it leads different people to have sharply opposing views about what policy ought to be, so policymakers cannot possibly satisfy everyone; and those conflicting opinions sometimes are expressed with great passion. Topics related to abortion policy—legislative action, court decisions, and so on—receive considerable media coverage, and however policymakers act regarding abortion is likely to become widely known and is sure to anger at least some people.

However, hot-button issues like abortion are atypical. Much policymaking is almost invisible. We can presume that an agency in the federal government sets standards for, say, the composition of the concrete used in federal highways. This is basically a technical matter: most of us don't know anything about the chemical and physical properties of concrete. We probably prefer that the government build the best-quality highways (so that the roads won't deteriorate quickly) at the lowest possible cost, but we have no idea what sort of concrete composition is required, and we expect somebody else—presumably experts in that agency—to handle the matter. On the other hand, we might imagine that the people who manufacture concrete—who doubtless view the federal government as a major customer—will have strong opinions about concrete policy: they probably want to encourage concrete consumption, but they don't want those policies to cut into their profits. Probably the industry employs lobbyists to work with legislators and officials in the various agencies that determine concrete-related policies. This sort of insider claimsmaking leads to policies being made almost entirely out of the public view.

This is why policy domains (Burstein, 1991) are so important. Each domain contains the people who are most interested in—and most knowledgeable about—a particular set of issues. Although we might agree that, as taxpayers, we all have an interest in whether the government buys the best concrete at the lowest possible price, few taxpayers have the time or energy to pay attention to that policy domain, let alone to play an active part in that policymaking process. This means that, within some domains, policymakers have a relatively free hand: they aren't closely watched, and they aren't subjected to strong, competing pressures.

Policymakers respond to this freedom in different ways. At least sometimes, policymakers adopt relatively activist stances to take advantage of their powers. For example, when Congress passed the Rehabilitation Act of 1973, the law contained a section prohibiting discrimination against "handicapped" persons (Scotch, 2001). This was a minor provision in a much larger, apparently routine bill designed to renew a federal vocational rehabilitation program; the antidiscrimination section attracted little notice while the bill was being considered in Congress.

However, officials at the Department of Health, Education, and Welfare's Office of Civil Rights (OCR) took an active role in interpreting the new law's provisions very broadly. They argued that the law's antidiscrimination section required altering a wide range of social arrangements previously taken for granted, such as modifying curbs and other physical barriers to wheelchair access. The OCR found allies in the emerging disability rights movement, and the agency's broad interpretation led to far-reaching changes, such as requirements that public buildings be refurbished to be accessible to the disabled. It is quite possible that, without the OCR's decision to promote an expansive interpretation of the new law, disability policy would not have changed as dramatically or as quickly as it did. In contrast, we can imagine occasions when agencies might choose to turn away from potential policymaking opportunities and decide simply to continue administering ongoing policies.

Of course, there is always the possibility that officials will suddenly find that what in most years would be routine, virtually invisible decisions suddenly are subjected to the glare of publicity. How a state's wildlife agency manages, say, its river otter population, is not ordinarily a major public issue, but under the right circumstances, it can become a contentious topic, with people who enjoy fishing arguing that otters are a pest and need to be eliminated, while environmentalists demand that otters be protected (Goedeke, 2005). In such cases, policies that usually might be shaped by insider claimsmaking may be subjected to countervailing demands by all sorts of insiders and outsiders, the policymaking process now made visible through media coverage (see Box 7.3).

It is also not certain how policymakers will respond to such conflicting demands. Although at first glance it might seem obvious that officials are influenced by lobbying efforts, the evidence on this score is relatively weak (Burstein & Linton, 2002); and perhaps contrary to popular belief, a fair amount of evidence suggests that legislators are responsive to public opinion (Burstein, 1998). We might suspect that insider claimsmaking is most likely to be effective when policymaking is not especially visible. This does not mean that policies are necessarily made in secret or that the process is always corrupt, but simply that much policymaking occurs outside the spotlight of media coverage. When policymaking attracts more media attention, policymakers probably become more responsive to public opinion (Burstein, 2006).

Box 7.3 Does Congress Listen?

Although many people assume that organized interests directly affect votes in Congress, the social scientific evidence for this effect is relatively weak. Most studies focus on a few high-visibility issues; however, recent research tries to measure the effects of testimony at congressional committee hearings on a broader range of issues.

Typically, hearings are called to draw attention to problems and muster support for specific solutions. Most of those invited to testify at hearings support the proposed legislation under consideration; the hearings become an arena where claimsmakers—including activists, experts, and representatives of interest groups—can argue for a problem's importance, and also endorse the policy proposal under consideration as likely to solve or at least improve the problem. Opponents may also appear at hearings; they rarely challenge claims about the problem's importance, but rather, restrict their claims to critiques of the proposed solution.

Does hearing testimony actually make a difference? The evidence is that testimony—both proponents' claims about the importance of a problem and the efficacy of the proposed solution, and opponents' raising doubts about the solution—have measurable effects on the chance of legislation passing. Congress needs information, and the testimony offered at hearings can provide information that affects policymaking decisions.

Source: Burstein & Hirsch, 2007.

Note, too, that policymaking on an issue can occur in multiple arenas. More than one congressional committee may be involved with legislation related to a particular policy domain; proponents can launch proposals before each committee and then, depending on how the different committees respond, choose to concentrate their efforts in those arenas that seem to offer the best prospects. In addition, policymaking arenas may be found at both the state and federal levels. Advocates can press for new policies at both levels: success at the federal level can provide momentum for further state-level campaigns; on the other hand, a successful state campaign or two may help persuade federal officials that they need to act. Similarly, those dissatisfied with the laws that are passed can press agency officials for interpretations that will shape policy implementation in particular directions; or if the agencies aren't responsive, it may be possible to appeal either the law's content or its implementation through various courts. Many doors offer openings to policymaking, so there are multiple opportunities for modest beginnings that get an issue's foot in the door and might lead to greater policy changes.

Although we tend to equate policymakers with government officials, remember that policymaking also can occur in the private sector. Corporations, churches, or other organizations can devise their own responses to claims about troubling conditions. Unlike government officials, who may be subject to countervailing pressures, private policymakers are less accountable to those outside their organizations. Foundations, for example, may donate money to encourage certain social policies (Bartley, 2007; Silver, 2006).

As private entities, foundations have considerable latitude in choosing which projects to support; and they are flexible, able to make decisions and even shift their priorities relatively quickly. In earlier decades, major foundations sometimes worked in partnership with the federal government: foundations funded experimental social programs, and then evidence that those programs had been effective was used to justify establishing federal social policies based on similar models, much as examples of successful state or local government programs can be used to promote federal legislation (Silver, 2006). In recent years, however, the federal government has tried to reduce its involvement in social programs by arguing that private, "faith-based" (that is, church-sponsored) programs can provide social services more efficiently or effectively than government agencies can. Thus, today's private efforts seem less likely to inspire larger public programs.

Box 7.4 Agreeing on a Frame Isn't Enough

The dozens of city agencies, social service providers, social movement organizations, and community organizations that seek to shape San Francisco's policies toward the homeless can be grouped by their political ideologies–left, center, and right. Those on the right tended to frame the problem in terms of individual failings: the homeless chose to be homeless, they had drug and alcohol problems, and so on. In contrast, those on the left and in the center largely blamed social structure—poverty, inequality, and a lack of opportunities for stable jobs that paid reasonable wages—for causing homelessness. These structural frames were shared by a great majority of those concerned with homeless policies.

Although those in the center favored the left's frames, when it came to policymaking, they tended to ally with those on the right. The right had more resources and influence; they had money to pay for political advertising (when ballot propositions asked voters to approve policies) and for campaign contributions (to foster the election of politicians sympathetic to their views). As a consequence, those in the center sought to maintain ties and avoid open conflict with the right. At the same time, some on the left favored social movement tactics involving demonstrations and confrontations that the center found unacceptable. The consequence was that those on the right, although they framed the issue in terms that the left and center largely rejected, nonetheless had the ability to shape the city's policies toward the homeless.

Source: Noy, 2009.

As we have seen, myriad organizational considerations can shape the direction of policymaking. Particular instances of policymaking will depend on the constellation of parties—claimsmakers, legislative committees, interest groups, official agencies, and so on—who are willing to weigh in on a particular issue (see Box 7.4). These actors become elements in Kingdon's (1984) policy proposal and political streams. But we should never forget that policymaking also depends on the problem recognition stream, on how social problems and their proposed policy solutions are constructed.

SYMBOLIC POLITICS AND THE RHETORIC OF POLICYMAKING

Policymakers must explain and justify their actions; that is, they must convince others that their policies are wise and appropriate. Such persuasion necessarily involves rhetoric—efforts to convince others that the new policies are the best courses of action. Why is this policy needed? What problem is it intended to solve? Why is this particular policy the most appropriate means for addressing the problem? To the degree that policymaking is a public act, policymakers need to anticipate and address such questions. This task requires yet another reconstruction, one that highlights certain aspects of the troubling condition and explains how and why a particular policy will solve the problem.

The political scientist Deborah A. Stone (1989) argues that policymaking involves the construction of **causal stories**. After all, a policy solution is most likely to be effective in solving a problem if it reflects an understanding of what causes that problem. Causal stories classify troubling conditions into familiar categories according to the nature of their causes. Different categories of causes invite different policy remedies. For example, a troubling condition might be depicted as having an accidental cause (which is to say that neither the events leading to the troubling condition nor their consequences were intentional). Put simply, accidents cannot be helped, so no one is blamed for them.

Other causal stories have other implications. Another popular explanation depicts social situations as caused by intentional action; this is, for example, how we think of most crimes—that people know they are supposed to obey the law, but sometimes they deliberately break laws. A third causal story emphasizes inadvertent causes: people do things intentionally, but their actions have unintended consequences.

It is possible to devise competing constructions of the same troubling condition using all three types of causal stories. Consider Hurricane Katrina, in 2005, which broke the levees in New Orleans and resulted in catastrophic flood damage. It is possible to construct the effects of the hurricane as an accident (the storm just happened to strike the city); or as a product of inadvertent causes (officials built the city's flood control system to withstand less severe storms because strong levees would have been much more costly, and it seemed unlikely that such a powerful storm would directly strike the city); or even as intentional (such stories might involve human intent [politicians willingly constructed levees that left the city's poorest districts at grave risk] or divine will [God was deliberately punishing New Orleans for its sinful ways]). Different causal stories carry different policy implications: Should the city be rebuilt? If so, who should pay for the rebuilding? Should anyone be blamed for the disaster?

Note that the choice of a causal story also affects the characterization of the people affected by the troubling condition—the policy's **target population**—in very different ways (Schneider & Ingram, 1993, 2005). Some causal stories depict troubling conditions as affecting vulnerable but morally worthy people—victims who deserve the policymakers' help and support. At the other extreme, stories can characterize target populations as villains—individuals who embody the troubling condition, and whose bad behavior needs to be controlled through the new policy's implementation. Note that different causal stories can construct the same target population in various ways, so, for example, drug addicts might be depicted either as villains (people who knowingly break the law) or as victims (whose hopeless lives lead to despair that causes them to turn to drugs).

Target populations can be relatively powerful (that is, politically influential), or relatively weak, and their status shapes policymakers' constructions. Contrast the differences in the ways politicians talk about Social Security (a program that benefits older citizens— one of the population segments most likely to vote) and welfare programs (which benefit poorer people, who vote less often): whereas Social Security recipients are generally described as having a right to expect that their benefits will be protected, when it comes to welfare some politicians express skepticism that welfare recipients actually need—or deserve to receive—their benefits.

It is important to appreciate that there is nothing inevitable about these constructions; the same troubling condition could lead to policymakers devising very different causal stories and characterizing the target population in very different ways. A causal story that is widely accepted and is taken for granted at one time may fall out of favor, pushed aside by a rival construction that might have once been unthinkable but now has wide acceptance.

When new constructions take hold, people throughout the social problems process may begin to rework their positions to fit the new story. Prior to the environmental movement's rise, for instance, pesticide manufacturers marketed products under tough, militaristic brand names, such as Arsenal or Torpedo (Kiel & Nownes, 1994). However, once policymakers began to respond to claims about the dangers posed by pesticides and the need for tighter regulation of the industry, the companies began describing their products as "crop protection chemicals," and devised less threatening brand names, such as Accord or Green Mountain. The rise of a new causal story can force many parties to adapt.

Not all causal stories and their associated policies are equally attractive, equally compelling. Ideally a causal story needs to be easily understood. That is, a good causal story should be easy to tell, simple enough to be conveyed by the media (which—as described in Chapter 5—prefer stories that can be converted into relatively straightforward secondary claims), and easy for audiences to follow (see Box 7.5). It also helps if the problem can be presented as having a straightforward, easily understood solution, and if that solution can be promised to be economical. Policymakers would prefer to construct their policies as effective and inexpensive: "this should solve the problem once and for all." Of course, such policy claims create expectations among the policymakers' audiences.

Policymakers typically emphasize the *instrumental* purposes of their policies. That is, they claim that the policy is intended to make a difference, to correct or improve a particular troubling condition in society. Of course, such claims make sense. The content of policymakers' claims—the causal stories, the definitions of the target populations, and so on—depict the troubling condition as having particular sorts of features, and also present the policy as the appropriate measure needed to address the troubling condition's causes, the target population's needs, and other aspects of the policymakers' constructions.

However, analysts often argue that policies can serve *symbolic* purposes as well. That is, policies embody values, serving to promote particular constructions of the world. Consider drug laws. The historical record is filled with examples of efforts to ban the distribution and use of illegal drugs, and most of those efforts have failed. The classic example is the United States' experiment with Prohibition, the period when alcohol was treated as an illegal drug. During Prohibition, an illegal trade in alcohol flourished; it created new opportunities for organized crime and led to considerable corruption. After about a dozen years, policymakers reversed course, legalized alcohol, and sought to regulate drinking through various liquor control laws limiting the conditions under which alcohol could be sold and consumed. Of course, alcohol problems did not disappear; alcoholism remains a major health problem and drunk drivers continue to kill people, but most policymakers consider the problems associated with legalized alcohol to be less troubling than those that might emerge if alcohol again became a target of prohibition.

Box 7.5 Constructing Abu Ghraib as an Isolated Incident

In April 2004, about a year after American troops invaded Iraq, CBS News broadcast photographs of U.S. troops abusing Iraqi prisoners at Abu Ghraib prison. Congress responded to the scandal by scheduling a series of committee hearings to determine what had happened, and what ought to be done.

The photographs—apparently taken by the troops for their own amusement—offered incontrovertible evidence that the abuse had occurred; denial was impossible. Still, the policymakers might construct Abu Ghraib in various ways: Should it be understood as a single, aberrant event, or was it an instance of a larger problem of Americans' mistreatment of prisoners, or perhaps Iraqis more generally? And what about the officers who commanded the misbehaving troops—how far up the chain of command did responsibility extend?

In general, those officials who supported the war sought to construct the problem narrowly, while the war's critics argued that the problem was much broader than the Abu Ghraib incident. New evidence continued to become public that revealed other instances of harsh methods of interrogation and ill treatment of prisoners, demonstrating that the problem was not confined to Abu Ghraib. However, congressional hearings and official inquiries downplayed the idea that these incidents represented a larger pattern. Instead, military commanders and officials who supported the war managed to construct an interpretation that there was no systemic problem, no larger culture of abuse, but rather evidence that a few dozen prisoners had been mistreated by a small number of troops—that these were isolated incidents that did not require new policies.

Source: Del Rosso, 2011.

It is easy to make parallel arguments about the problems associated with laws against other illegal drugs (MacCoun & Reuter, 2001). However, many policymakers insist that legalizing drugs is unthinkable. Legalization might be interpreted as constituting approval of drug use; it would "send the wrong message"—that is, it would seem to endorse the wrong values. Maintaining a strong commitment to the prohibition of drugs may not have particularly positive instrumental effects; experts disagree, but it is at least possible to argue that the effects of legalizing drugs would be no worse than the consequences of our current prohibitionist policy. However, antidrug laws also serve important symbolic purposes: they affirm society's commitment to sobriety and other moral principles.

Symbolic considerations are important, particularly when policymakers are elected officials. Topics that become contentious public issues—alcohol in the decades leading to Prohibition, or such contemporary topics as abortion, drugs, and welfare—encourage policymakers to adopt positions that play well as symbolic politics. Such policies affirm that one is standing up for the right values, and policymakers can assert that, at least in principle, these policies should work (even when their track record suggests that, in practice, such policies do not work as anticipated).

The notion of symbolic politics reminds us that policymaking is also a form of rhetoric, that it can be intended to persuade audiences—a category that can include the media, the public, and even claimsmakers (whom the policymakers may hope to placate, so they will stop calling for further policy changes)—that the policymakers have done the right things for the right reasons. We need to be alert to the dramatic nature of policymaking, to watch for the ways that policymakers—particularly elected officials—put policymaking to symbolic uses.

The competition for policymakers' attention and the policymakers' own desire to get favorable publicity for their activities encourages dramatizing the creation of new policies. Thus, policymakers often announce new policies with considerable fanfare; for instance, the new policy may be given a distinctive name, in order to convey the sense that this policy represents a dramatic change from past practices. For example, American political leaders have a fondness for "declaring war" on social problems; there have been heavily publicized wars on poverty, cancer, drugs, and most recently, of course, terrorism (J. Best, 1999). War rhetoric conveys a sense of widespread commitment for eradicating a social problem; calling a particular policy a "war" serves symbolic, not instrumental, ends.

The problem with this sort of war rhetoric is that it creates very high expectations. Americans tend to think of wars as relatively brief struggles that are supposed to end in total victory (for example, U.S. involvement in World War II lasted less than four years, and the Axis powers all surrendered). Our history is characterized by a series of short, generally successful wars; it is not marked by a Thirty Years' War or a Hundred Years' War. In fact, military conflicts that seem unlikely to be resolved quickly—Vietnam is the most obvious example—quickly become unpopular.

Of course, social problems are not clearly identifiable enemies that can be defeated and driven to public surrender. There isn't one form of cancer; there are dozens. Curing cancer would actually require many different cures. Similarly, people are poor for lots of different reasons, and no single policy is likely to address all of those causes; eliminating poverty is likely to require attacking many different causes over a long period. Solving social problems usually takes time and often occurs piecemeal (see Box 7.6).

Because successful policies often proceed gradually, their contributions may go almost unnoticed, although they can transform society's face over time. Consider the impact of childhood vaccination programs, stricter fire codes, or mandatory educational requirements—all policies that we take for granted. Such policies do not result in dramatic year-to-year changes, but over decades they can produce profound transformations. A look back in time can produce surprising revelations: in 1900, measles was one of the ten leading fatal diseases (U.S. Census Bureau, 1975, p. 58); today,

Box 7.6 The Undeclared War on Traffic Fatalities

In 1966, 50,894 Americans died in traffic accidents; in 2010, there were only 32,788 such deaths. In fact, the decline has been much more dramatic than those numbers suggest: deaths fell even as the population grew by 55 percent, the number of drivers more than doubled, and the miles driven tripled. The number of traffic fatalities per one hundred million miles driven dropped from 5.5 in 1966 to 1.1 in 2010 (National Highway Traffic Safety Administration, 2011).

Numerous apparently mundane policy changes account for this improvement, including the following:

- **Better cars.** Various safety features (such as seat belts, padded dashboards, electric turn signals, and air bags) became mandatory.

- **Better roads.** Various road improvements were made, including additional lanes, controlled-access highways, broader shoulders, and better signs.

- **Better drivers.** Tougher limits were imposed on alcohol consumption, and licensing was both delayed and made a graduated process for beginning drivers.

No one declared war on traffic fatalities, and no single policy change can account for the declining death toll. Rather, lots of minor policy changes nibbled away at the problem, but the cumulative effect is impressive.

This example serves as a reminder that often social policies are effective because of the combined effect of many small improvements, rather than dramatic policy pronouncements—such as heavily promoted wars on social problems—designed to get politicians favorable headlines.

of course, measles has virtually been eliminated. It is a shock to realize that this disease—now easily managed through childhood vaccinations—was once a serious threat to life. The policy's success is simply taken for granted.

Compare such quietly effective policies with the noisy announcements heralding many new policies. The announcement of a new war on a particular social problem raises expectations and thereby creates opportunities for prospective critics. After four or five years—roughly as long, remember, as Americans expect a war should last—it will be possible for critics to point to evidence that poverty or drug use or whatever the current pressing issue is continues to exist, and to argue that the new policy has failed. In other words, policies enacted with an eye toward symbolic politics are often vulnerable to critiques that are themselves grounded in symbolic arguments.

In summary, policymaking has important sociological dimensions (see Figure 7.2). Policies emerge only under favorable social conditions, and they involve yet another reconstruction of the trou-

Figure 7.2 POLICYMAKING IN THE SOCIAL PROBLEMS PROCESS

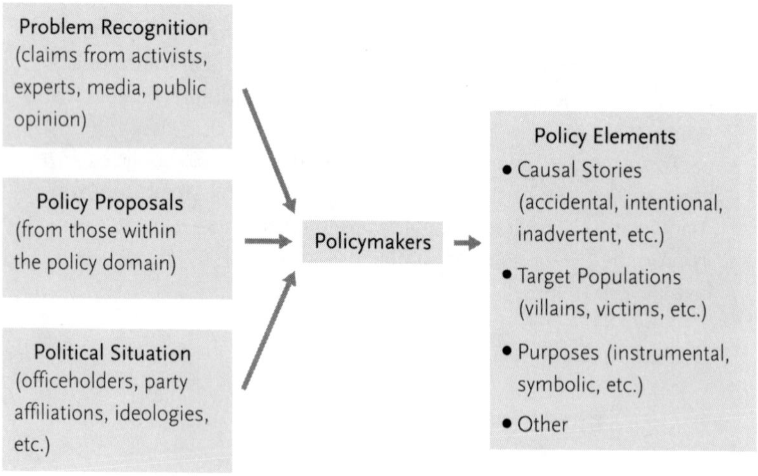

Problem Recognition
(claims from activists, experts, media, public opinion)

Policy Proposals
(from those within the policy domain)

Political Situation
(officeholders, party affiliations, ideologies, etc.)

→ Policymakers →

Policy Elements
- Causal Stories (accidental, intentional, inadvertent, etc.)
- Target Populations (villains, victims, etc.)
- Purposes (instrumental, symbolic, etc.)
- Other

bling conditions—this time by policymakers who must devise a plausible causal story, depict a suitable target population, and so on. Nor is this the end of the matter. We have already noted that the tendency to herald new policies in dramatic terms, as the means by which a troubling condition can be defeated or eliminated, sets the stage for future critics. We will have more to say about the process of evaluating social policies in Chapter 9. Before examining the construction of those critiques, however, we need to explore how policies are implemented through social problems work—the topic of the next chapter.

MAKING CONNECTIONS

- *Activists compete for attention from policymakers. Chapter 3 describes how these outsider claimsmakers try to influence the policymaking process.*

- *Policy changes frequently result from a shift in how the public or the media construct a troubling condition. See Chapter 6 for more on the role of public reactions in the social problems process.*

- *After policymakers ratify a new policy, it still must be implemented. The next chapter explores how social problems workers put a policy into action.*

CASE STUDY
HEALTH CARE AS A POLICY CHALLENGE

Health care has been a challenge for federal policymakers for decades. On the one hand, American health care has achieved real accomplishments: life expectancies continue to increase (about a month per year), thanks to changing lifestyles (reduced smoking) and medical innovations (such as drugs that reduce fatalities from heart disease and strokes). However, health care costs are much higher in the United States than in all other nations with advanced economies (such as Canada and most western European countries), and these costs rise at a faster rate than inflation so that, because most Americans rely on health insurance to help cover their medical bills, insurance premiums have been rising. The costs of maintaining an insurance policy are high for individuals who are not insured through their employers, and employers find it increasingly costly to arrange insurance for their employees; consequently, growing numbers of individuals and companies find it necessary to cancel their insurance programs. As a result, a increasing proportion of Americans are uninsured, and they tend to be poorer (less able to afford insurance), sicker (because, on average, health problems increase as income declines), or unemployed (because illness caused them to lose both their jobs and their insurance) so that, even as the quality of health care improves, a declining proportion of the population can afford it.

These trends have been apparent for decades, and plenty of claimsmakers have drawn attention to the rising cost of health care as a social problem (Jacobs & Skocpol, 2010). Yet efforts to devise new policies have met with great resistance. In most other advanced nations, the government is more involved in managing basic health care. In contrast, most American health care depends on doctors, hospitals, pharmaceutical manufacturers, and insurance companies that operate as for-profit businesses; they pay higher salaries, charge higher prices, and have higher administrative costs than their counterparts in other countries—reasons why health care costs more in the United States than elsewhere. This means that many of the people and organizations that make up the health care system have a strong economic interest in preserving the current arrangements, and in fighting any effort to increase government involvement in health care.

In addition, those opposed to expanding federal health care policy have little difficulty devising rhetoric to justify their opposition. They appeal to values of liberty and self-reliance, and associate reforms with socialism. They warn that any new policies will prove to be expensive, and that taxes to pay for the programs will inevitably rise; the history of Medicare—a program that essentially guarantees health care for all senior citizens, and that has a long record of costs exceeding expectations—serves as a warning for what might happen. They also suggest that the quality of health care will decline, that patients will be unable to get the services they want as quickly as they need them, and that without the financial incentives that for-profit medicine provide, there will be fewer innovations that might improve health care. In short, increasing the federal government's role in health care will provide poorer care at higher costs.

Proponents of expanding federal health care policy counter with their own arguments. They note the lower costs of government-managed health care in other countries, and point to statistics that suggest that those countries' populations may be even healthier than Americans. They can also point to polls showing that large numbers of Americans are worried about the costs of medical care, find it too costly to get the care they need, and favor some sort of health care reform. And, of course, they emphasize the trends: each year, the proportion of Americans with health insurance is declining. They invoke values of humanitarianism, suggesting that access to health care is a basic human right.

This division has proved to be a policymaking nightmare. There are vocal claimsmakers calling upon different values (liberty, humanity), and advocating opposing policies. There are experts on all sides insisting that their proposals are superior to all others. There are powerful interest groups lobbying. Public opinion offers unclear guidance: in 2007, the Gallup Poll showed that 69 percent of Americans agreed that "it is the responsibility of the federal government to make sure all Americans have healthcare coverage" and President Barack Obama made health care reform a top priority when he took office in 2009; following a brutal political debate that led to the passage of a bill in 2010—called "Obamacare" by its opponents—new Gallup Polls found that the percentage agreeing with the same question had fallen to 47 percent (Gallup, 2011). A 2011 poll of public reactions to the new law found that 24 percent favored expanding its coverage, 13 percent favored keeping it as is, 25 percent favored scaling it back, while 32 percent called for its repeal. At the same time, polls showed that more than four-fifths of Americans reported being personally worried about the availability and affordability of health care.

It is worth remembering that the passage of Medicare inspired a very similar debate, and that the policy continues to be a subject for debate (Oberlander, 2003). Its proponents argue that it has been a successful program, guaranteeing health care for most older Americans. It is also relatively popular: at least some of the people opposed to expanding the federal government's role in health care warned that Medicare should not be touched (apparently under the impression that it was not a federal program). However, Medicare's critics have continually warned that the program's rising costs will eventually break the federal budget, and some have called for converting the program into private insurance policies. Even a health care program that has been in effect for nearly fifty years remains controversial.

In short, health care illustrates how competing constructions can make it nearly impossible to agree on policymaking.

QUESTIONS

1. How does Kingdon's three-stream model apply to policymaking for health care?

2. What sorts of causal stories do health care claimsmakers present? How do they depict target populations for the policy?

3. Health care policy is not just symbolic politics. How does this affect the policymaking process?

8

Social Problems Work

The previous chapters explored the initial stages of the social problems process: claimsmaking, media coverage, public reaction, and policymaking. At each of these stages, people construct and reconstruct social problems: claimsmakers first draw attention to troubling conditions; the media then transform the claimsmakers' primary claims into secondary claims; next the public adds its own interpretations; and finally policymakers reframe issues in ways that can be addressed by new social policies.

This chapter concerns social problems work—the next stage in the social problems process. In this stage, too, people reconstruct the meaning of the troubling condition—but with a difference. The earlier constructions—during the stages from claimsmaking through policymaking—tended to characterize social problems in fairly abstract, general terms, as widespread, even society-wide problems. For instance, claimsmaking about the problem of poor people without medical insurance is likely to discuss the numbers of the uninsured poor, whether those numbers are rising or falling, how much caring for the uninsured costs, and so on. These claims may feature a typifying example or two, but the focus tends to be broad—on the implications of the troubling condition for the larger society.

That is, claimsmaking, media coverage, and policymaking tend to take what sociologists call a **macrosociological** approach.

In social problems work, the focus narrows. *Social problems work* consists of applying constructions of social problems or social policies to their immediate, practical situations (Holstein & Miller, 2003b; Miller & Holstein, 1997). Instead of discussing, say, crime, in the abstract, people doing social problems work construct specific events as instances of crime, even as they conclude that other events should not be treated as crimes. Social problems work is how people apply constructions of social problems in their everyday lives.

Most obviously, people engage in social problems work when their jobs require that they implement social policies. For example, medical professionals such as doctors and nurses will encounter sick people who don't have medical insurance, and they must decide what to do in such cases—whether to provide care or turn the ill away. Such social problems work is where "the rubber meets the road"—occasions when general, theoretical constructions about social problems or social policies must be applied to real-world situations. Although some sociologists define social problems work more broadly, to encompass any occasion when people apply their constructions of social problems (for instance, in everyday conversations), this chapter will emphasize the social problems work done by "street-level bureaucrats" (Lipsky, 1980): people who work as police officers, teachers, social workers, doctors and nurses, counselors, and so on—those who have to implement whatever policies have been devised for dealing with troubling conditions.

Social problems work often occurs in face-to-face interactions—for example, when a doctor examines a patient, a teacher instructs a student, or a police officer questions a suspect. To describe the participants in these interacting pairs, we will refer to **social problems workers** (that is, the doctors, teachers, and others whose jobs involve carrying out social policies) and their **subjects** (the people—variously called *addicts, clients, offenders, patients, suspects, victims,* *defendants*, and so on—who in some way embody a socially constructed social problem). Therefore, parts of this chapter will adopt a more **microsociological** perspective, focusing on the dynamics of these interactions between individual social problems workers and particular subjects. In order to understand these face-to-face encounters, however, we must also consider the larger social context within which these interactions develop. This chapter will begin by considering this context and, in particular, the nature of the jobs that social problems workers do. Then, after exploring the nature of interactions between social problems workers and their subjects, we will expand our focus to consider the sorts of social problems work that occur in everyday life.

ON THE JOB

Social problems workers find themselves squeezed between great expectations and mundane reality. The expectations travel from the top down; they are imposed on social problems workers by the larger society, by policymakers, and particularly by those who directly supervise what social problems workers do. At the grandest level, these expectations come from the larger culture's understanding of social problems work. In general, we expect doctors to heal the sick, teachers to help their students learn, police to fight crime by enforcing the law, and so on. These expectations are reaffirmed by popular culture. Think of all those television series featuring dedicated doctors and nurses, cops and prosecutors, teachers, and so on. In general, these heroic figures confront and solve instances of social problems in each episode: patients are healed, criminals are brought to justice, or whatever. Because most of us have fairly limited real-world contacts with social problems workers, these idealized images may shape how we think of social problems work; we may imagine that social problems work is as straightforward and effective as these melodramas imply.

Further, social problems workers operate within broad-based institutions—such as medicine or the legal system—that state both general principles and specific rules that should govern the social problems workers' actions. Police, for example, enforce the criminal laws that define not just the nature of various crimes, but also boundaries for legal police conduct. The activities of different social problems workers are governed by various institutional sets of rules—professional codes of conduct, standards for appropriate behavior, and so on. These rules provide another layer of expectations that constrain how social problems workers should act.

Finally, most social problems workers belong to particular organizations—a police force, hospital, or welfare agency—that have bureaucratic hierarchies, including supervisory personnel who have their own expectations for their subordinates. Organizations vary in the importance they place on implementing particular policies; for instance, some police departments assign a much higher priority to enforcing hate crime laws than other departments do (Jenness & Grattet, 2005). A police chief may decide that traffic offenses are becoming a problem in the community and order the department's officers to be especially vigilant about ticketing traffic offenses, or a hospital administrator may discourage medical personnel from ordering expensive tests. In these examples, officers who fail to issue tickets and doctors who continue to require lots of tests may become targets of their supervisors' disapproval. Obviously such organizational expectations act as further constraints on social problems workers.

The combination of cultural, institutional, and organizational expectations may be thought of as pressing social problems workers from above; these are all ways in which the larger society tries to shape how social problems work is conducted (see Figure 8.1). At the same time, social problems workers find themselves confronting the realities of the particular people and situations they encounter. Police officers observe minor traffic violations, or see a group of youths congregating on a street corner or an intoxicated person

Figure 8.1 SOCIAL PROBLEMS WORKERS IN THE MIDDLE

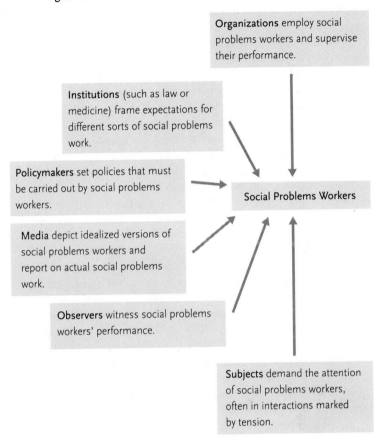

shambling down the sidewalk, or answer a call about a domestic dispute. These are all occasions when the officers face choices: Should they ignore what they see? Should they investigate further, by speaking to the individuals involved? Or should they take official action, such as issuing a ticket or making an arrest? During any day on the job in social problems work, lots of decisions of this sort will need to be made (see Box 8.1).

Box 8.1 Weather Forecasting as Social Problems Work

At first glance, meteorologists might not seem to be social problems workers; they predict the weather, rather than process individual subjects. However, the National Weather Service is a federal agency, established to provide weather forecasts that can help farmers, businesses, and local communities. Weather forecasting's social importance is particularly evident in warnings about tornados, blizzards, and other forms of severe weather; timely warnings can allow people to make preparations that can save many lives.

The problem is that meteorologists deal in probabilities, rather than certainties, and they must make public predictions. Errors—both failures to issue warnings for severe storms that do occur, and warnings about storms that turn out to be much less severe than predicted—lead to complaints and criticisms, not just from individual citizens, but also from local agencies (such as police and transportation services) that make plans based on weather forecasts. Like other social problems workers, meteorologists find themselves standing in the middle. They are scientists, who use computer models based on weather records from the past, but they are making predictions. Their data suggest the likelihood of particular outcomes (such as "there is a 60 percent chance of rain"), but they must weigh probabilities against potential costs of being wrong—particularly the consequences of failing to issue a timely warning of severe weather. As a result, weather forecasting is a product of scientific knowledge, experience with previous weather patterns, and an appreciation of the social institutions being served.

Source: Fine, 2007.

All this means that most social problems workers have considerable discretion. Their supervisors cannot oversee all of their actions, and on many occasions a social problems worker may conclude that "going by the book"—following the institutional and organizational rules—isn't the wisest, or best, course. Society tends to idealize social problems work, but social problems workers recognize that what they do must be practical. They may have reservations about the wisdom of the policies that they are expected to execute—those policies may seem too idealistic to fit the gritty, practical world that the social problems workers confront—and they may choose when to invoke, and when to ignore, particular policies (Åkerström, 2006). In short, they must draw upon their own experiences, as well as their conversations with other social problems workers about how best to do their jobs, in order to decide what to do in any given instance.

Social problems workers vary in the amount of decision-making discretion they have; the lone police officer on patrol is harder to supervise than a social welfare case worker whose supervisor's desk is only a few feet away. In general, the historical trend has been for institutions and organizations to try to reduce the independence of individual social problems workers in the name of ensuring a higher standard of performance. For example, it used to be common for new police officers to learn on the job, by being partnered for a time with an experienced officer who could show the ropes to the newcomer; increasingly, this sort of informal apprenticeship has been replaced by academies where officers-in-training receive weeks of classroom training on criminal law and police procedure.

Similarly, medicine changed during the early twentieth century: medical schools began being accredited, states established procedures for licensing physicians, and there were other formal developments designed to ensure that all doctors would have at least a minimum set of qualifications and be able to provide at least a minimum standard of care (Starr, 1982). In much the same way, recent efforts by the federal government to use standardized testing to measure the performance of students in the nation's schools are an effort to improve the caliber of instruction in individual classrooms.

In other words, the discretion of social problems workers can itself be constructed as a social problem in that it can lead to inconsistent work that may be, among other things, corrupt or incompetent. Therefore, reformers devise policies to press social problems workers to be more consistent, and to meet higher standards of performance. Such reforms emphasize professionalism; they encourage social problems workers to think of themselves as having special training and qualifications, and to aspire to meet their professions' high standards (Freidson, 1986). These reforms often require paperwork: social problems workers are required to provide records of their actions, or even to apply for approval to proceed—measures intended to give supervisors more control over the individual social problems worker's performance. Still, there is an inherent problem: grand principles, whether they are laws or professional standards, must be translated into practical actions. The social problems worker remains the front-line figure, the person who has to have some discretion to assess particular situations involving particular subjects and decide what ought to be done (see Box 8.2).

The tendency toward the professionalization of social problems work has other consequences. Our discussion of claimsmakers (particularly in Chapter 3) noted that claimsmaking campaigns often originate with activists who may have personal experiences with a particular troubling condition, or who may hold ideologies that help them frame critiques of existing social arrangements. Such activists invest time and energy in claimsmaking because they feel strongly that this issue is important and must be addressed. In some cases, activists may even engage in private policymaking by establishing their own grassroots programs to address troubling conditions. For example, after some members of the hippie community became concerned about the vulnerability of adolescent runaways, they established shelters to provide runaways with food, shelter, and other basic necessities (Staller, 2006); similarly, early feminists created centers for rape counseling and shelters for battered women.

Such grassroots operations tend to be staffed by volunteers and equipped through donations, but it is difficult to maintain them on that basis. The need for stable funding—to cover salaries and other

Box 8.2 How Police on the Beat View Compstat

Since the mid-1990s, the Compstat model has been adopted by many police departments. Compstat emphasizes the need for police administrators to collect and analyze statistics about crime, and to allocate resources to address problems that those data reveal. For instance, reports that there have been a lot of burglaries in a particular neighborhood should cause administrators to allocate more resources to address that problem.

Compstat encourages ranking officers to keep track of criminal activity and make decisions based on evidence, and many top administrators believe that it is an effective method for managing their police forces. However, the value of Compstat policing is lost on many patrol officers, who translate their orders into a simple call for more arrests. That is, while administrators may allocate additional resources to dealing with an increase in burglaries, the justification for shifting those resources may not reach or be understood by the beat officers. Similarly, the demand for careful reporting—necessary to assemble the statistical information that Compstat requires—is experienced by officers as pressure to produce more arrest reports. Officers trying to please their supervisors assume that officers' work will be judged primarily by this one standard.

Many social problems workers belong to large organizations; an urban police force may have thousands of officers. Understandings of what a policy is intended to do and how it should be carried out are likely to vary a good deal among people occupying different positions in the organization's hierarchy.

Source: Dabney, 2010.

costs—eventually leads these agencies to request government support. But this support usually comes at a cost; the agency may be expected to demonstrate that it is a professional operation, staffed by social problems workers who hold the appropriate credentials (rather than sharing the ideological positions of those who started the grassroots operation) and who can be counted on to abide by whatever legal constraints come with government funding.

There are exceptions to this pattern of professionalization. The obvious example is Alcoholics Anonymous (and the other twelve-step programs modeled on AA) that consist solely of people "in recovery." AA is an all-volunteer organization that refuses to acknowledge the relevance of professional credentials; its members turn to one another for support because AA's ideology insists that only those who have experienced alcoholism and recovery are qualified to guide those with drinking problems toward sobriety (Rudy, 1986). Even here, however, the emergence of health insurance provisions to cover alcohol and drug rehabilitation treatment has led to the creation of careers in alcohol and drug counseling, in which individuals who have themselves passed through the recovery process can become "professional ex-s" employed by rehabilitation centers to lead AA-like groups (J. D. Brown, 1991). Thus, the practical problems of maintaining the funding needed to support a stable program of social problems work tend to foster at least a sort of professionalism among social problems workers.

All this means that social problems workers have difficulty maintaining the ideological and emotional edge that helps motivate primary claimsmakers. At earlier stages in the social problems process, troubling conditions have been constructed and reconstructed, often in melodramatic terms, to make claims as persuasive as possible. In the construction of new crime problems, the crimes tend to be depicted as terribly harmful, and the criminals who commit those crimes tend to be characterized as callous, brutal, terrible people. Similarly, other troubling conditions, such as poverty, tend to be characterized as grave threats that inflict harm on innocent, good victims. Most claimsmaking portrays a melodramatic world, populated by evil villains and innocent victims.

In contrast, the people whom social problems workers actually meet on the job present more variety, complexity, and ambiguity than most social problems constructions promise. Police officers find themselves dealing with lawbreakers who may be hurt, frustrated, angry, sick, drunk, desperate, and so on—in other words, very different sorts of people from the melodramatic evildoers who must be brought to justice by, or the sympathetic victims who require the protection of, television's heroic cops. Similarly, other social problems workers meet people who are less admirable, less noble, and less innocent than the victims portrayed in many claims. Social problems work is not so clear-cut, so unambiguous, as claimsmakers and policymakers imply it will be.

CONSTRUCTING CASES

Typically, social problems work entails dealing with a series of individuals, subjects who require attention. On a given shift, a police officer encounters any number of people; the officer may stop some of them, others may hail the officer, or the dispatcher may send the officer to a place where someone thinks the police are needed. Similarly, a physician deals with a series of patients who feel sick, a social worker meets with various clients who may need assistance, and so on.

Each contact with a subject requires the social problems worker to assess the nature of the encounter: the police officer needs to decide whether a law has been broken and, if so, what the specific violation was (this was a robbery, that was an illegal turn); the doctor needs to decide whether the patient is actually ill, what the illness might be, and how best to treat it; and so on. Note that social problems workers may decide that there is really nothing wrong, or at least that there isn't anything wrong enough to require official action: the police officer may simply warn the person to stay out of trouble; the doctor may decide that further treatment is unnecessary.

A central theme in social problems work is the construction of **cases**; that is, social problems workers must decide whether particular subjects represent *instances* of a previously constructed troubling condition that requires attention through the application of an appropriate policy. Thanks to institutional and organizational expectations, social problems workers have an array of categories or labels that they might apply to the subjects who become their cases, as well as procedures for dealing with those cases (Chambliss, 1996). But first, subjects must be classified as cases; that is, individual people's practical problems must be translated into the categories (crimes, diseases, and so on) used by the social problems workers. Studies of social problems workers find that they consider a wide range of factors in making these assessments, asking questions such as:

- *What seems to be the problem?* Most obviously, social problems workers must label their subjects by categorizing their troubles. Such assessment involves yet another process of social construction. Consider a physician. Doctors are trained to recognize different diseases; a doctor who meets a new patient will ask questions designed to identify a familiar pattern of symptoms, such that the doctor can, with some confidence, declare that the patient suffers from a particular disease. Labeling the patient's disease will, in turn, allow the doctor to prescribe the appropriate treatment for that illness. Just as doctors construct individual patients as having particular maladies, other social problems workers classify their subjects into familiar categories: police officers must decide whether a crime has been committed (and if so, which crime) and whether there is sufficient evidence to make an arrest; educators must determine which students are having trouble learning, and then seek to identify the source of the difficulty (perhaps by diagnosing a particular learning disability); and so on.

    Often a social problems worker is able to conclude that a particular subject does not meet the standards to become a case, or that the subject represents a sort of case that a different kind of social problems worker handles. Such rejections or referrals may frustrate both subjects and social problems workers. If a physician proves unable to classify a patient's symptoms, the patient is likely to be dissatisfied with the doctor (and the doctor may conclude that there is nothing really wrong—that the patient is just a hypochondriac, someone who complains without a valid medical reason).

- *Which aspects of the case are relevant?* The need to classify each case into a familiar category leads social problems workers to focus on those features of the cases that are relevant for purposes of classification or treatment. For example, a doctor trying to diagnose an illness will be interested in particular symptoms that can help distinguish between different possible diagnoses, but may be uninterested in hearing about other symptoms that can't help with the diagnosis. These narrowly focused concerns may produce tension between the social problems worker and the subject: the social problems worker may dismiss some of the subject's concerns as irrelevant (which may frustrate the subject), and the social problems workers may in turn be frustrated by the subject's failure to grasp which information needs to be reported.

- *Does this seem to be a serious matter?* (For example, has someone been seriously injured?) Obviously, the more serious the problem, the more likely it is to be pursued—and to be assigned a higher priority—by the social problems worker. Differences regarding these judgments also can lead to tension between subjects and social problems workers. People may try to convince police officers, for example, that a fight was just a minor misunderstanding, that everyone has calmed down and that there's no need to make an arrest; on other hand, patients may insist that their symptoms are serious, and that the doctor needs to take action.

- *What is the nature of the subject?* Social problems workers may classify subjects by race, gender, social class, age, education, or any of the other status categories commonly used to locate individuals within their larger social context. Often cultural expectations dictate that different kinds of people should be treated differently—most people would doubtless agree that a police officer ought to treat a child of six differently from someone who is sixteen, or sixty-six for that matter. In other instances, subjects may suspect that the social problems worker is unjustly focusing on race or class; for example, an African American motorist who has been stopped may suspect that the police officer has engaged in racial profiling. Subjects and social problems workers may disagree about the relevance of the subject's characteristics for doing social problems work; for instance, subjects may complain that people of their status receive more—or less—attention from social problems workers than the circumstances of their cases warrant.

Social problems workers often are more concerned with other, nondemographic aspects of their subjects. For instance, an individual's demeanor may affect the social problems worker's actions. Is the person calm or upset? Is the social problems worker being treated respectfully? Those who challenge the authority of police officers are more likely to wind up arrested than those who remain calm and respectful. Another consideration is the individual's career as a subject. Some subjects come to the attention of social problems workers again and again; they become the equivalents of students repeatedly sent to the vice principal's office. Social problems workers often become frustrated with such repeaters, particularly if those subjects seem to have ignored earlier advice or admonitions.

- *Are other people watching?* The knowledge that there is an audience observing the social problems worker's interactions with a subject can make things more complicated for both parties. During a conversation between a police officer and a teenager, the presence of other youths may make it harder for either party to back down. In particular, audiences may make social problems workers more careful, so as to avoid criticism for their conduct. Here, too, both parties may become frustrated because the other is, in a sense, playing to the gallery.

• *Are there work-related considerations?* Is the social problems worker's shift about to end? No one is eager to spend after-hours time filling out paperwork. Has the social problems worker's boss encouraged—or discouraged—particular practices? All manner of organizational and individual considerations can shape social problems work.

In particular, a social problems worker's job is often complicated by a heavy case load. For example, doctors may be expected to deal with many different patients, just as social workers or public defenders are assigned many clients. There may be a constant influx of new cases—new patients, new arrests, and so on—that need to be addressed by social problems workers. A social problems worker can ill afford to devote too much time to any one case, lest the flow of new cases create an unmanageable backlog, a queue of other people needing that worker's services. This pressure to deal with cases in an efficient, expeditious manner encourages social problems workers to focus on just the professionally relevant features of each case. But, of course, this narrowing of focus creates yet another source of tension: subjects may feel that their cases are not receiving the careful, individualized attention they deserve (see Box 8.3).

In short, social problems work is complicated; many factors can influence how social problems workers decide to deal with particular cases. At the same time, they usually find themselves under pressure to be efficient, to deal with cases as quickly as possible, so as not to get backlogged. Social problems workers typically resolve this dilemma by devising *routines*, standard practices that allow them to sort through cases, classify them, do what needs to be done, and then move on to the next case. For example, both prosecutors and defense attorneys learn to deal with their heavy criminal court caseloads by negotiating guilty pleas (so that many cases can be handled in a relatively short amount of time). Lawyers on both sides must review the record to identify the key relevant features of each case; this evaluation allows them to classify these

Box 8.3 Managing Dignity in Nursing Homes

Caring for nursing home residents is a difficult form of social problems work. Most nursing homes are for-profit operations, often part of large chains of homes, and each home's manager presses the nursing assistants to work efficiently (that is, to care for many residents, which reduces the amount of time that can be devoted to any one person) and to keep careful records of what they've done (to reduce liability and guarantee reimbursement for services). The residents—particularly recent arrivals—are often unhappy about having to live in the home, and their relatives who visit may criticize how the resident is being treated. Nursing assistants find themselves dealing with competing demands from managers, family members, and residents.

While some social problems workers maintain distance from their subjects, this is hard for nursing assistants—who have close, intimate contact with residents—but the assistants find meaning in investing emotion in their work. They find dignity in what the larger society views as low-status labor, by helping residents and establishing emotional ties to them as individuals. Helping new residents come to terms with the frustrations of finding themselves in a nursing home, maintaining individualized relationships with residents under their care, and helping individual residents come to terms with impending death allow nursing assistants to view their work as meaningful and dignified. Social problems work is often more than a technical, by-the-book activity, because it involves emotions on the part of both the social problems worker and the subject.

Source: Rodriquez, 2011.

cases not just in terms of which law was violated, but also in terms of the seriousness of the defendant's particular offense, which in turn enables them to figure out reasonable terms for negotiating an appropriate guilty plea.

In the course of dealing with many cases, social problems workers may become aware of deficiencies in the policies they are charged with implementing. Perhaps a policy's language is ambiguous; perhaps it fails to address particular sorts of cases; perhaps social problems workers realize that the policy isn't producing the desired results—there are all sorts of possible problems. As the people with the most firsthand experience with these issues, social problems workers may devise practices that modify the policy in hopes of making their work more effective, so that the boundary between policy implementation and policymaking may blur (see Box 8.4).

THE SUBJECT'S VIEW

As the preceding discussion has made clear, social problems workers are encouraged to view the people they deal with as cases, as instances of a particular disease, crime, or other troubling condition, rather than as unique individuals. But, of course, the people who constitute those cases—those who, depending on the particular kind of social problems work, are termed *patients, complainants, defendants, students, clients,* and so on—do not see things that way. These subjects tend to view their experiences as special, unique. They want to discuss their particular symptoms, the reasons they had for making particular choices or taking particular actions, the specific series of events that led them to the social problems worker.

A person who feels sick and goes to the doctor experiences illness as a personal, unique series of events and wants the doctor to return his or her body to good health. People's perspectives as subjects within the medical system—or with any other form of social problems work—are personal, individualistic. We would prefer not to be treated as "just another case." It can therefore be shocking to discover that, among themselves, social problems workers may refer to their subjects not as individuals, but as types of cases. For example, hospital personnel may speak of "that stomach ulcer in Room 313"; such depersonalization violates the subject's expectations for individualized social problems work (Chambliss, 1996).

Box 8.4 Human Resource Workers Shape Policy

The Civil Rights Act of 1964 outlawed discrimination in employment, but how should this rather abstract policy principle be translated into practice? What constitutes discrimination, and what should employers do to avoid breaking the law? Devising the rules and procedures that would comply with the law fell to corporations' human resources (HR) professionals. Firms' HR offices had evolved to oversee hiring and benefits—necessary but peripheral functions—now they had the additional responsibility of devising practices that would not lead to violating federal antidiscrimination law.

The federal government had not tried to create a set of specific rules that firms could follow, and most civil rights activists had stopped focusing on employment discrimination and had turned their attention to other issues. Therefore, it fell to HR professionals to not just deal with particular cases of hiring and firing, but also develop the standards for understanding what should be considered discriminatory, and for establishing procedures that would be nondiscriminatory—and that would be accepted by the courts as being nondiscriminatory. These came to be understood as technical issues, something that required the special knowledge of HR professionals. The definition of what constituted equal opportunity evolved: the emphasis was less on avoiding discrimination, and more on the advantages of managing diversity; sexual harassment came to be understood as a form of discriminatory treatment; and so on. HR wasn't just social problems work; it was shaping the very policies it was enforcing.

Source: Dobbin, 2009.

We have already noted that tensions may arise because social problems workers and their subjects are likely to view their interaction in very different ways. The differences in the perspectives of the social problems worker who needs to classify subjects into cases of familiar categories, and the subjects who want to have social problems workers acknowledge them as individuals with unique problems creates another, familiar tension. Subjects often criticize social problems workers for being uncaring or insensitive, even as social problems workers complain that subjects expect individualized treatment for what, in the social problems workers' view, are common, routine problems.

Often, then, social problems work requires guiding subjects to redefine both their selves and their problems. An individual whose drinking has led to difficulties at work or at home is likely to explain those difficulties in idiosyncratic terms: if only my boss weren't so unreasonable, if only my spouse were more understanding, if only people could recognize that sometimes I need a drink; oh, maybe sometimes I drink a little too much, but it doesn't really hurt anyone else; and so on. The individual subject is likely to present a unique, autobiographical account of the circumstances that brought him or her to the social problems worker's attention: if only people would try to understand my point of view, they would recognize that what I did was reasonable.

The social problems worker's task is to help the subject rework that idiosyncratic account into a more general construction. The subject needs to reinterpret whatever unique combination of events led to the encounter with the social problems worker, to learn to construct those events as instances of a larger troubling condition— excessive drinking, family violence, criminal activity, or whatever. Ideally, the subject will adopt the new identity offered by the social problems worker: "I am an alcoholic"; "I am a battered wife, and my husband is an abuser"; and so on.

Twelve-step programs, for example, demand that subjects undertake this sort of redefinition of self: Alcoholics Anonymous meetings begin with participants' identifying themselves as alcoholics, and the program's first step is to admit to being powerless over alcohol. In other words, subjects are urged to identify themselves as instances of a general type of problem (so that they say, in effect, "I am an alcoholic, and my personal troubles are just one instance

---

Box 8.5 New Identities for Drug Addicts?

Dissatisfaction with simply imprisoning drug addicts has led to new policies, such as drug courts and methadone maintenance, that strive to reduce the harms to addicts and the larger society. Drug courts supervise offenders through a sequence of drug treatment and required courtroom appearances to describe their progress; those who successfully complete the program can avoid imprisonment. Drug court personnel continually evaluate their clients' progress, encourage them when they seem to be making good progress, or warn them when they are in danger of failing the program. Considerable emphasis is placed on getting the clients to construct their own lives in terms of the categories the drug court workers use. In ideal cases, people who graduate from drug court will continue to avoid using drugs, and come to define themselves as respectable citizens.

Drug courts prefer to work with first-time offenders, who might be diverted from a life of addiction. In contrast, methadone programs are defined as a last resort, a way of reducing harm for individuals who are seen by social problems workers as incapable of ending their addiction. While addicts receiving methadone may commit fewer crimes and be healthier than those using illegal drugs, they are viewed—by both drug center staff members and themselves—as people who are permanently dependent and vulnerable. For most participants, being in a methadone program precludes thinking of themselves as normal, equal members of society.

Sources: Järvinen & Miller, 2010; Makinem & Higgins, 2008.

---

of the larger problem of alcoholism"). The subjects are helped to understand that what once seemed to them to be their personal, unique circumstances can be understood—and are understood by the social problems workers and others—as just another case of a general problem (see Box 8.5).

Social problems workers not only find it necessary to convert individual subjects into cases in order to do their jobs effectively, but they also may believe that subjects need to identify themselves as cases if they are to benefit from the process. Some social problems work is based on force, or *coercion*: people who are arrested by police, brought to trial by prosecutors before judges, and sentenced to prison or probation are usually reluctant participants in the process; most would prefer to avoid the social problems workers' attentions. Even so, coercive social problems workers try to gain their subjects' cooperation using a combination of sticks ("You don't want to make this any harder on yourself") and carrots ("Be cooperative, and you may get a break"). Subjects who constantly offer maximum resistance make the social problems worker's job difficult; it is usually preferable to convince subjects to go along with the process, at least to the extent of accepting being defined and treated as a case.

Of course, not all social problems work is coercive; many social problems workers offer desired *services* to subjects who seek them out, providing different sorts of aid, assistance, or therapy. For example, physicians, social welfare workers, drug counselors, and so on see themselves—and are probably seen by their subjects—as helping the subjects deal with their difficulties. Yet again, a key to these services is persuading the subject to accept the social problems worker's construction of the case, first to concede that the social problems worker has correctly defined the problem and to adopt the suggested identity ("Okay, you're right, I'm an alcoholic"); and second, to follow the social problems worker's recommendations for addressing the problem. Following the prescribed program often involves adopting the social problems worker's construction of the situation, so subjects ideally acquire a new view that is supposed to help reduce or even solve their personal difficulties.

This process of subjects accepting the social problems workers' constructions is not always smooth. The social problems workers' redefinitions may be resisted by some subjects who insist on alternative interpretations. In general, subjects who have more resources (more money, more education, more social support, and so on) find it easier to resist whatever pressures the social problems workers apply, but even subjects with limited resources may be able to resist. A homeless person may insist on living on the street and refuse to enter a shelter, or someone arrested for violence against an abortion clinic may insist that this was a moral act in accordance with God's law (a view that even many abortion opponents would reject). Note that these subjects' acts of resistance may have different degrees of social support: on the one hand, for example, a homeless person may be unable to explain the decision to live on the streets in terms that make sense to anyone else; on the other, some abortion opponents may endorse the morality of antiabortion violence.

Much resistance, though, is less active, less visible. Doctors advise countless patients to eat less, stop smoking, drink in moderation, and get more exercise. To the doctors' frustration, many patients fail to follow this sensible advice and continue to suffer deteriorating health. Most forms of social problems work have these sorts of repeat subjects: most people who go through drug treatment programs return to drug use, most inmates released from prisons wind up back in prison, and so on. Often, of course, it is possible to construct these repeaters in sympathetic terms, as victims of larger social forces (for example, not only do ex-inmates retain the disadvantages [such as limited education and job prospects] that initially encouraged their involvement in crime, but having been imprisoned usually further reduces their options, making recidivism more likely). Still, many social problems workers place much of the blame on the subjects, arguing that, if only the subjects had been sincere, determined, and otherwise virtuous, they might have avoided becoming repeaters.

In general, social problems workers prefer their subjects to be compliant, willing to adopt the workers' constructions, so that their interaction with the subjects can be cooperative, and the social problems work effective. However, at least some social problems workers anticipate resistance and noncooperation; the police, for example, have the power to arrest and restrain suspects, regardless of whether those subjects acknowledge the officers' authority. Other subjects may choose to go through the motions, viewing temporary submission to the social problems workers' authority as a necessary annoyance. Social problems workers, in turn, may watch for—and insist on—evidence of the subject's genuine cooperation. For instance, a drug court that offers clients the possibility of avoiding imprisonment by participating in therapeutic programs may expel clients who fail to participate fully in the program, sending them back into the penal system. Because so many tensions are built into the relationships between social problems workers and their subjects, the social problems workers' hopes often are disappointed and it is not surprising that they may develop a certain cynicism about their work.

LOOKING OVER THEIR SHOULDERS

Social problems workers face an additional consideration: they know that they may be held accountable for their performance. Figure 8.1 illustrated how social problems workers find themselves in the middle, experiencing pressures from many directions. In particular, individual workers have supervisors, bosses who oversee how social problems work is done. These supervisors have expectations: they probably expect social problems workers to be productive (that is, to deal with their cases quickly and efficiently, so that the agency's work doesn't back up); they may assign priorities, telling their workers to treat some cases as more important, deserving more careful attention than others; they want their workers to avoid mistakes or other actions that might result in critical attention being focused on the agency; and so on. Most social problems workers understand their supervisors' expectations, and they usually try to avoid displeasing their bosses.

Similarly, supervisors have others looking over their shoulders, and not just their own superiors within their organization's hierarchy (very large agencies may have several levels of authority between the agency head and the lowly, street-level social problems workers who actually deal directly with the agency's subjects). But agencies operate within a larger environment: most depend on a legislative body or other outsiders for their funding; there may be professional bodies that oversee professionals' conduct (such as state boards that license physicians); and an agency may become the subject of media coverage, or even a target of claimsmakers' criticisms. It is very easy for attention to turn to criticism, and for criticism to lead policymakers to begin interfering with an agency's operations.

Therefore, everyone involved at all levels of social problems work—for example, from the police chief to the cop on the beat—must consider not just how best to deal with the subjects of social problems work, but also how those dealings might be regarded by others. The responses of social problems workers to these considerations revolve around two central principles.

First, social problems workers try to control the flow of information about their activities. They generally prefer that others learn about the work they do directly from them. Thus, agencies issue formal reports summarizing their activities, and they may employ public relations specialists to help guide media coverage of the agency's activities. Having control over information means that social problems workers may try to choose what they report; they may even try to cover up some information, to keep it secret. Not surprisingly, social problems workers may seek to release information that portrays their activities in the best possible light, even if doing so requires distorting what they report. This sets the stage for an ongoing struggle between various levels of supervisors who want to know what social problems workers do so that they can be held accountable, and the social problems workers who seek to manage what others learn about their work.

The second principle is that social problems workers try to limit outsiders' authority over their activities. Here, their argument is that only social problems workers can truly understand the nature of their work and the pressures under which they operate. To the degree possible, they want their performance judged by others who share their views of the job—that is, colleagues, fellow social problems workers who can be expected to sympathize with their position and endorse their actions. For example, teachers' unions often object to outsiders' proposals to award teachers merit pay on the basis of their students' test performance (the teachers argue that test results reflect too many things the teachers can't control), just as police often resist reforms that would create review boards with civilian (nonpolice) members overseeing complaints of police misconduct (on the grounds that outsiders cannot understand the real-world pressures that police face). Social problems workers object to such proposals because they give outsiders a measure of power over social problems work.

Social problems workers vary in their ability to control information and ward off outsider interference with their activities. In general, the more resources the subjects of social problems work command, the more likely it is that social problems workers will be scrutinized by outsiders and the more carefully they need to monitor any behavior that might be observed. For example, whereas police in an upper-middle-class suburb may view themselves as providing services to the community's residents and strive to maintain good relations with the local press and with the community generally, police in lower-class urban neighborhoods may have a freer hand because their work tends to be more hidden from public view.

When social problems work—such as health care, teaching, or policing—is directed toward subjects who are relatively poor and powerless, what happens is far less likely to attract public attention and concern than when comparable services for wealthier subjects are seen as failing. Moreover, poorer populations tend to have more problems that require more services, so social problems workers who deal with poorer subjects often find themselves swamped with work, compared to those working with better off, less needy subjects. At the same time, policymakers tend to be more responsive to middle-class demands for improved social problems work, so resources tend to flow to those social problems workers who need them relatively less. All this ensures that the quality of social problems work suffers—particularly work directed at less advantaged subjects—so social problems workers feel an even greater need to manage information. The result is a cycle of disappointment and fresh complaints about failing schools, unprofessional policing, and so on.

EVERYDAY SOCIAL PROBLEMS WORK

This chapter has focused on police, social workers, and other people who do social problems work for a living, carrying out the formal policies enacted to address claimsmaking about troubling conditions. However, we should recognize that we all sometimes become amateur social problems workers. Chapter 6 noted that the public reconstructs social problems claims in their everyday conversations. Similarly, ordinary individuals become aware of shifting construc-tions of troubling conditions, particularly via media coverage of claimsmaking and policymaking, and they find countless occasions to apply these constructions in their everyday lives.

Consider, for example, changing expectations regarding race and gender. The everyday world has become less segregated. Discrimi-nation can take many forms; the southern states' legalized systems of racial segregation that were the targets of the civil rights move-ment (that is, laws that segregated everything from schools and hospitals to drinking fountains) are only the most obvious example; other forms are less blatant. For instance, prior to the emergence of the women's movement, women made up only a small minor-ity of admissions to medical schools and law schools. Things have changed; most careers—like most neighborhoods, most schools, and most other settings—are more open to people of different races and both sexes. This is not to imply that there is absolute equality everywhere we turn. There is not. But expectations—and complaints—have shifted; for example, where activists once campaigned to open business schools to women students, they now complain that women in business confront a "glass ceiling" that makes it hard for women to move into the upper reaches of corporate leadership.

Everyday life is filled with occasions when people's behavior reflects changes in the larger culture, such as increasingly widespread assumptions about racial and sexual etiquette—the growing sense, for example, that blacks or women deserve to be treated with respect. Such changing manners, regarding how people respond to all sorts of differences—homosexuality, disabilities, unmarried couples cohabitating, and on and on—may be seen as one of the most common forms of social problems work, even if much of it has come to be taken for granted, as simply the way people think they ought to act. Of course, managing such reactions may be quite conscious, as when women having abortions must decide how to think—and feel—about their experience (see Box 8.6).

One form of everyday social problems work, then, is to smooth over what once might have been awkward occasions. Close personal relationships—ties between friends or family members—may offer the most extreme examples. Here, people know one another well; each person is understood to be a unique individual, with his or her own character and patterns of behavior. Such relationships can be seen as the opposite of the efforts of professional social problems workers to classify their subjects into cases belonging to particular categories.

A consequence of such highly personalized understanding of one another is that families and friends are often slow to construct those they know well as instances of larger troubling conditions. Cousin Joe may get drunk a lot and even hit his wife, and Jane next door may often get moody, but it is possible for those who know Joe and Jane to tell themselves that these are just personal

---

Box 8.6 Managing the Abortion Experience

The debate over abortion is intensely emotional, and women who seek abortions find it difficult to ignore the claims and counterclaims made about the issue. They need to do personal social problems work, to consider how what is happening in their personal lives relates to the social issue of abortion.

Women vary in their emotional reactions to abortion, and their reactions are shaped, in part, by their ideologies. The abortion experience poses different challenges for women who consider themselves pro-choice, and those who are pro-life (yet have nonetheless decided on abortion). Pro-life women are most likely to deal with difficult emotions: they may feel ashamed or guilty; in some cases, they even welcome these feelings as a sort of punishment that they believe is deserved. The abortion experience tends to be less difficult for pro-choice women; when they do experience negative emotions, they may define those emotions as the problem and work to keep them under control.

Having an abortion may involve various moments that require emotional attention: Will there be pro-life demonstrators outside the clinic? Will there be an ultrasound (required in some states)? Which aspects of the procedure will be remembered? How should one react to encountering pregnant women or babies? Any of these can be treated as routine moments, or as emotionally intense experiences that need to be managed. How a woman reconstructs the meaning of her own abortion varies from one individual to the next, but all women who have an abortion engage in social problems work of one sort or another.

Source: Keys, 2010.

---

quirks: "Joe's under a lot of strain"; "That's just how Jane is." It often takes time for friends and family to begin to use the larger culture's vocabulary of social problems—to speak of alcoholism, or domestic violence, or depression.

The media offer guidance for such everyday social problems work: many television talk show episodes are designed to help viewers reinterpret interpersonal problems as instances of larger social problems, and to offer advice—where to seek help, and so on. For example, friends, family members, and coworkers may be urged to stage an "intervention" to pressure an individual to acknowledge and do something about his or her drinking problem. In this way, ordinary people are encouraged to think that they, too, can assist professional social problems work, that they can recognize things that happen as instances of troubling conditions and respond appropriately, by guiding the subject toward professional social problems workers.

Social problems work, then, is a key stage in the social problems process because it connects general discussions of macrosociological social problems with the practical realities of individuals' lives. At one time or another, all of us experience troubling conditions, either personally or through our contacts with other people, and we all come into at least occasional contact with professional social problems workers. On these occasions, the currently available constructions of troubling conditions can affect us in many ways—through media messages, through the policies interpreted by social problems workers, and so on. What happens to us, what happens to those around us, and how we understand what's happening when we become involved with social problems work are all part of the social problems process. And, in turn, people's experiences with social problems work can lead to various reactions, which will be addressed in the next chapter.

MAKING CONNECTIONS

- *Through their jobs, social problems workers transform the meaning of a social problem from an abstract, general condition to a specific or immediate situation.*

- *The measurement of social problems workers' success will be discussed in the next chapter, on policy outcomes.*

● *Social problems workers frequently become targets themselves of claims by activists and experts and are subjected to new policies to address repackaged social problems. Chapters 3 and 4 explain how claimsmakers frame troubling conditions.*

CASE STUDY
LOAN APPLICATIONS AND FINANCIAL COLLAPSE

At first glance, the process of applying for a home loan seems routine, something that most people wind up doing at least once—or even a few times—during the course of their lives. It seems so normal, so uneventful, that it should hardly be considered an example of social problems work.

Up until fairly recently, someone who wanted to borrow money to buy a home would approach a lender (a bank, savings and loan, or some other financial institution that made home loans). The lender would ask for evidence that the would-be borrower was likely to be willing and able to repay the loan: for instance, borrowers had to have a down payment equal to, say, 10 percent of the price of the home; they needed good credit histories (evidence that previous loans had been repaid); and they had to show that they were employed and earning an income sufficient to allow them to cover their mortgage payments. Lenders took this seriously because it was their money; if a borrower refused to pay the lender back, the home would default to the lender, who would then have to find another buyer. Once we think about these arrangements, screening loan applicants can be understood as a process in which lenders/social problems workers apply policies for allocating credit to a series of would-be borrowers/subjects, in order to determine who is trustworthy.

Like other social problems workers, lenders operate within an institutional context (Lewis, 2010; Shiller, 2008). Each financial institution has its own policies to ensure that it isn't making risky loans, and these businesses are constrained by various laws. The system was relatively stable—until the rules were relaxed in several key ways:

- New policies encouraged lenders to bundle loans. When a financial institution makes a loan, that money is tied up—often for decades—as the loan is gradually being repaid. However, if the loan can be sold to someone else, the lender can recover the money and lend it again. Lenders who had made large numbers of loans could package them together, and sell them as securities to investors. As interest rates reached historic lows, this became an attractive investment: a bundle of sound loans made to low-risk borrowers could be counted on to bring in a steady income from all the regular payments on the loans. At the same time, there was little oversight on how those loans were valued, so that high-risk loans could be bundled with low-risk loans, and the bundle sold as a low-risk investment. Selling these bundles became a profitable business for financial institutions.

- Relaxed regulations also allowed financial institutions to keep less money in reserve. In the past, they were required to keep 10 percent of their assets on hand (that is, for every nine dollars they loaned, they needed to hang on to one dollar—a reserve in case some loans were not repaid). However, these rules were relaxed, so that the lenders needed to keep only 3 percent of their assets in reserve (one dollar in reserve for every thirty dollars loaned). As long as things went well, this change would not matter, but if large numbers of loans could not be repaid, the institutions could find themselves without enough money to continue doing business.

- The federal government found itself promoting home ownership, on the grounds that home owners had a stake in the larger society. Expanding the proportion of Americans who owned homes meant relaxing the rules for borrowers, so that people who had less savings, lower incomes, or poorer credit histories—people who would have had trouble qualifying for loans in the past—might be able to get a piece of the American Dream.

- In order to have more loans that could be bundled and sold to investors, financial institutions began working with firms that were in the business of arranging loans and then selling them to lenders. These companies were paid commissions for each loan they arranged, but they were not putting their own money at risk. They began relaxing the standards for qualifying for loans, until some were offering what came to be called "NINJA" loans (because they required No Income, No Job, and No Assets).

Why would someone sign a mortgage agreement they could not hope to repay? Prospective borrowers were told that this was a sure thing, because house prices were certain to rise. A person might borrow, say, $300,000 to buy a home, using a loan structured so that there would be minimal initial payments at a very low interest rate (although the interest rate—and the payments—would rise dramatically in a year). One year later, just before the payment would become unmanageable, it would be possible to sell the home (now worth perhaps $330,000), or arrange a more favorable loan based on the fact that the borrower now owned a larger share of the home.

These arrangements depended on finding ever more borrowers, which meant continually increasing the proportion of dubious loans, and they worked—until house prices peaked, borrowers couldn't repay their loans, and the values of all those bundled securities plummeted. This set off the global great recession.

Once the scope of the economic crisis became clear, many people explained the crisis in terms of "greed," but they could not agree on just who had been greedy. Was it the borrowers who had signed mortgage agreements that they could not fulfill, on the assumption that they would be bailed out by continually rising home prices? Or was it the lenders, who viewed mortgages as something they could sell for a quick profit, and who passed along the risks of bad loans to investors? Or was it government agencies that agreed to relax lending standards? Or was it the rating agencies that took commissions to certify that bundles of dubious loans were low-risk investments? Different constructions led to blaming very different people.

The great recession illustrates the importance of apparently mundane social problems work. The importance of the institutional rules that governed the standards for home loans became visible only after the dangers of relaxing them became apparent.

Questions

1. How do the pressures on lenders resemble those experienced by other social problems workers?

2. How did changing the rules governing lenders contribute to the global financial crisis?

3. How can a sociological imagination help connect the individual experiences of lenders and buyers with the larger economy?

9

Policy Outcomes

The social problems process can be lengthy. In its typical form, as described in earlier chapters, claims lead to media coverage, public reaction, and policymaking, and the resulting policies shape social problems work. At each stage in this process, actors reconstruct the troubling condition: just as media workers repackage the primary claims of activists and experts into secondary claims that fit the media's requirements for suitable news or entertainment, social problems workers must figure out how to bring the idealized generalities that inspired the social policies to bear on the gritty, practical situations they confront. At every stage in the social problems process, there are likely to be shifts in how the troubling condition is understood, as it is constructed and reconstructed by different people.

This chapter concerns what we can view as the final stage in the process: its *policy outcomes*, reactions to the way that social problems workers have implemented policies. There is a broad range of possible outcomes. At one extreme, we can imagine everyone agreeing that a particular policy solves the problem; perhaps all interested parties smile, dust off their hands, and turn their attention to something else. The Nineteenth Amendment to the Constitution, which granted women the vote throughout the United States, might be an example; women's right to vote became a part of the political landscape that is now simply taken for granted. However, this sort of complete satisfaction with social policy is probably rare. At the other extreme, a policy may be completely rejected, perhaps because it is seen as having failed to work, or even as having made things worse. For instance, the Eighteenth Amendment, which established prohibition of alcohol as the law of the land, was quickly found unsatisfactory and repealed (via the Twenty-First Amendment). Most policies fall between these extremes and are seen as flawed—satisfactory in some respects, but unsatisfactory in others.

In most cases, policies fail to make the troubling conditions that they are intended to address vanish. This should not come as a surprise. Crime, racism, poverty, and most other troubling conditions are unlikely to disappear simply because a particular policy has been implemented. These conditions tend to have multiple causes—consider all of the various things that might lead someone to commit a crime—and it is unlikely that any one policy can address them all. It is almost certain that more will remain to be done. This helps explain why so few social policies are regarded as completely successful.

It is significant that our culture speaks of social *problems*. The very term implies that there must be a solution; after all, schoolchildren learn to *solve* arithmetic *problems*. We might use other terms to characterize society's troubling conditions. We might call them **social conditions**, an expression that does not seem to imply the same confidence that there must be a solution; or **social issues**, a term that draws attention to disagreements or debates without necessarily raising expectations that they can be resolved. But because we think in terms of social *problems*, people often judge social policies as falling short if they don't solve everything; they tend to criticize policies that don't work, construct interpretations for those policies' shortcomings, and make recommendations regarding what ought to be done differently.

This chapter will focus on such critiques—what we will call *policy outcomes*. As we will see, the range of such outcomes is very broad. Even when people agree that a policy is flawed, they may have very different interpretations about what the flaws are, what causes those flaws, and how the flaws might be repaired. This chapter cannot possibly explore all of the many ways that people respond to social policies; it can only sketch some key features about policy outcomes. The discussion will begin by considering how policy outcomes can evolve into new claims, then turn to the types of people who participate in constructing policy outcomes, as well as the rhetoric they tend to favor.

NEW CLAIMS BASED ON POLICY EVALUATION

As suggested already, general acceptance of a social policy's success may be relatively rare. Certainly our attention is drawn to cases of vocal critical reactions, in which people charge that the policy is somehow imperfect. These reactions can be viewed as new claims, claims that the flawed social policy itself now constitutes a troubling condition that needs to be addressed. Although such claims about policies' flaws can take many forms, we can identify three general types of critiques about social policies.

Critique #1: The Policy Is Insufficient

The first critique is that the policy is *insufficient*. Here, critics argue that the policy was a step in the right direction, but that it doesn't do enough and, as a result, has fallen short of what is needed to eliminate the troubling condition that it was intended to address. For example, critics might argue that an antipoverty program, although it may help some poor people, is insufficient to end poverty; or that a civil rights law does not do enough to eradicate the legacy of racism. An insufficient policy, according to its critics, does too little.

The critique of insufficiency is often promoted by those who supported the original claims that led to implementation of the social policy. Having identified a particular troubling condition and having successfully urged policymakers to act, they now claim that the policy just wasn't enough, that the policy needs to be extended or expanded to better deal with the troubling condition. Often these new claims are part of a broader strategy. After all, when claimsmakers first draw attention to a troubling condition, they may anticipate considerable resistance from the press, public, and policymakers who find the claims too unfamiliar or the claimsmakers' proposals too radical. Although they may privately think that eliminating the troubling condition will require extensive—and expensive—policy changes, claimsmakers may fear that it will be impossible—at least at first—to convince the public and policymakers to buy into such far-reaching changes. It's better to call for specific, narrower—and cheaper—policies; that is, it's better to ask for something that others might be willing to give. And, as discussed in Chapter 7, policymakers may adopt a similar approach, settling for a modest initial program in hopes that it will be a foot in the door. Once many people accept the need to do something about the troubling condition, it may be possible to mount a new campaign, arguing that the original policy is insufficient, and that more needs to be done.

Critique #2: The Policy Is Excessive

The second critique, which is the opposite of the first, states that the policy is *excessive*. The argument is that the policy goes too far, that it does too much and needs to be rolled back. For example, some critics argue that laws protecting endangered species are too broad (in that they block economic progress in order to protect minor, unimportant species), too cumbersome (in that there are too many bureaucratic steps required to demonstrate compliance with the laws), and not in society's best interest (in that the requirement to protect endangered species impedes society from achieving other important goals). These, too, are claims—claims that policies have an inappropriate, damaging impact.

Those who present claims about excessive policies are likely to have resisted those policies in the first place. They may have seen the proposed policy as threatening their interests or their values, yet failed to block the policymaking process. Now they have returned to argue that the policy has, in fact, proved to be excessive, and they may seek to cut it back. In particular, they may try to convince media workers, members of the public, and policymakers who supported the initial policy that they made a mistake, that it is time to backtrack and undo the damage (see Box 9.1).

Critique #3: The Policy Is Misguided

Finally, policies may be critiqued as *misguided*. Once again, these evaluations are claims that the policy has led to a troubling condition, but in this case the claim is not so much that the policy goes too far or not far enough, but that it heads in the wrong direction. There are various bases for making such claims. For example, the critics can argue that the *construction of the troubling condition* that led to the original policy was mistaken, that the problem needs to be understood in completely different terms.

Such claims often offer alternative definitions of the troubling condition that are grounded in a different underlying ideology. For example, concerns about the spread of sexually transmitted diseases among adolescents and about teenage pregnancy have led liberals to advocate policies for sex education and for providing youths better access to contraception and abortion (Irvine, 2002). In effect, such programs of reproductive health services define the troubling condition as caused by society's failure to deal effectively with the reality of widespread adolescent sexual behavior. These programs had long met resistance from—and were sometimes blocked by—conservatives

Box 9.1 Alcohol, Risks, and Pregnancy

In the early 1970s, physicians identified Fetal Alcohol Syndrome—a rare but serious condition that affects some babies born to alcoholic women. The diagnosis was renamed Fetal Alcohol Syndrome Disorder and expanded to include a far broader range of symptoms. Although the research found these effects among the children of alcoholic women who drank quite heavily during pregnancy, and although the medical literature has found no effects on children born to women who drink in moderation during pregnancy (although there is some evidence that "low-to-moderate" drinking—less than 1.5 drinks per day—may increase the risks of miscarriage during the early months of pregnancy), medical and public health authorities began recommending that women abstain from all alcohol during their pregnancies. Some authorities have begun recommending that women who are trying to conceive should abstain from drinking alcohol.

Critics point to these recommendations as instances of excessive policies. Risk is a theme that guides much contemporary policymaking. Risks are probabilities: someone who smokes has a higher likelihood—a greater risk—of developing lung cancer and other health problems. While the evidence clearly shows that babies born to alcoholic women are at higher risk of having serious health problems, there is little evidence that moderate drinking during pregnancy threatens the fetus, which suggests that the risks are rather low. Does a low risk justify recommending abstinence? Medical authorities and their critics disagree.

Source: Lowe & Lee, 2010.

who worried that sex education and reproductive health services might promote adolescent sexual activity.

However, the emergence of HIV/AIDS as a major health risk led many schools and communities to adopt expanded new programs. After the programs were in place, some conservatives presented an alternative construction of the troubling condition by arguing that it was the liberals' policies that were promoting sexual activity among the young; the conservatives' counterclaims argued instead for abstinence-based programs designed to discourage premarital sexual behavior. There are many similar examples, cases in which critics argue that the assumptions behind social policies—such as those dealing with poverty or homelessness—are mistaken, and that only by reinterpreting the nature and causes of the troubling condition can effective policies be designed and implemented.

Other critiques may generally accept the initial construction of the troubling condition, yet argue that the *policies* that emerged were in some way misguided. For example, Lipsky and Smith (1989) argue that constructing social problems as emergencies often wastes resources. Emergencies are defined as short-term challenges for which policymakers tend to adopt short-term solutions, but it often might make more sense to establish long-term arrangements to deal with such conditions. For instance, instead of viewing home-lessness as an emergency that requires short-term shelter and other assistance, it might be less costly and more helpful in the long run to establish programs to make stable, low-cost housing available for longer periods. Just because people agree about the nature of a social problem doesn't mean they won't disagree about how best to deal with it.

One important theme in critiques about misguided policies is that the policies actually make things worse, that they exacerbate the troubling conditions they are designed to eliminate. That is, these claims often describe policies as having *ironic* consequences. For instance, critics argue that antidrug policies actually encourage the spread of illicit drugs (for example, they might argue that arresting drug dealers increases the risks of dealing and reduces the supply of drugs, leading to higher drug prices, which in turn attract more people to the now even more lucrative business of drug dealing), or that programs designed to lift people out of poverty actually increase the numbers of poor people (here the argument might be that the more generous social welfare programs become, the more likely it is that people will choose to remain dependent on welfare rather than working) (MacCoun & Reuter, 2001; Murray, 1994). Note that the former critique tends to be favored by liberals, while the latter usually is presented by conservatives; claims that policies have ironic consequences are not limited to particular ideologies. Such claims often describe a vicious cycle: a troubling condition leads to a policy that makes the condition worse; in response, the policy is expanded (because that's how people have agreed to address this issue), which in turn causes the condition to get even worse, and so on. Critics insist that the only way to break this cycle is to devise completely different policies that approach the problem from a fresh direction.

A somewhat different critique of misguided policies argues that the implementation of the policy—the *social problems work*—violates the policy's true intent or purpose. Here, critics claim that the initial construction of the problem and policy—perhaps what was intended by its advocates to be a supportive, generous plan to help the afflicted—is being subverted by social problems workers. Such critiques may contrast the public face of a policy with its hidden workings, arguing that, for example, job training programs usually do not help their clients to find good jobs so much as steer them into low-paying, dead-end jobs (Lafer, 2002). Alternatively, the critics may argue that the social problems workers are abusing their positions, wasting resources, or paying too little attention to the needs of those the policy is meant to help. Claims about police brutality or police corruption, for instance, are less about flawed laws than about problems with the ways the laws are enforced (see Box 9.2).

In short, there are various ways to construct the workings of social policies as imperfect—as troubling conditions in their own right. The social problems process does not usually come to an end after a particular social policy has been implemented. Rather, new social policies often provide the raw material for launching yet another social problems process, one in which critics construct

Box 9.2 When Should Pathologists Identify Abuse as a Cause of Death?

The campaign to raise awareness of child abuse has emphasized the risks to children of a failure to recognize and report abuse. In particular, pathologists who investigate the deaths of children have been encouraged to "think dirty," that is, to be suspicious and consider the possibility that the deaths might have been caused by abuse. However, defense attorneys for adults charged with fatally abusing children have argued that some pathologists have been too ready to designate deaths as caused by abuse, that some innocent adults have been charged in cases when the deaths had probably not been caused by abuse.

In these cases, the pathologist is asked to examine a child's body and give an expert interpretation of the cause of death—not just which injuries caused the death, but also what caused those injuries. Inevitably, there is ambiguity, and the social problems workers—the pathologists—are constructing interpretations that will be considered authoritative. What assumptions should guide them? *Thinking dirty* suggests that the need to protect children should be an overriding value, that pathologists should not be reluctant to blame a death on abuse. But what of the rights of the accused—shouldn't that person be considered innocent unless there is certain evidence that abuse caused the death? Whatever principles are chosen to guide policy, there will be vulnerability to criticisms that officials are either too slow or too eager to attribute children's deaths to abuse.

Source: Cradock, 2011.

claims that the policy is doing too little, too much, or the wrong thing; that this in itself is a troubling condition; and that something ought to be done about it. In fact, dissatisfaction with the operation of current social policy is an element in most claimsmakers' rhetoric. A glance back at the examples in earlier chapters will reveal that many of the claimsmaking campaigns we have discussed throughout this book have focused, at least to some degree, on the deficiencies of existing social policies. This means that social problems processes can be linked through time: when one runs its course, it often inspires one or more new claimsmaking campaigns, as illustrated in Figure 9.1.

ACTORS, EVIDENCE, AND EVALUATION

The previous section described several ways to criticize the workings of social policies. But who presents these critiques? And what sorts of rhetoric do they use to make their claims convincing? This section considers some of the actors who play prominent roles in constructing outcomes to the social problems process, as well as the sorts of evidence that they are likely to feature in their claims.

Most obviously, *social problems workers* can become critics. As noted in Chapter 8, it is not unusual for social problems workers to be ambivalent about the policies that they must implement. Moreover, they have a good sense of what is—and isn't—working. Social problems workers often have to report to their supervisors about what they have been doing. Because most social problems workers keep records, they have two important advantages in debates over social policy outcomes: they understand how social problems work is actually practiced, and they have access to those records. Again, Chapter 8 noted that social problems workers seek to control information about their work, and this desire shapes their claims. They have an interest in convincing other people that they're doing a good job and, perhaps, that they would be able to do an even better job if only they had more resources—more personnel, a bigger budget, and so on. Thus, social problems workers may be reluctant to challenge either the basic policies that they are supposed to implement, or the manner in which they actually implement those policies, unless they can, in the process, advocate receiving additional resources for their agencies.

Figure 9.1 ONE SOCIAL PROBLEMS PROCESS CAN INSPIRE OTHERS

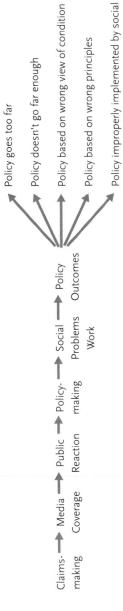

Claims-making → Media Coverage → Public Reaction → Policy-making → Social Problems Work → Policy Outcomes

Policy goes too far

Policy doesn't go far enough

Policy based on wrong view of condition

Policy based on wrong principles

Policy improperly implemented by social problems workers

A Social Problems Process

Possible Claims for Launching a New Social Problems Process

Because they control their agencies' records, social problems workers are particularly likely to support their claims with evidence of organizational activity—that is, measures of how much work they do. It is relatively easy for them to compile this information: police departments can tally the number of arrests made during the previous year, hospitals can count the number of patients, and so on. Social problems workers can use these data to demonstrate that they have been busy doing what they are supposed to do, and they often argue that the fact that they are busy is evidence that they need bigger budgets and additional personnel to handle the demand for their services. In other words, social problems workers are particularly likely to use measures of organizational activity to support claims that existing policies are insufficient, and that they need to be expanded to give social problems workers more resources.

Sometimes the social problems workers' *subjects*—the people whose lives constitute the troubling condition that the policy is supposed to address—offer their own evaluations. For example, poor people may criticize antipoverty programs for not doing enough to help poor people, just as both people who have been arrested and crime victims may complain about mistreatment at the hands of the criminal justice system. Again, as noted in Chapter 8, subjects often are frustrated in their dealings with social problems workers, and they may be dissatisfied with the actual implementation of social policies.

Like social problems workers, subjects have the advantage of firsthand experience with how policies work, and they are most likely to draw upon these experiences for evidence to support their claims. Thus, they tend to favor anecdotal accounts—this is how the policy failed to work in our particular cases, or in the cases of people we know—which then serve as typifying examples for what are constructed as larger policy failings. (Recall a lesson from Chapter 2: typifying examples are rarely typical; they are chosen because they offer compelling illustrations of claims.)

Whereas social problems workers usually argue that policies are insufficient, subjects' critiques can be more varied. Subjects, too, may claim that the policy is insufficient; for example, they might argue that there are long waiting lines and other delays because there aren't enough social problems workers to aid the subjects who need services. Or they may warn that policies are excessive; for instance, they may charge that people who commit minor criminal offenses may suffer unreasonably harsh, life-damaging penalties. Or subjects may insist that the policies are misguided; for example, they may claim that social problems workers ought to help their subjects, rather than coerce them. Properly chosen typifying examples can support any of these critiques.

Compared to social problems workers, subjects tend to have significant disadvantages when critiquing policies. To the degree that subjects draw upon their own personal experiences to document the policy's shortcomings, audiences may dismiss the subjects' claims as self-interested. High-status subjects' claims may receive careful attention (see Box 9.3). But the subjects of many kinds of social problems work have relatively few resources (that is, they have limited money, education, and social status), and the very fact that they are subjects can be stigmatizing (in that they may have been labeled as criminals, mentally ill, and so on). Although it is not impossible for low-status or stigmatized subjects to devise claims criticizing how a particular social policy operates, these disadvantages can make it much harder to get the media, policymakers, and other audiences to attend to the subjects' claims.

The prospects are better for a third set of critics, those whose claims launched the initial social problems process—the *original activists and experts* who first drew attention to the troubling condition and the need to do something about it. These people may already have the advantage of ownership; that is, the media and policymakers may be used to listening to what these claimsmakers have to say about this troubling condition. In particular, experts' critiques may seem more credible because they have professional

Box 9.3 Holding Colleges Accountable for Crime on Campus

American colleges and universities have never been free of crime, but in recent decades, campus policies have come under attack from a variety of critics. In cases of young people who have been victimized by sexual assault, hazing, and other forms of violence, parents have charged that campuses haven't done enough to protect their students; and public health claimsmakers have warned about the dangers of acute alcohol poisoning and other consequences of binge drinking. What once might have been viewed as tragic incidents have been redefined as policy failures.

Colleges and universities take these complaints seriously, in part because there have been cases where individual campuses were held legally liable for harm to students. New policies have evolved to enhance campus security and reduce risks. Tighter security systems for dormitories and programs to educate students about safe sexual practices and the risks of drug use and binge drinking are designed to make students safer, but also to demonstrate that the institutions have taken reasonable precautions to protect those students. New incidents—such as the 2007 shooting spree at Virginia Tech—inspire new criticisms (in that case, that the university did not take advantage of cell phones to warn students), which in turn lead to new preventative policies (such as improved systems for relaying warnings to the campus community). In this way, campuses seek to prevent further tragedies—and the blame that might come from having failed to take adequate precautions against known dangers.

Source: Sloan & Fisher, 2011.

credentials, and these experts may be seen as offering authoritative assessments. Claimsmakers' criticisms that the policy they promoted has somehow failed to deal effectively with the problem, then, stand a somewhat better chance of being heard than do critiques from other people.

In fact, such dissatisfaction from claimsmakers may be expected. As noted in Chapter 7, policymakers may have altered the claims-makers' original proposals; social policies often are products of compromise, as policymakers try to placate both claimsmakers who are calling for action and opponents who want to do nothing, or as little as possible, or perhaps something very different. To the degree that a policy was a compromise measure, everyone may anticipate that the initial claimsmakers will still be dissatisfied and want more, that they are likely to argue that the policy was insufficient and call for further reforms.

Activist and expert claimsmakers alike may draw upon both anecdotal responses and measures of social problems workers' activity to document their claims that policies are insufficient. Like subjects, they can use typifying examples to show that the policy doesn't do enough to help those affected by the troubling condition. Expanding the policy may require nothing more than increasing resources (bigger budget allocations and so on), but it may also involve domain expansion (see Chapter 2). Here the claimsmakers argue that the policy defines the troubling condition too narrowly, that a broader definition is needed so that a larger share of those affected can be helped.

Alternatively, like social problems workers, claimsmakers can point to statistical evidence (perhaps collected by social problems workers) to demonstrate that there is a growing problem requiring further action. After social policies are established to deal with previously neglected troubling conditions, social problems workers' statistics often display a marked jump. For example, the campaign to draw attention to child abuse led to laws requiring that doctors, teachers, and others report instances of suspected abuse; not surprisingly, the number of reported cases increased dramatically. But child abuse claimsmakers could then use these statistics to argue that the increased numbers of reports proved that child abuse was a growing problem, that current policy responses were insufficient, and that additional resources were needed to fight child abuse.

Policies may be critiqued not only by the claimsmakers whose efforts led to policymaking, but also by *rival activists and experts*. These are people who opposed the original claims and the resulting policy, whose counterclaims proved unsuccessful during the social problems process. They are, of course, predisposed to be critical; and they are particularly likely to argue either that the policy is excessive, or that it is misguided. In their view, the policy was a failed experiment: it didn't work, and it may even have made things worse. These rival claimsmakers call upon policymakers to undo the damage, and they warn that expanding the policy will only exacerbate matters.

These rival claimsmakers also can draw upon both anecdotal and statistical evidence. Their typifying examples point to subjects whose lives have been harmed by their contacts with social problems workers implementing the policy (for instance, a nice middle-class college student who suddenly faces felony charges for possessing a small amount of drugs, or a welfare recipient who is discouraged from finding work by a system of benefits that encourages dependency). Similarly, they can interpret the available statistical evidence as showing that the policy is having negative effects (that, say, the war on drugs has imprisoned large numbers of people, and a disproportionate share of these are African Americans; or that people are remaining welfare recipients for longer periods of time than under the preceding policy). Note that, just as initial claimsmaking campaigns can be mounted by either liberals or conservatives, these critiques by rival claimsmakers who opposed those campaigns are not restricted to one ideology: both liberal and conservative claimsmakers can frame parallel critiques of policies that each opposed.

Thus far, we have examined policy critiques by four different groups: (1) social problems workers, (2) subjects, (3) the initial claimsmakers whose activities led to the policies, and (4) opposition claimsmakers who stood opposed to the original claims. Each group tends to favor particular arguments, and to rely on particular sorts of evidence. Although some successful policies can lead to social problems work that attracts minimal criticism, other, more contentious issues inspire prolonged, visible debates. Topics such as abortion, gun control, drug law enforcement, environmental regulation, health care, and welfare policy are widely known to be issues about which people have disagreed in the past, disagree at the present, and in all probability will continue to disagree in the future. Such contentious policies attract many critics—sometimes from all four groups—but often their critiques tend to be discounted because each group is widely understood to have a vested interest in a by now predictable position in the debate, and therefore cannot be counted on to be an impartial judge of a policy's effectiveness. Is there no way to develop accurate, objective assessments of how social policies work?

THE SEARCH FOR IMPARTIAL EVALUATIONS

Doubts about whether interested parties can be trusted sometimes lead to efforts to solicit impartial evaluations of how well policies work. The most obvious of such efforts take the form of **evaluation research** (Rossi, Lipsey, & Freeman, 2004). Evaluation research usually involves some sort of social scientific assessment of a policy's effectiveness; the hallmarks of such research are efforts to create objective measures of a policy's costs, benefits, and outcomes. Often the evaluators are outsiders, chosen because they do not come from within the ranks of social problems workers, although such evaluations also can be done by insiders. The real issue is not who does the evaluation, but whether the methods used to produce the evaluation can lead to information that others will find convincing.

In theory, the most compelling evidence would come from careful experiments to assess the policy's effectiveness. At a minimum, two matched groups of subjects would be compared: social problems workers would apply the policy to the experimental, or treatment, group; and the control group would experience something else (usually whatever social problems workers did before the policy was implemented). In practice, experimental designs are often more elaborate: there may be several treatment and control groups that undergo slightly different conditions. Well-designed experiments can provide fairly convincing evidence regarding whether a policy works better than whatever preceded it.

There are, however, significant problems with experiments. One problem is that experimental research tends to be time-consuming, in part because designing the research, carrying it out, and then analyzing the results can take a long time. But experiments also take time because the evaluators may want to wait to follow up the subjects who experience the policy. It may take time for the policy's effects to be felt, or a policy's early effects on the subjects' lives may wear off over time; since it takes a while for either of those consequences to become apparent, researchers may prefer to make their final measurements years after the subjects' contacts with social problems workers end. In addition, experimental designs, because they can be elaborate and take years to complete, are often costly. As a practical matter, people engaged in policy debates are often too impatient to wait for experimental results that may not be available for years, as well as unwilling to pay for such expensive research.

Therefore, evaluation research usually winds up using less compelling, nonexperimental methods to study policy effectiveness. Often such studies consist of two sorts of comparisons. The first is across time: the evaluators compare a particular measure of the old and new policies' effectiveness (for instance, under our old policing policy the crime rate was X, whereas under our new policy it is Y). Second, evaluators may compare different places (other cities, states, or countries) to see whether our policy seems to be more effective than those used elsewhere.

The evidence produced through such comparisons is weaker than the findings of experiments because the differences between the old and new policies may actually have been caused by another factor (such as the economy booming or declining), or perhaps the other places used for comparison aren't really comparable (for instance, City A's agencies are known to be corrupt, City B has a very different ethnic composition, and so on). Such comparisons pose complicated problems for researchers: both the troubling conditions that the policies are designed to address and the policies themselves are likely to vary from time to time and place to place; in addition, policymakers, social problems workers, and others may insist that they already know whether and why a policy works, so the evaluators' findings may not be welcome (see Box 9.4).

There is another problem: to hold down costs, nonexperimental research often winds up measuring policy effectiveness using whatever data have already been collected. In practice, this usually means using the records kept by the social problems workers—the measures of organizational activity discussed earlier, such as the number of arrests or the average amount of time that clients continue to receive welfare benefits. This information may be suggestive, but it often doesn't answer the key questions: Do lots of arrests mean that crime is under—or out of—control? Do clients stop receiving welfare benefits because they have been helped out of poverty, or because they have become frustrated with the policy and have given up?

Since it is difficult to produce high-quality, inexpensive data quickly, evaluation research rarely provides the last word in assessing policies' effectiveness. Too many questions remain. Typically, such research depends on the records compiled by social problems workers, and those records have limitations. Imagine an effort to evaluate a new antidrug policy. Evaluation researchers might try to compare available measures of organizational activity, such as the number of drug arrests or the value of the drugs seized before and after the policy's introduction. But note that this approach raises various questions: Are those records accurate? (How, for example, is the value of the drugs seized calculated?) Were the records kept in the same way before and after the policy was introduced (or was

Box 9.4 Do Sex Offender Policies Work?

In recent decades, a variety of laws have been passed to deal with sex offenders: those convicted of these offenses must register with authorities; there are restrictions on where offenders can live; and those living near registered offenders must be notified. Proponents of these measures have used frightening typifying examples of children murdered by known violent offenders, and few people have been willing to speak out against these laws. But attempts to evaluate the laws raise doubts about how well they work.

Although the laws seem to assume that the danger of sexual victimization comes from strangers, it is generally agreed that most instances of child sexual abuse involve family members or others known to the child. The laws also assume that sex offenses are committed by repeat offenders, although research shows that sex offenders have far lower recidivism rates than people imprisoned for other offenses. Most important, laws assume that notifying neighbors will allow them to take precautionary measures to protect their children, yet studies suggest that those who have been warned don't become more protective. There is also evidence that the laws impede efforts to rehabilitate sex offenders; it is harder for them to find work or even places where they can legally live, making it more likely that they will be unemployed and homeless.

Although evaluation research calls the effectiveness of these laws into question, it is difficult to alter these policies, which do work as symbolic statements of concern.

Source: Leon, 2011.

there perhaps a more systematic effort to count every case once the policy went into effect)? And, after all, what do such measures mean? Do more drug arrests and more drugs seized mean that the policy is working (because, presumably, drug dealers and drugs are being taken out of circulation), or do they suggest that the policy is failing (because there seem to be more dealers to arrest and drugs to capture)?

In short, evaluation research tends to rely on imperfect, ambiguous data, and the correct interpretation of its results is often unclear. Depending on the assumptions that evaluators bring to their work and the choices that they make in deciding how to measure the policy outcomes, it is often possible for evaluators to come to very different conclusions. And although evaluation research is theoretically impartial, evaluators can be "hired guns," brought in to buttress a particular tale. A policy's advocates may commission research that allows them to point with pride at evidence of their policy's success, while the policy's opponents may present their own research suggesting the policy's shortcomings. Not surprisingly, then, evaluation research often fails to gain acceptance as the authoritative, impartial, last word on a policy's impact.

The knowledge that evaluators may design research that seems to affirm their prejudices sometimes leads to efforts to devise special high-status, impartial bodies to evaluate policies and issue recommendations. At the highest level, the president or Congress often appoint national **commissions**; and state or local authorities may appoint similar bodies (Zegart, 2004). The commission members tend to be visible figures known for their integrity and chosen to represent a range of interest groups (for instance, leaders from business, labor, law, the media, and religion; members from both political parties; males as well as females; individuals from different regions and ethnic groups; and so on). In other words, the commissioners are meant to represent a broad range of those concerned with the policy. Such "blue ribbon" commissions may be appointed with great fanfare with the expectation that the commission's findings will also be well publicized, accepted as authoritative, and used to guide future policy.

Of course, selecting commissioners who already hold important positions and lead busy lives means that they will have difficulty devoting much time to the commission's work. The actual work tends to fall upon the less well-known staff members, who assemble evidence about the policy's workings and guide the commissioners in making their recommendations. Moreover, a commission's recommendations may prove unpopular. Commissions tend to be appointed precisely because an issue is seen as divisive, so it is almost inevitable that whatever is recommended will prove controversial. Although commission recommendations sometimes receive considerable media coverage, they often fail to lead to the significant policy changes that the commission hoped to achieve (see Box 9.5).

One other category of actors who play an important role in evaluating policy outcomes deserves attention: the *appellate courts* (see also Chapter 7). Policymaking often involves creating new laws, and social problems work often leads to legal actions. In turn, the people who find themselves targeted by new social policies can appeal their cases to higher courts. These appellate courts may rule on the constitutionality of the policies, affirming some, striking down others, and clarifying still others. In turn, *legal scholars* may try to influence courts' decisions by writing law review articles that criticize the legal basis for policies (Malloy, 2010). In the United States, a bill passed by legislators and signed into law by a president (in the case of federal legislation) or a governor (in the case of state legislation) may be modified—even ruled illegal—by appellate courts. Such court rulings may reject the policy itself, or the ways in which social problems workers implement that policy. This power makes courts important players in shaping policy outcomes.

Legislators are supposed to represent the popular will (recall Chapter 7's discussion of the various pressures they face), while courts are intended to provide a check on legislative enthusiasm. This means that even the most successful claimsmaking campaigns— those that elicit media coverage, mobilize public concern, and see their claims translated into new policies—may be constrained or rejected by the courts. For example, legislators often promote laws against burning the American flag, laws that have considerable vote-getting appeal (Welch, 2000). However, the courts have tended to recognize flag burning as protest, a form of political speech, protected under the First Amendment. Similarly, courts often constrain overly broad interpretations of new policies, restricting the grounds

Box 9.5 Commissions Explain Disasters

Dramatic disasters, such as the accidents that destroyed the space shuttles *Challenger* and *Columbia*, or the terrorist attacks of September 11, 2001, often lead to the appointment of special commissions to investigate the disaster's causes and make recommendations for policy changes that can prevent similar events from occurring in the future. These commissions' reports attract a good deal of attention, and are widely seen as authoritative verdicts regarding what went wrong and how policies should be changed.

Commissions, then, construct explanations. But this involves making choices, which, in turn, constrain commission findings. It turns out to be relatively easy for commissions to focus on individual decisions that, in retrospect, can be seen as mistakes (for example, overriding the advice of engineers who warned that cold weather might endanger the *Challenger*'s launch). It proves to be somewhat more difficult to criticize the organizations involved (thus, the 9/11 Commission noted that many agencies had failed to focus sufficient attention on the terrorist threat, but the commission did not blame them for what happened). Commissions tend to avoid institutional explanations (for instance, the commissions investigating the space shuttle accidents downplayed or ignored pressures from Congress and the White House for NASA [the National Aeronautics and Space Administration] to launch shuttles more regularly, although these pressures arguably encouraged the agency to treat risks as tolerable; while the 9/11 Commission did not ask how American foreign policies might have fostered the rise of terrorists). Having been appointed by high government officials, commissions tend to treat those officials carefully.

Source: Vaughan, 2006.

for defining, say, hate crimes (Jenness & Grattet, 2001) or sexual harassment (Saguy, 2003). The courts' rulings, in turn, may be denounced, constructed as new troubling conditions by assorted claimsmakers, media workers, policymakers, or social problems workers.

In sum, courts, like evaluation researchers and commissions, are often seen as failing to resolve debates over policy outcomes. However much we might like to imagine that an impartial interpretation will resolve people's differences in policy debates, such solutions prove elusive. People continue to disagree about which policies can best address troubling conditions.

IDEOLOGICAL PREDISPOSITIONS

As we have seen in this chapter, there are many possible bases for criticizing how social policies are being implemented, as well as many types of people who might be moved to offer such critiques. From this we might conclude that all sorts of debates over policies are theoretically possible, but in fact, many policy discussions take fairly predictable forms.

Key to many policy debates is ideology. Within contemporary America, many people—including activists, experts, media workers, members of the general public, policymakers, and social problems workers—can locate themselves on a political spectrum that is understood to run from left to right—that is, from those who have relatively liberal views to those who hold relatively conservative views. Precisely how individuals construct this ideological spectrum varies: just as conservatives may lump together people who variously think of themselves as liberals, progressives, or radicals, and who recognize these as important distinctions, liberals may not appreciate the range of positions among those on the right.

In general, however, when discussing social problems, those on the left tend to emphasize the importance of equality and worry that society discriminates too much on the basis of race, class, and gender; they favor social policies that promote equality and discourage discrimination. And in general, those on the right emphasize the importance of liberty and social order; they worry that excessive social policies may constrain liberty and, in the process, damage overall societal well-being. Of course, these are questions of emphasis: few Americans would denounce either equality or liberty, yet they may disagree about their relative importance, or the best ways to achieve these values in particular situations.

This means that debates over social policies often break down into those favoring a more liberal position opposed to those favoring a more conservative stance. Each ideological side has its own activists in social movement organizations, think tanks filled with experts, media commentators, and policymaking politicians; the same people tend to find themselves allied over a range of policy debates. In fact, when individuals thought to be associated with a particular side break ranks on an issue and agree with those they usually oppose, the split is considered remarkable, something worth mentioning. Thus, when discussions about a particular policy outcome begin, it is often possible to predict who will line up on which side of the issue.

Not all ideologies fit neatly on the familiar liberal-conservative continuum. Think of libertarianism (usually viewed as a form of conservatism, but one that leads to what are typically thought of as liberal positions on issues related to drug use or sexual behavior), various religious doctrines (which can vary a great deal, depending on the theological interpretations being advanced), or feminism (which is centrally concerned with improving women's place in society). In addition, there are professional ideologies; professions have distinctive views of troubling conditions and how these conditions ought to be addressed. For example, recall Chapter 4's discussion of medicalization: medical authorities tend to favor constructing troubling conditions as medical problems that ought to be solved through medical solutions.

Ideologies are not unrelated to *interests*. Ideologies allow individuals to appeal to principles, such as equality, liberty, or women's rights, to argue that these values *should* guide how society responds to troubling conditions (for example, a liberal might criticize a particular social policy because it fails to alleviate the inequalities at the root of the troubling condition, and a conservative policy critique might focus on how the policy unreasonably constrains people's liberty). In other words, ideologies allow their adherents to construct principled arguments, to claim that this is the right thing to do because it is consistent with a particular value. At the same time, people frequently adopt ideologies that support their interests (for example, a large share of feminists are women whose interests the ideology advances, just as medical authorities often stand to benefit from medicalizing troubling conditions). The link between ideology and interest creates rhetorical opportunities for those who oppose a particular ideology: they can charge that proponents of a particular claim may be motivated less by a principled sense of what is right than by their self-interest, by the advantages they stand to gain if their claims succeed.

The tendency for ideological critiques to invoke values creates a range of questions that might be addressed in policy debates. On the one hand, critics can focus on practical questions: Is the policy effective? Does it do what we want it to do? Does it work better or cost less than alternative policies? On the other hand, critics can emphasize principles: Is this policy consistent with important values? Is it morally sound? Is it the sort of thing we ought to be doing? Policy debates often conflate these two approaches, so that opponents denounce one another's practical claims for being unprincipled, while rejecting the opposition's principled claims as impractical. Of course, an inability to agree on the questions that ought to be asked virtually guarantees that people will be unable to agree on the answers (see Box 9.6).

Ideologies, then, can be seen as predisposing how people may respond to policy outcomes. When people are allied with particular ideological stances—whether of a political, professional, or other nature—it is often possible to predict how these individuals will respond to a particular social policy. Those whose ideology led them to favor the policy in the first place are likely to claim that any shortcomings are due to the policy's being insufficient,

Box 9.6 PARTICIPATION AS AN OUTCOME OF
SOCIAL PROGRAMS

Debates over the effects of social policies that target the poor are common. One possible effect of such policies is to foster civic engagement among those receiving assistance. People with low incomes are less likely to vote, less involved in community organizations, and less able to speak for themselves. Some advocates argue that increased civic involvement is a desirable outcome for these social programs. But what sorts of programs encourage their beneficiaries to become more active in society?

Comparisons of Head Start (preschool programs designed to promote social and cognitive development) and Temporary Assistance to Needy Families ([TANF] the current name for federal "welfare," that is, cash assistance to the poor) suggest some answers. Head Start actively encourages parental participation in its programs. In contrast, TANF is more paternalistic, in that the program's workers decide who qualifies for which benefits. Research shows that those who become involved with Head Start are more likely to vote, more likely to join social movements, and more likely to participate in local social organizations (such as churches), than those who receive TANF. TANF rules vary from state to state, and the same pattern emerges among different states' programs: the less paternalist the program, the more it fosters civic participation. This leads some critics to argue that promoting civic participation is an important policy outcome, and that policies should be designed to be less paternalistic, and encourage greater involvement by their subjects.

Source: Bruch, Ferree, & Soss, 2010.

and to argue for expanding or extending the policy to make up this shortfall. In contrast, those who stood ideologically opposed to the initial policy are more likely to claim that the policy is excessive or misguided, that it needs to be cut back or redirected. Although ideologies do not control how everyone approaches policy outcomes, they often shape the responses of at least some participants in the discussions.

Once again we see the subjective nature of the social problems process. Just as claimsmakers must construct troubling conditions so that people become concerned enough to do something, and just as policymakers and social problems workers must construct practical responses to that concern, so, too, must critics devise interpretations of the workings of policies. They may decide that a policy is a great success (remember granting women the vote; no one now advocates disenfranchising women), or they may decide that it works pretty well and just needs a bit of fine-tuning (maybe we ought to install another traffic light at that dangerous intersection). Or, of course, some people may argue that the policy isn't working all that well and that we ought to do significantly more, or maybe a lot less, or perhaps something completely different. At the stage of policy outcomes, the social problems process comes to an end—unless it inspires an entirely new round of claimsmaking.

MAKING CONNECTIONS

- *Policy outcomes are reactions to policies after they have been implemented by social problems workers. However, as this chapter and the following chapter explain, the social problems process is cyclical, so policy outcomes become the basis for new claims.*

- *Social problems workers can become compelling critics of policies. As Chapter 8 explained, they understand how social problems work is actually practiced and see policy flaws firsthand.*

- *Both activists and experts frequently use typifying examples (discussed in Chapter 2) to make new claims that criticize policies.*

CASE STUDY
TECHNOLOGICAL CHANGE AND POLICY OUTCOMES

It is easy to think of social change in terms of technological developments, particularly new methods of transportation (such as the railroad and the automobile), communication (such as the telegraph and television), and production (such as developed during the Industrial Revolution). Our abilities to travel farther, communicate faster, and produce more, new material goods reverberate throughout society; they change social arrangements and lead to the construction of new social problems. This process continues with each new technological development; consider how the Internet, smart phones, and other recent innovations have forced people to reassess a variety of social policies.

Patents and copyright are protected by the U.S. Constitution, which gives Congress the power "to promote the progress of science and useful arts, by securing for limited times to authors and inventors the exclusive right to their respective writings and discoveries." Many historians agree that these protections established a culture of innovation in nineteenth-century America that enabled a small, rural society to become an industrial powerhouse. But the policies that emerged reflected particular technological arrangements; thus, copyright laws were designed to protect authors and publishers from printers who might otherwise publish their own bootleg editions of books without paying royalties to the authors. These policies worked reasonably well as long as reproducing copyrighted works was itself an expensive, highly skilled process.

However, thanks to the Internet, the means of reproduction have been widely disseminated. An individual with a personal computer, the appropriate software, and a little know-how now has the ability to make personal copies of not just books, but also photographs, music, movies, and pretty much anything else that can be digitally encoded. Downloading unauthorized files has become a sort of folk crime—a widespread form of individual rule-breaking, much like breaking the speed limit, or drinking during Prohibition. At the other extreme, the spread of industrial capacity around the world has led to the rise of global counterfeiting, ranging from reproductions of all sorts of consumer goods to the unauthorized production of medical drugs (Lin, 2011).

Policies to protect intellectual property—the rights of its creators to copyright or patent the fruits of their ideas—are therefore under attack. Critics demand that existing regulations be enforced, but it is difficult to confront every factory that is producing fake designer sunglasses, let alone every individual who illegally downloads a song. Moreover, there is growing resistance: some countries may choose to turn a blind eye to counterfeiting firms that generate economic growth (to say nothing of bribes for cooperative officials). Some governments in less developed countries have claimed the right to allow firms to produce cheap, generic versions of anti-HIV/AIDS drugs when Western pharmaceutical firms that hold the patents insist on charging high prices. In some cases, this resistance leads to broader critiques of policies to protect intellectual property. Critics argue that patents that protect high prices, which in turn effectively make it impossible for patients in less developed countries to receive lifesaving drugs, are inhumane. Similarly, the claim by Internet enthusiasts that "information wants to be free" challenges the very notion of copyright. A generation ago, policies to protect intellectual property may have seemed secure, but technological changes have unsettled that stability.

Take a second example: the spread of cell phones and smart phones has changed many aspects of social life, and in the process has inspired claimsmaking. Initial criticisms focused on etiquette—overheard phone conversations being viewed as an intrusion. Soon, however, people began worrying about the possibility that drivers using cell phones posed a danger, among other examples. In some cases, these fears led to policy changes, such as some states passing laws against some sorts of cell phone usage while driving. And as phones got smarter, new problems were constructed.

In particular, sexting—sending sexually explicit messages, especially pictures—drew particular attention (Chalfen, 2009). There were reports of junior high and high school students using their phones to take sexually provocative pictures of themselves, and then sending the images to others (for instance, a girl taking a partially nude picture of herself, and then sending it to her boyfriend). In some cases, when these reports reached law enforcement officials, the young people discovered that they were in considerable legal trouble: the pictures were technically child pornography (an offense that the law treats as a serious felony); further, in many states anyone convicted on a child pornography charge must register as a sex offender, a label that can follow the individual throughout life. Critics were soon arguing about what would be an appropriate policy regarding sexting: Did protecting children from predators require that child pornography laws be left unchanged? Should sexting—at least consensual sexting within a romantic relationship—be defined as a personal, noncriminal matter, or something that ought to be dealt with through educational programs warning young people that it was impossible to ensure that a digital image would not become public? Or should policymakers split the difference by defining sexting as a minor legal offense, perhaps some sort of misdemeanor?

Policy outcomes emerge when people find fault with how a policy is being applied. In some cases, opposition is predictable: people opposed to the initial policymaking are likely to criticize the policy as soon as it is in operation. In other cases, social changes alter how people think about policy. Technological innovations affect—often in unexpected ways—social arrangements. In some cases, a policy previously thought to be working pretty well (such as copyright law) suddenly is defined as needing significant modification. In other cases, entirely new uses for technology (such as sexting) reveal unanticipated policy problems.

Questions

1. What sorts of warrants do competing claimsmakers offer when debating intellectual property issues?

2. Why have cell phones inspired so many policy debates?

3. What is another example of a technological change affecting how people think about policy outcomes?

10

■

Claims across Space and Time

■

The previous chapters have traced a six-stage social problems process from (1) the initial claimsmaking, through (2) media coverage, (3) public reaction, and (4) policymaking, and on to (5) the social problems work that implements the policy, followed by (6) policy outcomes. This sequence of stages should be seen as the natural history that a typical social problem might follow. To be sure, not every social problem fits the pattern exactly. Most important, many claims fail: they don't attract media attention, or they don't lead to public concern, or they don't lead to policy changes, or the policies are never implemented. The model of a six-stage sequence that has guided this book depicts a successful campaign to draw attention to a particular troubling condition and to get the larger society to try to do something about it. Many claims may follow different trajectories, but the model remains a useful framework for understanding the course taken by those claims that have the greatest impact.

There are, however, additional complexities that require some attention. Thus far, we have been thinking about social problems one at a time: here is how the U.S. Bureau of Narcotics constructed marijuana as a social problem in the 1930s, here is how today's authorities are constructing the crystal meth problem, and so on.

Such **case studies** are useful, but it seems obvious that the marijuana and crystal meth cases might have some important features in common, even though they occurred decades apart. After all, both cases involve claims that a particular drug is harmful and ought to be prohibited. This similarity raises important questions: Are such drug problems constructed completely independently; that is, does each set of claimsmakers start from scratch in assembling its claims, and do policymakers adopt a fresh approach each time they encounter claims about a new drug problem? Or are there underlying similarities in the way drug problems and drug policies are constructed, and if so, what are they, and why do they occur? Does the history of previous claims about drugs affect current claimsmaking? Do claims about similar troubling conditions always take the same form, or are they affected by the social circumstances in which they emerge?

This chapter explores some of these issues; in particular, it considers how claims vary from place to place, and from time to time. It begins with comparative research, in which analysts compare what happens when claimsmakers raise claims about the same troubling condition in different places—in different cities, or in different countries. Then it examines diffusion, the way claims spread from one place to another. The third section of the chapter asks how claims evolve over time; it explores apparently cyclical claims—issues that attract considerable attention for a time, then fade from notice, only to be revived in a new wave of claimsmaking. The chapter concludes with a discussion of progress: claimsmakers tend to emphasize that things are getting worse, but is envisioning societal decay the best framework for thinking about social problems?

COMPARISON

Usually sociologists who study the construction of social problems conduct case studies. That is, they examine one instance, one case of the social problems process—how and why a particular problem was constructed in a given place at a given time. In fact, many studies focus on specific aspects of a particular case, so different analyses of the same case might consider, for example, just how the claims' rhetoric was assembled to make a persuasive argument, who made those claims, or how the media covered the topic.

The main advantage of the case study is that it permits a careful, detailed analysis of how one particular instance of the social problems process developed. Most of the points raised in the earlier chapters of this book are the product of sociologists' case studies, and a large share of the sources cited in this volume's references present such case studies. But case studies have a major disadvantage: there is no way of knowing whether the case being studied is fairly typical or quite unusual. Throughout this book we have been discussing things that can happen during the construction of social problems. When we first diagrammed the social problems process in Figure 1.1, the picture seemed simple and straightforward. But later chapters featured more detailed, more complicated diagrams of the various stages in the social problems process. These complications reveal that not all social problems follow exactly the same trajectory; there are important differences in how social problems can develop, so the particular case being studied may not always be all that typical.

The simplest way to study such differences is to compare two cases that we might expect to be fairly similar. For example, Cynthia Bogard (2003) examined how the problem of homelessness was constructed in two major American cities—New York City and Washington, D.C.—during the early 1980s. She found important differences. In Washington, activists—a self-styled group of "Christian anarchists"—promoted homelessness as a moral issue; they devised clever protests designed to attract media attention (in a city filled with media workers), and they sought to involve nationally prominent politicians in the issue. While acknowledging that many homeless individuals were troubled by mental illness or substance abuse, the Washington activists constructed the homeless as rational figures, who would stop living on the streets if only they had access to safe, nonintrusive shelters. In contrast, in New York City the issue of homelessness centered around a struggle between city and state officials over who ought to be held responsible for the condition—and pay the costs of fixing it. The state blamed the city for encouraging gentrification that had eliminated low-cost housing units and thereby had made their former residents homeless; the city, on the other hand, insisted that many of the homeless were seriously mentally ill individuals who now found themselves on the streets after the state had closed many of its mental hospitals. In New York, the homeless were typified as incapable of caring for themselves, and as a threat to public order. In short, the two cities featured different claimsmakers, with different interests, who constructed the homelessness problem in different ways.

Bogard's study shows that, even in dealing with the same problem during the same years, the social problems process can develop along different paths—with different claims made by different claimsmakers leading to different policies. There are all sorts of possible bases for making such comparisons:

- *Geography.* Bogard compared the social problems process in two cities, but it is possible to compare other geographic entities. Most obviously, analysts can compare how the same troubling condition is addressed in two or more countries (J. Best, 2001b).

- *Time.* Many social conditions have been around for a long time, so it is possible to compare two or more efforts to construct the same social problem in the same place during different times. For example, there have been a series of anticult campaigns in American history (Jenkins, 2000).

- *Similar conditions.* Some troubling conditions are understood to belong to the same category of social problems, so the basis for comparison seems obvious. For example, there are parallels in the ways that different drugs have been constructed as social problems (Reinarman, 1994).

● *Similar constructions.* Sometimes analysts compare problems that seem to be constructed with similar claimsmaking rhetoric. For instance, freeway shootings, stalking, and other crimes characterized as "random violence" can be compared, as can how claimsmakers construct different problems that involve "victimization" (J. Best, 1999).

● *Other bases for comparison.* Analysts might compare different campaigns by the same claimsmakers (for instance, examining how feminists—or medical authorities—construct various social problems), how different media construct the same problem, and so on. The bases for comparison are limited only by the analysts' imagination.

Figure 10.1 illustrates some of these forms of comparison among social problems processes. The top of the figure displays one six-stage social problems process (for a particular problem—call it Problem X). The same process is shown in reduced size at the center of the figure, where it is surrounded by other social problems processes that suggest various bases for comparison between the construction of Problem X and the construction of other social problems. Note that it is not necessary to compare the entire sequences of stages in two social problems processes; a sociologist might focus on comparing particular, even very narrowly defined topics (such as the use of statistics in two claimsmaking campaigns).

Comparison is a powerful method of analysis because it can help us discover both underlying similarities and unexpected differences. People involved in the social problems process sometimes assume that things have to be the way they are; they take it for granted that the problem pretty much has to be constructed in the terms with which they're familiar. One of the most important lessons from comparing social problems processes is that whatever we understand about social problems is a product of people's choices, that people—claimsmakers, media workers, policymakers, social problems workers, and so on—have chosen to highlight some aspects

Figure 10.1 BASES FOR COMPARISON AMONG SOCIAL PROBLEMS PROCESSES

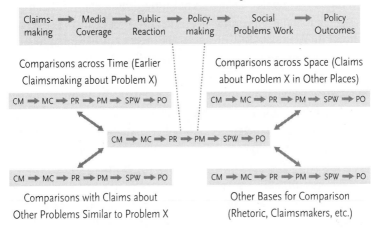

Social Problems Process Concerning Problem X

Claims- ➡ Media ➡ Public ➡ Policy- ➡ Social ➡ Policy
making   Coverage   Reaction   making   Problems Work   Outcomes

Comparisons across Time (Earlier   Comparisons across Space (Claims
Claimsmaking about Problem X)   about Problem X in Other Places)

CM ➡ MC ➡ PR ➡ PM ➡ SPW ➡ PO   CM ➡ MC ➡ PR ➡ PM ➡ SPW ➡ PO

CM ➡ MC ➡ PR ➡ PM ➡ SPW ➡ PO

CM ➡ MC ➡ PR ➡ PM ➡ SPW ➡ PO   CM ➡ MC ➡ PR ➡ PM ➡ SPW ➡ PO

Comparisons with Claims about   Other Bases for Comparison
Other Problems Similar to Problem X   (Rhetoric, Claimsmakers, etc.)

of a troubling condition while downplaying others. It can be hard to notice what those people have ignored, but comparisons often can help us recognize that choices were made, and to ask how and why those proved to be the favored choices.

Consider the issue of sexual harassment. Americans take it for granted that sexual harassment is a type of gender discrimination, and that it should be defined broadly to encompass not only demands for sexual favors but also inappropriate joking and other behaviors that create a "hostile environment" (Saguy, 2003). In France, however, sexual harassment has been defined not only more narrowly (encompassing only demands for sex), but also very differently (as sexual violence involving the abuse of hierarchical authority). These different definitions evolved through different processes: in the United States, court rulings gradually established the domain of sexual harassment; in France, courts cannot establish the law, so an act of Parliament was required—which was important because policymakers had to find a legislative consensus, and there was not enough support for a broader definition of what constituted sexual harassment. Press coverage also differed in the two countries. The American press devoted a large share of its coverage to scandals—claims implicating prominent politicians in sexual harassment. In contrast, considerable French media coverage focused on the "excesses" of *Americans'* treatment of sexual harassment; commentators argued that France should avoid copying the Americans' example. In other words, there were numerous differences in how sexual harassment was constructed in the two nations.

Comparative studies often reveal such differences in how social problems are constructed, even when we might imagine that the issue would have to be constructed in the same way. If cell phones pose a threat of exposure to radioactivity, as some claimsmakers suggest, presumably the physical processes that produce those risks ought to be the same everywhere, exposing cell phone users throughout the world to the same dangers. Yet different countries construct health risks from cell phones in very different ways (Burgess, 2004). Comparative analyses, then, can expose the social processes that underpin the construction of even physical threats. Risks of radioactivity—usually thought of as understandable in terms of physics and biology—are socially constructed, as are all other social problems. Comparative research can help make such social processes visible.

DIFFUSION

Comparative studies reveal that the social problems process can lead to different outcomes in different places: two countries may construct a given problem in much the same way; or they may construct that problem in rather—sometimes dramatically—different terms; or one country may define the troubling condition as a big deal, while the other may dismiss it as unworthy of concern (see Box 10.1). However, it is especially interesting when a prob-

BOX 10.1 RELIGION, DEMOCRACY, AND ISRAELI SOCIAL ISSUES

Israel's government resembles other Western democracies, but cultural differences make it possible to construct different social problems in different places. In Israel, the ultraorthodox *Haredi* community campaigns to steer the nation away from secularism toward a more theocratic state, one where citizens' behavior follows strict religious guidelines. The *Haredi* are a relatively small minority—probably less than 10 percent of Israel's population—but they are vocal claimsmakers. Their claims, rooted in religious doctrine and interpretation, lead them to attack—even violently—conditions that they define as social problems, even when those conditions are not seen as troubling by the country's secular majority. These disputes can impinge on everyday life; for instance, women wearing what *Haredi* view as immodest clothing may be criticized or harassed.

Religion and democracy can be understood as ideologies, each with its own values and guidelines for behavior. They may generally coexist, but there are always likely to be tensions (consider debates in the United States over school prayer or teaching evolution). In Israel's case, there is a substantial, built-in tension: the country was established as a democratic, Jewish state, intended to respect both ideologies. Judaism has many interpretations, but the *Haredi* conviction that their interpretation is correct, and their willingness to act on their convictions, coupled with a reluctance of other groups to engage in theological disputes, allows a small group to have a disproportionate influence on discussions of social issues.

Source: Ben-Yehuda, 2010.

lem attracts attention in different places at about the same time. Although it is possible that the social problems processes in different countries are completely independent, unrelated to one another, another possibility is that claims have spread from one country to another, and we can study this process (J. Best, 2001b).

Diffusion is the term used by social scientists to describe the spread of innovations. New things—new ideas, new inventions, and so on—emerge in particular places, but then they spread from one group to another. If one group figures out a better way to, say, make arrowheads, that group's neighbors may copy or adopt the method for their own benefit. The process of diffusion involves sources, or **transmitters**, passing the innovation along to **adopters**. Successful innovations can spread across many societies and over thousands of miles.

Diffusion can occur in the case of social problems claims. A claim may originate in a particular town, region, or country but then spread to other places. Not all claims experience diffusion, and of those that do spread, some travel farther and more widely than others. What accounts for these differences?

All social problems claims argue that a particular condition exists and that it is troubling. Successful diffusion of a claim requires that adopters accept that these basic ideas apply to the adopters' setting—their community or nation. Certainly diffusion requires accepting the notion that the condition exists; a society whose members doubt the existence of a condition is unlikely to be receptive to claims about that problem. For instance, being worried about witches requires that people believe in witches; regardless of how worried about witches a society of believers may become, they will find it hard to spread their concern to a society of nonbelievers. Similarly, the condition must be seen as troubling: a society with a traditional aristocracy might view a decline in deference as quite troubling, but their claims probably would have little appeal for members of democratic societies, who might agree that the condition exists but view this as a cause for celebration rather than concern.

For a claim to spread from one society to another, then, potential adopters of the claim must come from cultures and social structures that allow them to recognize both that their society has the condition about which claims are being made, and that that condition is troubling. This means that claims are less likely to spread to societies very different from those in which the claims originated. In particular, adopters need to view their society as similar to the society where the claims originated (Strang & Meyer, 1993). When similarities are harder to recognize, diffusion becomes less likely.

For example, it is easier for social problems claims to spread among countries with a common language and interwoven histories. In recent decades, many successful claimsmaking campaigns have originated in the United States and then spread to England, Australia, and Canada (for instance, concerns about satanic ritual abuse traveled from the United States to all three other English-speaking countries). In addition, claims that originated in those countries have traveled to the United States (concern about both bullying and road rage, for example, spread from Britain to the United States) (J. Best, 2001b). On the other hand, American constructions of social problems often meet resistance in France; French media tend to criticize American policies and present alternative constructions for social issues such as sexual harassment, immigration, or obesity (Benson & Saguy, 2005; Saguy, Gruys, & Gong, 2010).

Diffusion must occur through channels; that is, there need to be links, connections between potential transmitters and prospective adopters. Theorists of diffusion make an analytic distinction between **relational channels** involving interpersonal contact between transmitters and adopters, and **nonrelational channels**, such as mass media, that do not involve personal ties (McAdam & Rucht, 1993). In practice, the diffusion of claims usually combines both relational and nonrelational channels. Through informal ties (such as acquaintanceship) and more formal ties (such as memberships in the same professional organizations), people in different countries get to know one another well enough to establish relational channels: this person got to know foreigners while attending school abroad; these folks met at international conferences for police officers, or social workers, or whatever.

At the same time, information about social problems flows through nonrelational channels—through the press and entertainment media, through books and news broadcasts and the Internet. Relational and nonrelational channels are mutually reinforcing. Once again, it should be clear that a common language makes it easier for diffusion to occur through both sorts of channels. Translating claims into another tongue takes time; claims can travel faster when transmitters and adopters share a language.

All diffusion ultimately depends on the actors in the process—the transmitters and, especially, the adopters. Transmitters may make deliberate efforts to disseminate social problems claims to other countries. Drawing attention to troubling conditions is, of course, central to social problems claimsmaking, and some claimsmakers explicitly seek to spread their message to other nations. This is particularly true when claims depict large-scale, even global problems, such as population growth, ecological degradation, or economic globalization. Such claimsmakers become missionaries, seeking to spread their message abroad, through both relational and nonrelational channels. International social movements, for example, offer a way of spreading claims about troubling conditions to countries that might be expected to resist those claims.

In other cases, transmitters are more passive; their concern may be limited to their own country, even to a particular locality; they make no effort to promote the diffusion of their claims. Still, their claims may reach other countries, particularly via such nonrelational channels as media coverage, professional publications, and the like. Nonetheless, the key actors in diffusion are adopters. Prospective adopters must define conditions in their society as being sufficiently like those depicted in the transmitters' claims before they will join in spreading those claims.

Of course, societies have differences as well as similarities. There are likely to be both cultural differences (people in the transmitting society and those in the prospective adopting society are likely to construct the world in at least somewhat different terms), as well as differences in social arrangements (such as different legal or educational systems). Such differences are potential obstacles to diffusion; they make it easier for prospective adopters to conclude that a particular claim is not really applicable to their society. For example, tobacco smoking is much more common among males in Japan than in the United States or western Europe (Ayukawa, 2001). Whereas other countries' governments have launched vigorous public health campaigns to reduce smoking, Japan has been slower to take such actions. Why? In Japan, the government controls tobacco distribution and derives considerable revenue from smokers. Also it is hard to mobilize social movements in Japan to campaign against government interests. What is—and what is not—considered a social problem depends on a society's culture and social structure (see Box 10.2).

Therefore, diffusion is easier when claims are phrased in relatively abstract or theoretical language. **Theorization** is the presentation of claims that emphasize general, abstract principles and arguments: for instance, claimsmakers might describe sexism generally in terms of male, or patriarchal, domination rather than in terms of specific discriminatory practices; the former construction offers a general principle that might be detected at work in many different social settings, whereas the latter may seem applicable only in countries where those particular practices are common—and seen as troubling (Strang & Meyer, 1993). Theorization abstracts and simplifies. In the case of social problems claims, theorization smooths out the argument. It reduces specifics of limited, local relevance and rephrases the claim in broader, more general terms that make it more widely acceptable. The theoretical becomes significant; the practical, less important. Thus, a theorized claim is more easily spread to new societies, where it can be reformulated to take local culture and social structure into account.

As a result, claims about the same social problem often take somewhat different forms, depending on the social arrangements in different societies. In some cases, differences in social arrangements

> ## Box 10.2 Sexual Harassment Attracts Attention in Japan
>
> Through the process of diffusion, claims about sexual harassment—initially constructed in the United States—spread to other nations. In the process, the nature of the problem was often redefined. France, for instance, defined it as a abuse of power, whereas Americans had come to favor a broader definition that viewed sexual harassment as a form of gender discrimination. Even when claims spread across national boundaries, they must be transformed to fit the local culture.
>
> Claims about sexual harassment reached Japan relatively late; Japan passed its first law in 1997, after at least thirty-six other countries had taken action. Japan's definition resembled that used in the United States, just as the term *sekuhara* was derived from the English phrase. Still, the fact that Americans had anti–sexual harassment policies more than twenty years before the Japanese had an effect on who became aware of the issue. In Japan, concern with sexual harassment as an issue has been greater among younger women. This suggests that awareness of social problems spreads, not only geographically, but also within populations. Women who were entering, or getting ready to enter, the workforce when Japan began establishing policies against sexual harassment became more likely to be aware of and concerned about the issue, and more willing to lodge complaints if they were mistreated. In the United States, where the policies are well established and familiar, concern is spread more evenly across age groups. Thus whether an issue attracts attention, how it is characterized, and who considers it important can vary across national boundaries.
>
> Sources: Uggen & Shinohara, 2009.

may make it hard for claims to travel successfully. In recent years, for example, British claimsmakers have focused on various types of bullying—not just bullying in schools, but also bullying in other settings, including the workplace (Furedi, 2001). The British campaign against workplace bullying received considerable support from that country's powerful trade unions. In contrast, efforts to construct workplace bullying as a problem in the United States (where unions are less influential) have been markedly less successful. The abstract—and already familiar—problem of bullying (particularly among children) spread easily, but the more specific construction of workplace bullying did not. Similarly, the abortion issue evolved differently in the United States and Britain (Lee, 2003). British law has long regarded abortion as a medical matter, subject to physicians' authority, but Americans have come to view it as a question of rights.

Contemporary commentators argue that globalization has become a central concept for understanding the world. Countries are increasingly linked through trade, rapid transportation, and essentially instantaneous communications. Money and jobs—but also ideas—flow more freely across international borders. This means that the future is likely to feature even more diffusion of social problems claims. In part, this is because some claimsmakers seek to construct global issues such as global warming or terrorism. In part, it is because some troubling conditions, such as epidemic disease, may start in one corner of the world, yet spread great distances. In addition to these considerations, however, improved communications (such as through the World Wide Web) give people around the world access to claims made in distant places, and at least some of those claims will be theorized in terms that make it easier for them to spread.

CYCLES IN CLAIMSMAKING

Early in the social problems process, it is very common for claims-making rhetoric to describe a troubling condition as new, or at least as deserving new concern because the condition is growing much worse. After the issue begins to attract more attention and people want to know more about it, there may be an effort to trace the troubling condition's history. For instance, claims about child abuse might include brief historical accounts stating that although adults have abused children for centuries, we now know better; or a history of poverty might argue that previous efforts to eliminate poverty have been misguided, and that a totally new approach is needed. Even the most unlikely topics, such as Columbus and noise, can have elaborate histories of claimsmaking (Kubal, 2008; H. Schwartz, 2011). Still, claimsmakers tend to focus most intensely on the troubling condition's current manifestations, rather than on its distant past. Most claims concentrate on the present situation and pay relatively little attention to the past; to the degree they do remember an issue's history, they may simplify it (see Box 10.3).

This narrow focus is unfortunate, because careful study of the history of a social issue can often place today's claims within an illuminating context. In particular, many troubling conditions are the focus of *cycles* of concern. That is, a troubling condition may become the focus of intense claimsmaking, then slip out of the spotlight for a while before returning as the focus of renewed attention.

A cycle of concern begins when a troubling condition that has been receiving little attention becomes the subject of claimsmaking (Downs, 1972). As a result, concern increases until it reaches a peak, then interest falls off once more, until the topic is again attracting little notice. This cycle is another way of thinking about the social problems process: attention increases as claimsmakers, media, the public, policymakers, and social problems workers become involved. But why does interest decline? Why doesn't it remain high? Why are there cycles of concern?

Part of the answer is that the social problems process values novelty. Claims that seem new or fresh compete more easily in the social problems marketplace to attract attention from the media, the public, and policymakers. This is why claimsmakers who come to own particular issues find it necessary to constantly update and repackage their claims (as discussed in Chapter 3). But even when claimsmakers work to keep an issue visible, they find themselves at an increasing disadvantage because other, competing claims that

---

Box 10.3 Social Movements' Selective Memories

Collective memories—what groups choose to recall—inevitably are selective; they simplify complex events into more straightforward stories. Consider Rosa Parks, the African American woman whose 1955 arrest for refusing to move to the back of a bus launched the Montgomery, Alabama, bus boycott that drew national attention to Martin Luther King Jr. as a civil rights leader. Or take the 1969 Stonewall riots—the resistance to a raid by the New York City police on the gay bar the Stonewall Inn, the anniversary of which is commemorated in annual Gay Pride parades that celebrate the rise of the movement for gay and lesbian rights. Both are recalled as key moments in the histories of their respective social movements.

However, in both instances, there had been earlier parallel events: other black women who had been arrested for refusing to give up their seats on buses, and other instances when raids on gay bars had led to active resistance. Why are those events forgotten, while Parks and Stonewall are recalled? Collective memories are socially constructed by movements to be useful. Montgomery civil rights leaders decided to make an issue of Parks's arrest because she was well known and highly regarded in the city's black community— a symbol people would rally around. Stonewall rose to visibility in part because New York already had an active gay movement with its own press; the bar's location in Greenwich Village also meant that other alternative media, such as the *Village Voice* newspaper, were interested in covering the story. Such contingencies shape the form history takes.

Sources: Armstrong & Crage, 2006; B. Schwartz, 2009.

---

seek to draw attention to topics that have been neglected are likely to seem more novel. The fact that a particular claim has been occupying center stage for a while begins to make other claims seem fresher, more interesting, particularly to the media, which depend so heavily on presenting novel material (see Chapter 5). In addition, as noted in Chapters 8 and 9, once the social problems process reaches the stage of social problems work, there is likely to be some disillusionment. Very often the policies touted as the solution to the problem haven't caused the problem to disappear; instead, the troubling condition endures, and people begin losing their enthusiasm for those policies.

All of this means that, however successful claimsmakers have been in managing to raise concern about a particular troubling condition, that concern eventually is likely to decline, so the issue moves out of the limelight. However, that need not be the end of the matter; once enough time has passed, the previous wave of concern is likely to be forgotten, thanks to all of the competing claimsmaking campaigns that have captured the attention of the social problems marketplace in the meantime. Conditions may once more become ripe for drawing attention to what now again seems to be a neglected topic. Therefore, we should not be surprised to discover that the histories of many social problems display sequential waves of concern interspersed with periods when the topic receives relatively little attention.

For example, consider three waves of intense concern about delinquent gangs—youth gangs—in twentieth-century America. The first began in the 1920s, the second in the 1950s, and the third in the 1980s. Each period was marked by warnings that today's gangs were much worse—larger, better organized, more dangerous—than gangs in previous eras. Each wave featured claimsmaking by experts, such as sociologists, psychiatrists, and criminologists; each became the subject of both sensational news coverage and popular cultural depictions of gangs. Nor did these waves begin in the twentieth century; waves of concern about gangs date back to the 1840s in U.S. cities, and to the eighteenth century in London (Pearson, 1983).

We can spot similar sequential waves of concern regarding many other issues. The historian Philip Jenkins has described the oscillating attention given to the sexual exploitation of children (Jenkins,

1998) and to cults (Jenkins, 2000). The pattern turns up in surprising places; for example, Christian theologians periodically direct their attention to claims that there are "hidden gospels"—ancient manuscripts that were suppressed by religious authorities because they reveal that Christ's true message was antithetical to what the established church now endorses (Jenkins, 2001).

In each of these cases, a new set of claims attracts a great deal of attention for a time, but then concern begins to dissipate. When claimsmaking on the topic revives, usually people pay little attention to the previous wave of concern. The older set of claims—and the intense concern it generated—is often forgotten, as a new generation of claimsmakers reinvents the wheel. Even if the earlier claims are recalled, they tend to be dismissed: those people in the "good old days" may have thought they had a gang problem, but their gangs were nothing compared to ours.

What accounts for these waves of concern? One possibility, of course, is that the troubling conditions criticized by claimsmakers become more or less common over time, and claimsmaking merely tracks these shifts. Perhaps gang membership actually rises and falls in different historical periods. However, it is impossible to document such changes. There are probably always some gangs operating, but there is no long-term measure of such activity; in particular, in periods when gangs aren't a focus of attention, it is unlikely that anyone is charting gang involvement. When gangs attract concern, we have no way of being sure that the reason for the concern is that they have become more active.

Another possibility is that dramatic events attract media and public attention to particular social issues. For example, Jenkins (1998) notes waves of great concern over sexual crimes against children (as well as periods of much lower concern about these crimes). To be sure, during the waves of concern, heavily publicized news reports described terrible sex crimes against children; however, there were similar reports during the periods of low concern. During the waves of high concern, such crimes were depicted as *instances* of the larger problem of sexual violence against children—proof that something needed to be done. In contrast, during the periods of low concern, press coverage of such terrible crimes treated them as aberrant, exceptional behavior—not as representative of a larger phenomenon. It is difficult to make a strong case that claimsmaking activity simply rises and falls along with the increases and declines of a potentially troubling condition.

How, then, should we understand these waves of concern? One clue is that some of the same issues—gangs, cults, sexual crimes against children, even hidden gospels—appear again and again. Such recurrence might seem only sensible; it doesn't seem surprising that people would worry about these topics. But such wavelike patterns seem more striking when we realize that they occur in other societies and involve constructions that strike us as peculiar, such as waves of concern about vampires in East Africa (White, 2000). The variation in the types of concerns that are prevalent in different societies suggests that certain problems may be particularly easy to construct in particular societies—that some combination of cultural and social structural arrangements may foster such recurring claims (see Box 10.4).

It may help to think of societies as having the equivalent of fault lines—or "axes of variation" (Erikson, 1976). That is, social arrangements can create tensions between groups—between youths and older adults, between immigrants and the native-born, and on and on. Such tensions can flare into claimsmaking whenever self-identified groups find themselves competing for scarce resources, or whenever one group controls another's access to such resources. Claimsmaking is particularly likely to increase during periods of relative scarcity, when the competition between groups is more intense.

Such tensions can be expressed in lots of different ways. Probably most often, people complain about specific individuals or particular actions: "He shouldn't have done that!" But sometimes tensions can be linked to larger claims, so that particular actions

Box 10.4 Cycles Can Have Ironic Consequences

Cyclical concerns about many issues seem to repeat themselves, so that, for example, each new wave of anxiety about gangs tends to focus on the threat of violent youth. But some issues may be substantially reworked, so that different waves seem unrelated, at least at first glance.

Take the "brown scare" of the early 1940s. American entry into World War II had been opposed, particularly by some on the political right. Proponents of the war criticized their opponents as "pro-Nazi" fascist sympathizers, and warned that these opponents were endangering the war effort through espionage and sabotage. (The color brown—the color of Nazi uniforms—became shorthand for fascism, just as red was routinely associated with communism.) The federal government charged thirty defendants with sedition; ultimately the prosecution ended in a mistrial, in a largely forgotten episode in American history.

However, the principles behind the prosecution—that political dissent might be dangerous, a sign of conspiracies that needed to be rooted out by the federal government—survived. When the war ended, a new red scare, directed at the threats posed by communists, began (McCarthyism became the best-known aspect of this movement). The tables had turned: where the left had called for political trials for those on the right, the right was now promoting analogous investigations of the left. Fears of dark conspiracies formed a cycle, although the specifics of the successive waves of concern were quite different.

Source: Fine & McDonnell, 2007.

are understood as instances of a more general, troubling condition. At any given moment we can imagine that tensions inspire countless grievances—what we might think of as potential claims. Whether any particular grievance starts a full-scale social problems process will depend on contingencies: whether the grievance can be packaged as a rhetorically powerful claim, whether claims-makers can mobilize sufficient resources, the nature of the other claims currently competing in the social problems marketplace, and so on.

The level of tension along societal fault lines can be understood as another contingency. Periods of higher tension probably increase the receptivity of the press, the public, and policymakers to claims. In some cases, these claims may even—at first glance—seem oblique. Late nineteenth-century America, for instance, witnessed an active claimsmaking campaign against the English sparrow, a bird that had been imported to the United States in hopes that it would eat insects that infested urban areas (Fine & Christoforides, 1991). The sparrow was widely denounced in moralistic terms: it was lazy and dirty. The intensity of the antisparrow campaign seems surprising, until it is understood as part of the period's larger anti-immigrant claimsmaking. In the late nineteenth and early twentieth centuries, the United States was experiencing one of its periodic waves of opposition to immigration, and claims about the influx of a foreign bird paralleled worries about the country's ability to accommodate human immigrants. Although complaints about bird species aren't all that common, the larger tensions of the time gave the antisparrow claims visibility.

In addition to cycles of concern regarding particular issues, we can note periods when American society seems particularly open to claimsmaking. Three major periods of intense reform activity appear in U.S. history. First, in the decades preceding the Civil War (roughly 1830–1860), there was considerable social movement activity: the abolitionist campaign to abolish slavery, of course, but also intense interest in women's rights, new religions, the temperance movement against strong drink, opposition to immigration (particularly focused on anti-Irish sentiments), and so on. Second, the late nineteenth/early twentieth-century period featured a revived women's movement, further opposition to immigration (particularly from southern and eastern Europe), prohibitionist campaigns against alcohol and other drugs, and all of the other causes associated with the Progressive Era. And more recently, beginning in the 1960s and continuing to the present, there has been intense claimsmaking regarding civil rights, women's rights, a war on drugs, renewed concern about immigration (now from Latin America and Asia), and many other issues.

A comparison of these three periods shows that concerns with such fault-line topics as race, women's issues, immigration, and drug use do not just recur, but tend to emerge at roughly the same times. This concurrence suggests that conditions in some historical periods seem to foster claimsmaking. We might speculate that the impending Civil War left people unsettled and more open to the social problems claims of the first period. In the more recent period—as noted in earlier chapters—a new media environment and increasingly sophisticated claimsmaking methods have helped foster contemporary claimsmaking (see Box 10.5). Again, examining the social problems process across time reveals surprising similarities and differences that can help us better understand our contemporary arrangements for constructing social problems.

THE PROBLEM OF PROGRESS

Comparisons of claims across time raise another comparative question: Do things ever get better? That is, can we speak of social progress, or are things actually getting worse? It seems possible to make a strong case that there has been progress on many fronts: During the twentieth century, life expectancy rose markedly (a newborn male's life expectancy—46 years in 1900—rose to 78 in 2010, the improvement for females was even greater, and life expectancies for nonwhites grew more than those of whites). The percentage of young people graduating from high school climbed (from about 6 percent in 1900 to, according to some calculations, over 80 percent in recent years). The right to vote became more widely available

---

Box 10.5 TAKING A LONG VIEW OF SOCIAL MOVEMENTS AND PRESS COVERAGE

A study of coverage of social movements in the *New York Times* over the entire twentieth century identified a number of interesting patterns. Five movements received more than half the coverage: the labor movement, the black civil rights movement, the veterans movement, movements for women's rights, and the nativist/white supremacist movement. If the prominence of labor and veterans issues seems surprising, it is because those causes attracted more attention in the past than they have in recent times: attention to labor peaked immediately before and after World War II, while attention to veterans was concentrated between the 1920s and the 1950s; neither was receiving much coverage at the century's end. In contrast, the feminist and environmental movements were gaining more attention during the decades after 1970.

What makes a movement newsworthy? Three factors seemed to be most influential. First, movements with disruptive potential generated news; thus, the labor movement attracted attention when strikes were more common, just as coverage of the civil rights cause peaked during the 1960s—the decade with the most demonstrations and racial riots. Second, movements that embodied more active SMOs—more claimsmakers trying to draw attention to their causes—gained more press coverage. Third, once policymakers had enacted a policy, its workings (how it was being enforced) and the resulting debates over policy outcomes also received considerable attention. Taking a long view irons out some of the short-term fluctuations in press coverage and reveals larger historical patterns.

Source: Amenta, Caren, Olasky, & Stobaugh, 2009.

(in 1900, few women, few African Americans in the South, and no one aged 18–20 could vote). And the standard of living improved (so that, for instance, access to indoor plumbing, electricity, and phone service—all relatively rare in 1900—became nearly universally available) (J. Best, 2001c). Isn't all this progress?

Most people would say yes, but claims about troubling conditions tend to accentuate the negative. Claimsmakers' rhetoric often insists that things are worse than they seem and that they are deteriorating, that real catastrophe lies ahead, that progress is only an illusion. Claimsmakers rarely speak of progress; they seem to fear that acknowledging societal improvements may encourage complacency and discourage taking the actions needed to address troubling conditions. This worry is understandable: it is probably harder to arouse concern about a troubling condition if people are focused on how much things have improved. In addition, however, four aspects of the culture and organization of claimsmaking make it easier to downplay progress:

1. *Perfectibility.* Claimsmakers often invoke **perfectibility** as a standard. They declare that they won't settle for improving a particular troubling condition—that they are determined to eradicate the problem. As noted in Chapter 7, policymakers often "declare war" on social problems: heavily publicized wars have focused on such problems as poverty, cancer, drugs, and most recently, terrorism (J. Best, 1999). Similarly, our current education policy promises to "leave no child behind." But perfection is a very high standard; as long as one child is doing poorly in school, or one person is poor, there will be room for improvement—and therefore continued opportunities for claimsmaking.

2. *Proportion.* As big problems disappear, relatively smaller problems seem proportionally bigger than before. In 1900, many of the most common causes of death were infectious diseases. Vaccinations and antibiotics caused many of these threats to virtually vanish. Still, everyone is going to die from some cause, so attention can now focus on potentially fatal diseases—such as breast cancer—that received relatively little attention when influenza, pneumonia, and diphtheria were killing far more people. Similarly, ending the worst forms of racial inequality (such as lynching and institutionalized segregation in the South) allows attention to focus on those less violent, less systematic forms of racism that remain. This means that claimsmakers

need never run out of conditions that might be constructed as social problems.

3. **Proliferation.** Contemporary society encourages the proliferation of social problems claims. Chapter 5 discussed the growing number of arenas where claims can be mounted, including the increasing number of television channels and the Internet's endless reach, which have made it far easier to promote social problems claims. At the same time, most of these emerging arenas address segmented audiences, giving claimsmakers the advantage of being able to direct their rhetoric toward the homogeneous audience most likely to be receptive. Claimsmakers can therefore avoid confronting criticism and counterclaims, particularly during the early stages of a campaign, when they are seeking to mobilize support. The disadvantage, of course, is that in a world with more arenas, it is harder to gain general public attention for one's claims. For example, it has become easier to promote environmental causes by communicating in arenas filled with environmentalists, but harder to get the attention of the whole society and keep everyone focused on environmentalist concerns.

4. **Paranoia.** Finally, social progress fosters paranoia—fears of societal collapse. How can claimsmaking rhetoric be made compelling in a world characterized by social progress? One method is to warn that we are in terrible danger, that a collective catastrophe is on the horizon. Apocalyptic scenarios abound; claimsmakers warn about the threats of nuclear war, nuclear winter, global warming, overpopulation, pollution, resource depletion, epidemic disease, ethnic conflict, globalization, economic collapse, famine, genetic engineering, nanotechnology (tiny technological devices that might outcompete the natural biological system), or robotics (machines that might develop superior intelligence and eliminate people). Moreover, all of these fears focus on troubling conditions that have *social* causes and are therefore suitable subjects for claimsmakers. They can argue

that progress is a temporary illusion and warn that what seems to be progress will, in fact, lead to disaster.

In short, the experience of progress has, in some ways, made it easier to construct social problems: claimsmakers can insist that social arrangements remain imperfect; they find it easier to draw attention to previously neglected problems now that some of the big problems of the past have been resolved; they can target and reach audiences likely to be sympathetic to their claims; and they can warn that progress is illusionary, just a predecessor of far worse problems (see Box 10.6).

Given these patterns, it should not be surprising that social problems claims feature the most urgent rhetoric. Not only can claimsmakers draw attention to existing troubling conditions, but they also can predict alarming future problems. These are the secular equivalents of religious prophecies that the world will end on a particular date. It is worth noting that, in retrospect, these warnings often seem misguided. Consider alarmist warnings about AIDS in the late 1980s (in 1987, a leading television talk show host declared, "Research studies now project that . . . one in five heterosexuals could be dead from AIDS at the end of the next three years" [Fumento, 1990, p. 3]); and the furor about the Y2K problem (the concerns that the world's computers would be unable to cope when the calendar changed from 1999 to 2000, and that the resulting crisis might threaten civilization itself).

Apocalyptic rhetoric helps make claims stand out in the social problems marketplace. Every year brings a flu season, and it is always possible to speculate that this year's flu may turn into a devastating pandemic. Accentuating a positive record of progress rarely makes claims more competitive, whereas offering a dire forecast can help grab the attention of media workers, the general public, and policymakers. Terrible fears make for good headlines, create good

Box 10.6 Forecasting Future Problems

Claimsmakers often warn about a troubled future, about the terrible consequences of failing to address the problem they are constructing. But all claims about the future share a problem: it is always possible for skeptics to ask how the claimsmakers can possibly predict what's going to happen. In order to overcome such doubts, claimsmakers' rhetoric must convince their audiences that they can indeed foretell the future.

Most obviously, claimsmakers justify their predictions in terms of whatever authorities their society recognizes: in some societies, this may involve interpreting a holy text; in others, forecasts may be derived from sophisticated scientific models (compare claims that the Mayan calendar forecast the end of the world on December 21, 2012, with climate scientists' computer models for projecting global temperature increases during this century). But there are other ways of making future claims compelling. In general, predictions of huge problems—catastrophes that threaten life as we know it—are more likely to capture people's attention. Similarly, arguing that the problem has a high probability of occurring is a way of getting people concerned. And claiming that the problem will occur sooner rather than later also helps. A prediction, based on authoritative sources, that a catastrophe is certain to occur in the immediate future is likely to get the attention of the press, the public, and policymakers, while it is hard to arouse concern with other forecasts, grounded in questionable authority, for less serious outcomes that aren't especially likely and may not occur for some time. The rhetoric of future claims deserves critical examination.

Source: J. Best, 2011.

conversation topics, and offer policymakers opportunities to take a stand defending society from a threatening menace.

In short, the question is not whether there is or is not evidence of social progress. The point is that the social problems process pits claims against one another, and that claimsmakers can justify pessimistic rhetoric as a competitive strategy—the most effective way of arousing concern for their issues. This is one more way that the larger societal context shapes claimsmaking.

EXTENDING OUR FOCUS
ACROSS SPACE AND TIME

Although the case study is the typical method for studying the social problems process, this chapter has suggested that there is much to be gained from studying more than one case at a time. Comparisons allow us to compare and contrast social issues across space and time—to recognize that there are various ways to construct the same troubling condition, and that claims morph as they diffuse from one country to another, or as a new wave of concern breathes fresh life into a once visible issue that has since fallen out of favor.

Typically, claims emphasize troubling conditions in the here and now—and in the future. Claimsmakers warn that this is why things are bad now, and that there are reasons to worry that things might get much worse. Expanding our focus—thinking about claims more broadly, by considering how social problems were constructed in other places or during other time periods—can help us place those claims in context, to locate the social problems process within a larger framework, so that we can better understand how that process operates. Without such bases for comparisons, it is difficult to assess any particular set of claims.

MAKING CONNECTIONS

- *Although many troubling conditions follow the six stages of the social problems process, often claims fail to attract media attention (discussed in Chapter 5) or public concern (covered in Chapter 6).*

- Comparisons across time or between places are a useful way of evaluating social problems and the choices made by social problems workers and policymakers. See Chapters 7 and 8 for more about social policy and its implementation.

- Looking at cycles of concern across time or between different countries reveals how conditions in some historical periods foster claimsmaking. Chapter 3 explains how activists exploit cultural opportunities when conditions are optimal for drawing attention to their claims.

CASE STUDY

SEXUAL TRAFFICKING ACROSS SPACE AND TIME

Prostitution may not be the oldest profession, but it has a very long history. Lots of people—mostly males—desire sexual services and are willing to pay for them, and it should be no surprise that others, mostly females, can be found to meet that demand. In some cultures, these arrangements are not viewed as problematic; in others, they are constructed as social problems.

To gain some perspective on contemporary American views of prostitution, it helps to appreciate how the problem was constructed in the nineteenth century (Donovan, 2006). On the one hand, officials in many cities devised policies to manage prostitution: they tried to confine prostitutes to particular geographic districts, and conducted medical inspections to identify women with venereal disease. These arrangements were criticized by reformers, especially Protestant ministers who viewed prostitution as a moral problem and who campaigned for *social purity*, and members of the early women's movement who denounced the double standard that condemned female prostitutes while ignoring their male customers.

In the views of these activists, women were naturally innocent and pure. How, then, had these "fallen angels" become condemned to "lives of shame"? Surely the answer was that they had been tricked or forced into prostitution; antivice advocates told elaborate stories of respectable young women being fed drugged ice cream sundaes and then awakening to find themselves trapped in brothels, deflowered, and "ruined." This nefarious system for luring women into prostitution was termed *white slavery*, a phrase that linked the campaign against prostitution to the morally righteous cause of abolitionism. By the beginning of the twentieth century, claimsmakers routinely depicted white slavery as related to immigration; they insisted that recently immigrated males (particularly Jews and Italians) were preying on women, both by offering would-be immigrants passage to America in return for the women's serving as prostitutes, and by recruiting recent female immigrants to enter the brothels.

The problem with the white slavery stories was that most prostitutes denied that they had been victimized in this way. Rather, they consistently told a different tale: prostitutes came from poor backgrounds; their principal respectable job options were sewing, waiting tables, or working as domestic maids—all choices that involved hard work for little pay. Some made a calculated choice: it was not so much that they saw prostitution as a desirable job, as that the other options seemed worse. Some reformers argued that the solution to prostitution was not so much moral reform, as changing social arrangements to give poor and immigrant women more opportunities.

Fast-forward to twenty-first-century America. In most major cities, police antistreetwalking campaigns largely have driven prostitution from public view; increasingly, sexual services are sold in private settings, such as massage parlors, strip clubs, and apartments (Bernstein, 2007). At the same time, new antiprostitution claimsmaking has emerged to fight what is called *sexual trafficking*.

The key claimsmakers in this movement resemble their counterparts in the earlier campaign for social purity and against white slavery: the opposition to sexual trafficking involves an alliance between Christian conservatives and some liberal feminists, with the former viewing prostitution as a moral issue, and the latter seeing it as gender exploitation (Bernstein, 2010; Doezema, 2010). (This alliance is not unprecedented: opposition to pornography also led religious conservatives to ally with some feminists. Both issues created divisions among feminists, with some campaigning to eliminate pornography and prostitution, while others called for toleration and protection of "sex workers.") Moreover, these advocates stand opposed to familiar villains: just as earlier reformers blamed white slavers for leading women into prostitution, contemporary rhetoric focuses on the role of sex traffickers. Another similarity between earlier and contemporary constructions of the problem is the importance of immigration. Where earlier reformers worried that immigrant women were especially vulnerable to white slavery (and in the case of Asian women, what was termed *yellow slavery*), today's advocates view sexual trafficking as a global issue.

Sex trafficking claims, like earlier opposition to white slavery, downplay the importance of economic and social conditions in leading people into sex work. Young men and women in many less developed countries face bleak employment prospects (Agustin, 2007). Many decide they could improve their lot by migrating to more prosperous countries, often, but not only, to the United States, Canada, or Western Europe, where they might earn more money. Of course, immigration laws make it difficult for many of these people to migrate legally, so they pay people who help smuggle them across borders; often, those seeking to migrate cannot afford the passage and promise to pay from their earnings after they arrive. Some of them, once they reach their destinations, sell sexual services as a way to support themselves. None of this is very different from the reasoning that has always led some people to prostitute themselves; selling sex may not be a great way to make a living, but it may seem no worse than other choices.

In other words, it is possible to construct prostitution as an evil enterprise, in which villainous human traffickers force women into sexual slavery; it may even be possible to point to horrific typifying examples that fit this pattern. But other analysts argue that selling sex is a form of work that is chosen, mostly by those who find themselves disadvantaged by social and economic arrangements that constrain their choices. Essentially parallel debates about the nature of prostitution may be found across time and space.

QUESTIONS

1. What might explain the similarities between the constructions of the prostitution problem by today's advocates and those of their counterparts in the past?

2. In the past, people often saw prostitution as a local problem, but contemporary advocates emphasize its global dimensions. Why?

3. Why does it seem easier to construct prostitution as a moral problem, instead of emphasizing the role of economic and social conditions?

11

The Uses of the Constructionist Stance

Most of us find ourselves discussing social problems with friends or family members from time to time. In general, these everyday conversations focus on what we've called *troubling conditions*. People argue about the scope of conditions, or about what causes them (for instance, some may insist that poverty is caused by discrimination or a lack of good jobs, while others counter that poor people are at least partly to blame for their own problems). Reports from the media may be used to buttress one position or another (perhaps someone will refer to a radio talk show or a program on television about poverty). There may be disagreements about what should be done (should the government distribute more—or less—money to the poor?). In short, these conversations tend to treat social problems as though they are conditions that have an objective existence in our society.

Of course, this book has adopted a very different stance. It has been relatively uninterested in such social conditions, and has focused instead on what people think and say about social problems. Instead of treating social problems as social conditions, it has described a *process* in which people's ideas about social problems emerge and evolve.

Chapter 1 introduced a model of a social problems process with six basic stages: claimsmaking, media coverage, public reaction, policymaking, social problems work, and policy outcomes. That model (reproduced as Figure 11.1) provided the organizational framework for the chapters that followed, which, in general, dealt with successive stages in the social problems process.

While exploring the six stages in the social problems process, this book has remained focused on the subjective nature of social problems. Remember that what all phenomena that are considered social problems have in common is not a particular objective quality, some sort of harm or damage that they inflict on society. Rather, the one characteristic that all social problems share is subjective: people define them as troubling. Social problems are not conditions; they are *concerns*.

This subjective work—people's efforts to understand and draw attention to what they define as troubling conditions—occurs at every stage in the social problems process. It begins with claims-makers' efforts to construct claims that will convince others to share their concern about a troubling condition. And at each successive stage in the process, people—media workers, members of the public, policymakers, social problems workers, and those who evaluate and criticize policies—rework the claims that come to their attention, and reconstruct the problem again and again so that their new understanding will be appropriate for their purposes. News workers repackage primary claims into secondary claims to fit the demands and conventions of news coverage; members of the public respond by interpreting these secondary claims to correspond with their own understanding of how the larger world works; policymakers

Figure 11.1 BASIC MODEL OF THE SOCIAL PROBLEMS PROCESS

Claims- ⟶ Media ⟶ Public ⟶ Policy- ⟶ Social ⟶ Policy
making   Coverage   Reaction   making   Problems   Outcomes
                                          Work

make further alterations so that the troubling condition can be addressed through a formal policy; social problems workers try to apply abstract policies to practical situations; and various evaluators redefine what is needed according to their assessments of how well policies work.

In other words, social problems construction is not something that happens all at once, through the actions of a single set of actors at one stage in the social problems process. Instead, it is an ongoing process, in which different people work out different ways of making sense of the situations they confront. Any phenomenon can be understood in lots of different ways, and social construction is a process of making choices—of people in a particular situation choosing one perspective among all the possibilities. Each effort to construct or understand a social problem needs to meet two criteria: first, it needs to make sense to—and be useful for—whoever is producing the construction; second, it needs to be able to convince others—whoever the audience for that construction may be.

Social construction is thus an *interactive* process. People present their constructions to an audience of others (as when an activist holds a press conference, a legislator tries to convince colleagues to vote for a bill, or a case worker tries to persuade clients that taking a particular action will be in their best interest). Those others, however, may react in different ways (perhaps no reporters bother to attend the press conference, perhaps the legislature votes unanimously in favor of the bill, perhaps some clients reject the case worker's advice while others follow it). These reactions become feedback, and on the basis of the audience's response, the people offering the construction may continue pressing their claims, modify those claims to see whether a repackaged version might elicit a better response, or even decide to abandon the claims entirely. Although we may think of a claimsmaker addressing an audience, we should not imagine that that audience is passive. Rather, audiences react to claims, and claimsmakers are likely to revise their constructions in response to those reactions.

All of this means that our initial model of the social problems process, as illustrated in Figure 11.1, oversimplifies the process in some important ways. First, the arrows between stages imply that influence is unidirectional; they ignore the role of feedback and the interactive nature of the process. Second, the actors at the different stages in the social problems process do not necessarily limit their interactions to contacts with those in the next stage. Third, and very important, interactions also occur *within* each stage. That is, activists interact with others in their social movement organization, as well as with activists in rival SMOs, and with other sorts of claimsmakers, such as experts. Similarly, media workers interact with their colleagues and follow one another's coverage, and so on.

Moreover, when we look at interactions between actors in different stages, we realize again that the basic model's depiction of actors addressing only those at the next stage in the process is too simple. For example, the model suggests that claimsmakers will focus their attention on influencing media coverage, but claimsmakers may do far more. Sometimes claimsmakers bypass the media and directly address members of the public, policymakers, social problems workers, or even those who evaluate policy outcomes. There are many possible pathways through the social problems process. Figure 11.1 can be thought of as offering a simplified, fairly typical natural history—a framework for developing this book's argument. In contrast, Figure 11.2 gives a better sense of the complicated ways in which actors in different stages of the process can interact; it suggests the range of possible connections that might shape how social problems evolve.

Examine Figure 11.2 carefully, and note the following five features:

1. The five one-way stage-to-stage arrows found in the simplified model reappear in Figure 11.2 as thicker arrows—a reminder that these are particularly important links in the social problems process.

Figure 11.2 Interactions in the Social Problems Process

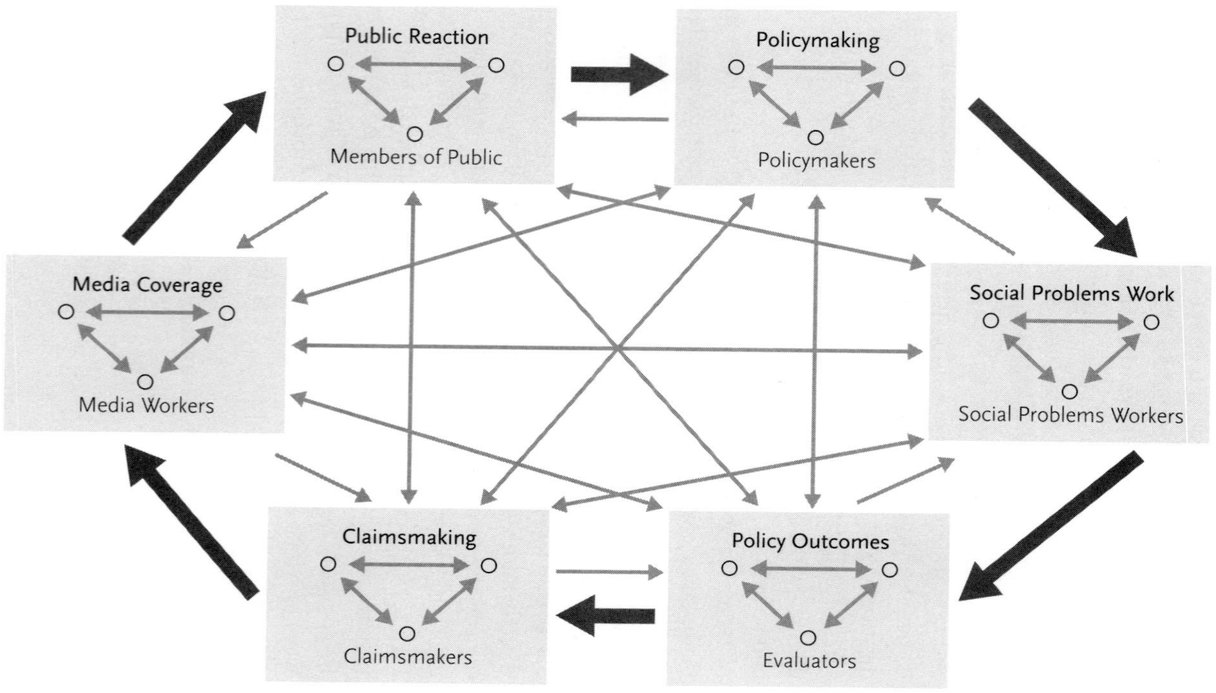

2. Each stage in the social problems process is now represented by a box, and small circles within each box denote the various actors in that stage (that is, different claimsmakers in the claimsmaking stage, and so on). In turn, those circles are linked by two-way arrows suggesting interactions among the people at each stage.

3. Arrows connect each stage with every other stage, illustrating possible connections, in that it may be possible for actors at any stage to communicate with people anywhere else in the social problems process.

4. The arrows linking all the different stages go in both directions, to illustrate that there is always the possibility of feedback and social interaction.

5. The figure is laid out as a circle, rather than along a straight line, and there is a thick arrow between "Policy Outcomes" (which the basic model presented as the final stage in the social problems process) and "Claimsmaking" (which was, of course, the first stage). This arrow denotes how reactions to social policies often lead to new claimsmaking campaigns (as discussed in Chapter 9). The figure's roughly circular shape reminds us that the social problems process need not end—that critiques of social policies often inspire new cycles of claimsmaking.

Figure 11.2 is complex, but that is because it reflects genuine complexities—the many possible pathways through the social problems process. The entire process is an example of what sociologists call a *complex system*, with many elements that affect one another (Watts, 2011). It is important to appreciate this complexity; spend some time examining Figure 11.2. Pick one particular arrow and consider the sorts of activities it might involve. Then pick another. Do this until you are comfortable, until you understand how this complex figure depicts the overall social problems process.

These complexities become especially apparent when we compare social problems processes across space and time (the subject of Chapter 10). For example, many campaigns raise concern about dangerous drugs. Some of these efforts are remarkably successful at attracting intense media coverage, arousing great public concern, and inspiring new policies; the 1986 campaign to warn Americans about the dangers of crack cocaine is an obvious example (Reinarman & Levine, 1995). On the other hand, some campaigns flop, such as the 1989 effort to draw attention to "ice" (smokable crystal methamphetamine), although later campaigns to raise alarm about this drug had more success; or the 1993 warnings about "Cat" (methcathinone, a drug that—so far—has not aroused great concern) (Jenkins, 1999).

We can imagine a continuum of outcomes for antidrug campaigns that ranges from widespread, intense concern to indifference. Only by comparing antidrug claimsmaking campaigns—targeting different drugs, at different times, or in different places—can we begin to appreciate the many possible ways that the social problems process can unfold. And, of course, various claims about other troubling conditions—racial discrimination, ecological problems, and so on—will display similar variability in their outcomes.

In other words, our constructionist model—both the simpler version depicted in Figure 11.1 and the more complex version presented in Figure 11.2—should be understood as a tool, a framework that can be used to help us think critically about the social construction of social problems. Most days, news media present various stories that report on claimsmaking, policymaking, or social problems work; very often they also run stories about public reactions and evaluations of different policies. (And, of course, all of those stories are themselves examples of media coverage.) The constructionist model can be used to place all those stories in their broader context, to view them as parts of the larger social problems process. And that's worth doing, because we are constantly surrounded by examples of the social problems process.

IS THIS STUFF USEFUL?

As noted way back in Chapter 1, the constructionist stance for thinking about the social problems process is not the traditional approach to studying social problems. Most books about social problems have been—and continue to be—organized around a series of chapters that deal with different conditions considered to be social problems—crime, racism, and the like. Each chapter summarizes information about its problem: statistics about crime rates, theories of crime causation, and so on. This book has presented very little information of that sort.

The justification for this book's constructionist approach is that it is intellectually coherent. Rather than letting our attention drift as we examine, one at a time, crime and other specific phenomena that people consider social problems, this book has focused on the general topic of the social problems process—on the insight that the only thing the various conditions called social problems have in common is that they are socially constructed—and it has explored the ins and outs of that process.

This approach is intended to give you some tools for recognizing, thinking about, and responding to social problems claims. Ten years from now—or maybe twenty or thirty—you will encounter warnings about a terrible new social problem of some sort. There is no way of predicting exactly what the topic of those warnings will be—perhaps a new crime, or a new disease, or a new form of drug abuse. But we can be reasonably confident that you will run into such claims, because such claims have been an important part of the social landscape for a very long time, and there is no reason to expect that they will vanish—particularly not in a world where twenty-four-hour television news broadcasts, the Internet, and other forms of electronic communication make it incredibly easy to promote new claims. If anything, claims are likely to spread via ever more channels as new media evolve (consider, for example, the relatively recent emergence of Facebook pages as forums for claims, and of news bulletins transmitted to cell phones and other portable electronic devices). People who pay even minimal attention to the media can expect to spend their lives bombarded by such claims.

Moreover, the historical record is full of warnings about terrible problems that—in retrospect—seem mistaken. In the 1970s, some environmentalists warned that civilization was jeopardized by global climate change—that humans faced an impending ice age brought on by global cooling. Fifteen years later, fears about the threat of global cooling would be replaced by what seem to be their exact opposite—concerns over the danger of global warming. In another example, in the early 1990s some commentators warned that violent crime was about to spiral out of control—that a generation of "superpredators" would be coming of age. Instead, crime rates fell fairly steadily during the years that followed. These claims received plenty of respectful attention when they first appeared, even though their forecasts proved to be quite wrong.

There are many other examples of urgent claims that hindsight lets us see as exaggerated, if not silly. There is a long history of critics warning that the amusements of the young—games, toys, dances, movies, television, music, and on and on—endangered the next generation. Each successive style of rock music, for example, has been denounced as threatening the moral fabric of young people. There is an equally long history of commentators charging that the current wave of immigrants threatens the foundation of American society, that some new recreational drug is spreading out of control, and so on. Such claims often acknowledge that earlier claims about similar problems exaggerated the threat, yet the claimsmakers insist that this new problem is different—the real deal—that it presents a genuine danger that must be addressed.

At one extreme, it is possible to treat all social problems claims as correct, true, accurate. When claimsmakers warn that a particular troubling condition is this serious, affects that many people, and so on, we might simply accept those claims, even though we may realize that, in the past, many such claims have proved to be exaggerated or even false. In other words, every time we encounter a news story that warns we should be worried about a new problem, we could decide to worry. An alternative, but equally extreme stance might be to approach all claims cynically, to presume that they are wrong, false, bogus. We could suspect that claimsmakers are interested parties who are quite willing to say anything, that media workers are just trying to attract an audience, that politicians are cynically pandering to voters' concerns, and so on. Knowing that some social problems claims have been exaggerated in the past, we might simply discount and ignore any claims we encounter in the future. The first possibility encourages excessive credulity; the second fosters cynicism, apathy, and ignorance.

Obviously it would be desirable to find a middle ground between those extremes—a stance somewhere between credulousness and cynicism. That is, it would be better to approach claims thoughtfully—critically—so that we could weigh what we're told about social problems and make our own evaluations about the nature of those problems and the best ways of addressing them.

The constructionist model of the social problems process can help in this regard. Understanding that claims need to be made persuasive—that claimsmakers are competing to be heard in the social problems marketplace so that they can bring their claims to the attention of press, public, and policymakers—offers a useful foundation for thinking about social problems as a process. In particular, it can help us to think carefully about how the problem is being constructed, about the rhetoric of claimsmaking, about who is making which claims, and so on.

By adopting a constructionist stance, we can identify interesting questions that we might ask about a set of claims. Is the problem clearly defined, or are we encouraged to understand it primarily through typifying examples? Is there any reason to suspect that those typifying examples may not be all that typical? If the claims feature statistics, where do those numbers come from, and how likely is it that they are accurate? What sorts of warrants are being used to make the claims compelling? How are the media covering the issue? What sources are they drawing upon, and how does what the media report differ from what the claimsmakers are saying? Are the media presenting different constructions of the problem, and what do those differences reveal?

Further questions arise at successive stages in the social problems process. Is the problem addressed in our everyday conversations? Is it a theme in stories or jokes that we hear from people we know, and if so, does the public seem to be constructing the problem in different terms from those that claimsmakers and the media are using? Which aspects of the problem do policymakers emphasize? Do their policy recommendations match their claims? Do they seem workable? How do social problems workers describe their activities and the clients with whom they work? Who criticizes social policies and why, and how do they frame their critiques?

Such questions give us tools that we can use to think critically about social problems. Note, however, that being critical sometimes does mean rejecting claims. The answers to some of the questions you ask may strike you as completely convincing; you may decide that some claims are quite correct, and you may even be moved to join some claimsmakers' causes. In other instances, though, questioning the claims might lead you to suspect that those claims are exaggerated or misguided. Thus, thinking critically can help you become a thoughtful consumer of social problems claims.

There is another way to use the constructionist approach. Studying how social problems are constructed—how some claims prove effective while others fall by the wayside—offers useful information for would-be claimsmakers. That is, constructionist research can be studied for its practical advice on how to arouse concern and mobilize action regarding whatever you might consider as troubling conditions (just as it can suggest how opposition to claims might be made more effective). Studying the social problems process offers lessons on how to assemble persuasive claimsmaking rhetoric, how to mobilize effective adherents, how to incorporate expert knowledge in campaigns, how to elicit media coverage and attract public attention, how to understand the concerns of policymakers and social problems workers, and so on. If you are inclined to take an active part in the social problems process, the constructionist stance can help you ask—and answer—very practical questions. It is a perspective that can benefit participants, as well as observers.

What constructionism cannot do is tell you which conditions ought to concern you. You have your own values, your own sense of what is or is not troubling, what needs to be changed, and what sorts of changes are needed. You may be attracted by the ideologies of liberals or conservatives, of feminists or fundamentalists. Those are choices you need to make, and the constructionist stance does not provide the grounds for preferring one choice over another. The goal of this book has not been to tell you *what* to think about various social conditions, but rather to offer guidelines for *how* to think about the social problems process. If this book advocates a moral position, it is that it is desirable for people to think critically about that process, to engage the claims they encounter.

I hope you will find these ideas useful in the years ahead. Good luck.

Glossary

abeyance A period when a social movement is relatively inactive.

activists Members of a social movement organization who make claims about social problems. Compare *experts*.

adopters The people who accept new innovations as part of the process of diffusion. Compare *transmitters*.

agenda setting Choosing which claims will receive the attention of media or policymakers.

arena A public venue where social problems claims can be presented.

audience The people whom claimsmakers seek to persuade with their claims.

audience segmentation Targeting media presentations for particular audiences.

beneficiaries People who stand to benefit from a social movement's success. Compare *constituents*.

bias A tendency for media workers' personal beliefs and views on an issue to interfere with balanced and impartial coverage.

biomedicalization The process of arguing that biological processes are the root cause of many troubling conditions.

carrying capacity The number of issues that can receive attention in an arena.

case An instance of a previously constructed troubling condition that requires attention through the application of appropriate policy.

case study An examination of a particular problem.

causal story A story that classifies a troubling condition in a familiar category according to the nature of its cause.

claim An argument that a particular troubling condition needs to be addressed.

claimsmakers People who seek to convince others that there is a troubling condition about which something ought to be done.

claimsmaking The process of making claims, of bringing a troubling condition to the attention of others.

commission A special, high-status group—often created at the national level—that evaluates policies and issues recommendations.

conclusion The part of a claim that specifies what should be done, what action should be taken to address a troubling condition.

condensing symbol A shorthand element—such as a landmark narrative, typifying example, slogan, or visual image—that evokes a package.

conscience constituents People who contribute money or even join demonstrations because they believe in a particular cause, although they do not expect to be direct beneficiaries of that cause.

constituents People who support a social movement. Compare *beneficiaries* and *conscience constituents*.

constructionism A sociological approach that focuses on the process of social construction.

contemporary legend A story, also called an *urban legend*, spread from one person to another and believed to be true by teller and listener.

counterclaim An argument that directly opposes a particular claim.

countermovement A movement that opposes a social movement by promoting counterclaims that challenge the opponent's claims.

cultural opportunity A situation when a shift in popular ideas makes it possible to change how a particular troubling condition is addressed. Compare *political opportunity*.

cultural resources Cultural knowledge that can be incorporated in claims.

diagnostic frame A social movement's depiction of the nature of a problem. Compare *prognostic frame*.

dialog An exchange of ideas between two or more persons.

diffusion The process by which innovations spread.

domain expansion Redefining a troubling condition to encompass a broader array of cases.

evaluation research A social scientific assessment of the effectiveness of a specific policy.

experts People—such as physicians, scientists, lawyers, and officials—who have special knowledge and claim to speak with special authority. Compare *activists*.

feedback The phenomenon in which a particular cause produces an effect that in turn affects the cause.

focus group A set of people that researchers select to discuss certain topics in order to learn what the public is thinking.

frame alignment Ways in which activists try to promote a social movement's frame to prospective members.

frame amplification Ways in which activists appeal to prospective members by arguing that a social movement's frame is consistent with popular beliefs.

frame bridging Ways in which activists appeal to prospective members thought to be already sympathetic to a social movement's frame.

frame dispute A disagreement between groups of activists about how to frame a particular troubling condition.

frame extension Ways in which activists appeal to prospective members by extending a social movement's frame to encompass the concerns of those prospective supporters.

frame transformation Ways in which activists appeal to prospective members by inviting them to reject familiar views of the world and adopt the activists' very different perspective.

framing The way in which claimsmakers construct claims about a troubling condition.

ground The portion of a claim that argues that a troubling condition exists.

ideology A system of beliefs regarding how society does and should operate.

inertia A reluctance to alter existing social arrangements.

insider claimsmakers Claimsmakers who have easy access to publicity and people in positions of power. Compare *outsider claimsmakers*.

joke cycle A set of jokes that share a form or topic and are popular for a period of time.

landmark narrative A typifying example that dominates news coverage of a troubling condition, shaping the terms in which the problem is covered and how the news audience understands the problem.

macrosociology Sociological studies concerned with whole societies. Compare *microsociology*.

master frame A broad construction that can be easily modified and applied to many troubling conditions.

media coverage Attention from mass media outlets, such as newspapers and television, that can bring claims to the attention of a wide audience.

medical model A general framework for thinking about medical matters as diseases that require treatment.

medicalization The process of defining a troubling condition as a medical matter.

microsociology Sociological studies concerned with interactions between individuals. Compare *macrosociology*.

motif A recurring thematic element in legends and jokes.

motivational frame A social movement's justification for taking action.

naming Coining a term to identify a troubling condition.

natural history A sequence of steps or stages often found in a particular process.

news work The job of locating and presenting news to the larger public.

nonrelational channel A link in diffusion that does not involve a personal connection between a transmitter and an adopter. Compare *relational channel*.

objectivism A school of thought that defines social problems in terms of objectively measurable characteristics of conditions. Compare *subjectivism*.

outsider claimsmakers People who lack easy access to publicity and to people in positions of power. Compare *insider claimsmakers*.

ownership Having one's construction of a troubling condition become widely accepted.

package A familiar construction of a particular troubling condition, including specifications of its causes and solutions.

perfectibility Using the eradication of a troubling condition—instead of its improvement—as the standard for evaluating a social policy.

pharmaceuticalization The process of defining prescription drugs as solutions to troubling conditions.

piggyback To link a new troubling condition to an already established social problem.

policy domain The part of the political system that focuses on a particular troubling condition.

policy outcome The result of how a particular social policy is implemented.

policy proposal stream A set of policy proposals that policymakers hear for addressing a troubling condition.

policymakers People who are able to establish a social policy of some kind.

policymaking The process of devising policy to address a particular troubling condition.

political opportunity A situation when a shift in power makes it possible to change how a particular troubling condition is addressed. Compare *cultural opportunity*.

political stream The current political situation recognized by policymakers in which a troubling condition might be addressed.

polity Groups and individuals who have easy access to policymakers.

popular culture Commercial entertainment.

population All those described by a statistic. Compare *representative sample*.

position issue A troubling condition about which people disagree. Compare *valence issue*.

primary claim One of the initial claims, usually presented by activists or experts, that begin the social problems process. Compare *secondary claim*.

problem recognition stream The set of claims that policymakers hear about a troubling condition.

prognostic frame A social movement's description of what needs to be done about a particular troubling condition. Compare *diagnostic frame*.

relational channel A link in diffusion that involves interpersonal contact between a transmitter and an adopter. Compare *nonrelational channel*.

representative sample A sample that accurately reflects the diversity of the population.

resource Anything that can be drawn upon to construct a claim.

resource mobilization Collecting and assembling money, members, and other resources needed by a social movement.

rhetoric The study of persuasion.

risk society Society in which social problems are often constructed in terms of risks.

sample A subgroup used as a basis for statistical generalizations about a population.

sample survey A poll administered to a sample in order to generalize about opinions or other characteristics of a population.

secondary claim The media's transformation of a primary claim. Secondary claims are usually shorter and more dramatic than primary claims.

segmentation See *audience segmentation*.

SMO See *social movement organization*.

social condition A social circumstance or arrangement.

social construction The process by which people continually create—or construct—meaning.

social issue A topic of social concern that is characterized by disagreement or debate.

social movement A general cause that motivates activists and social movement organizations to address a particular troubling condition.

social movement organization (SMO) A particular organization that belongs to a social movement.

social problems marketplace The public forum where claims are presented and discussed.

social problems process The process through which particular troubling conditions come to be constructed as social problems.

social problems work The application of constructions of a troubling condition or a social policy to practical situations.

social problems workers People who do social problems work.

sociological imagination The ability to see private troubles in terms of larger public issues.

statistic A number that measures or characterizes a particular situation.

subjectivism A school of thought that defines social problems in terms of people's subjective sense that something is or isn't troubling. Compare *objectivism*.

subjects The people (variously called addicts, clients, offenders, patients, suspects, victims, defendants, and so on) who in some way embody a socially constructed social problem.

target population The group of people intended to be affected by a social policy.

theorization The presentation of claims using abstract principles and arguments.

topical joke cycle A joke cycle about a particular event.

transmitters The people who promote new innovations as part of the process of diffusion. Compare *adopters*.

troubling condition A condition that becomes a subject of claims.

typifying example A particular instance chosen to illustrate a troubling condition—often a dramatic, disturbing, or memorable case.

urban legend See *contemporary legend*.

valence issue A troubling condition about which there is general agreement. Compare *position issue*.

variant A version of a contemporary legend or joke.

warrant The portion of a claim that justifies doing something about a troubling condition.

References

Abraham, J. (2010). Pharmaceuticalization of society in context: Theoretical, empirical, and health. *Sociology* 44: 603–22.

Agustin, L. M. (2007). *Sex at the margins: Migration, labour markets and the rescue industry.* London: Zed.

Åkerström, M. (2006). Doing ambivalence: Embracing policy innovation—at arm's length. *Social Problems* 53: 57–74.

Alterman, E. (2003). *What liberal media? The truth about bias and the news.* New York: Basic Books.

Amenta, E., Caren, N., Olasky, S. J., & Stobaugh, J. E. (2009). All the movements fit to print: Who, what, when, where, and why SMO families appeared in the *New York Times* in the twentieth century. *American Sociological Review* 74: 636–656.

Appleton, L. M. (1995). Rethinking medicalization: Alcoholism and anomalies. In J. Best (Ed.), *Images of issues: Typifying contemporary social problems* (2nd ed., pp. 59–80). Hawthorne, NY: Aldine de Gruyter.

Armstrong, E. A., & Crage, S. M. (2006). Movements and memory: The making of the Stonewall myth. *American Sociological Review* 71: 724–751.

Ayukawa, J. (2001). The United States and smoking problems in Japan. In J. Best (Ed.), *How claims spread: Cross-national diffusion of social problems* (pp. 215–242). Hawthorne, NY: Aldine de Gruyter.

Barnes, F. (2004, May 28). Liberal media evidence. *The Daily Standard.* Retrieved from www.weeklystandard.com.

Barrett, S. (2003). *Environment and statecraft: The strategy of environmental treaty-making.* New York: Oxford University Press.

Bartley, T. (2007). How foundations shape social movements: The construction of an organizational field and the rise of forest certification. *Social Problems* 54: 229–255.

Beamish, T. D., & Luebbers, A. J. (2009). Alliance building across social movements: Bridging difference in a peace and justice coalition. *Social Problems* 56: 647–676.

Beck, U. (1992). *Risk society: Towards a new modernity*. London: Sage.

Becker, H. S. (1995). The power of inertia. *Qualitative Sociology* 18: 301–309.

Beckett, K. (1994). Setting the public agenda: "Street crime" and drug use in American politics. *Social Problems* 41: 425–447.

Beckett, K. (1996). Culture and the politics of signification: The case of child sexual abuse. *Social Problems* 43: 57–76.

Benford, R. D. (1993). Frame disputes within the nuclear disarmament movement. *Social Forces* 71: 677–701.

Benford, R. D., & Hunt, S. A. (2003). Interactional dynamics in public problems marketplaces: Movements and the counterframing and reframing of public problems. In J. A. Holstein & G. Miller (Eds.), *Challenges and choices: Constructionist perspectives on social problems* (pp. 153–186). Hawthorne, NY: Aldine de Gruyter.

Benson, R., & Saguy, A. C. (2005). Constructing social problems in an age of globalization: A French-American comparison. *American Sociological Review* 70: 233–259.

Ben-Yehuda, N. (2010). *Theocratic democracy: The social construction of religious and secular extremism*. New York: Oxford University Press.

Berger, P. L., & Luckmann, T. (1966). *The social construction of reality: A treatise in the sociology of knowledge*. Garden City, NY: Doubleday.

Berns, N. (2004). *Framing the victim: Domestic violence, media, and social problems*. Hawthorne, NY: Aldine de Gruyter.

Berns, N. (2011). *Closure: The rush to end grief and what it costs us*. Philadelphia: Temple University Press.

Bernstein, E. (2007). *Temporarily yours: Intimacy, authenticity, and the commerce of sex*. Chicago: University Chicago Press.

Bernstein, E. (2010). Militarized humanitarianism meets carceral feminism: The politics of sex, rights, and freedom in contemporary antitrafficking campaigns. *Signs* 36: 45–71.

Best, J. (1990). *Threatened children: Rhetoric and concern about child-victims*. Chicago: University of Chicago Press.

Best, J. (1999). *Random violence: How we talk about new crimes and new victims*. Berkeley: University of California Press.

Best, J. (2001a). *Damned lies and statistics: Untangling numbers from the media, politicians, and activists*. Berkeley: University of California Press.

Best, J. (Ed.). (2001b). *How claims spread: Cross-national diffusion of social problems.* Hawthorne, NY: Aldine de Gruyter.

Best, J. (2001c). Social progress and social problems: Toward a sociology of gloom. *Sociological Quarterly* 42: 1–12.

Best, J. (2011). If this goes on . . . : The rhetorical construction of future problems. In T. van Haaften, H. Jansen, J. de Jong, & W. Koetsenruijter (Eds.), *Bending opinion: Essays on persuasion in the public domain* (pp. 203–217). Leiden, Netherlands: Leiden University Press.

Best, J., & Furedi, F. (2001). The evolution of road rage in Britain and the United States. In J. Best (Ed.), *How claims spread: Cross-national diffusion of social problems* (pp. 107–127). Hawthorne, NY: Aldine de Gruyter.

Best, J., & Lowney, K. S. (2009). The disadvantage of a good reputation: Disney as a target for social problems claims. *Sociological Quarterly* 50: 431–449.

Best, R. (2010). Situation or social problem: The influence of events on media coverage of homelessness. *Social Problems* 57: 74–91.

Bishop, G. F. (2005). *The illusion of public opinion: Fact and artifact in American public opinion polls.* Lanham, MD: Rowman & Littlefield.

Blumer, H. (1971). Social problems as collective behavior. *Social Problems* 18: 298–306.

Bogard, C. J. (2003). *Seasons such as these: How homelessness took shape in America.* Hawthorne, NY: Aldine de Gruyter.

Bronner, S. J. (1988). Political suicide: The Bud Dwyer joke cycle and the humor of disaster. *Midwestern Folklore* 14: 81–89.

Bronner, S. J. (2008). *Killing tradition: Inside hunting and animal rights controversies.* Lexington: University Press of Kentucky.

Brown, J. D. (1991). The professional ex-. *Sociological Quarterly* 32: 219–230.

Brown, P. (1992). Popular epidemiology and toxic waste contamination: Lay and professional ways of knowing. *Journal of Health and Social Behavior* 33: 267–281.

Bruch, S. K., Ferree, M. M., & Soss, J. (2010). From policy to polity: Democracy, paternalism, and the incorporation of disadvantaged citizens. *American Sociological Review* 75: 205–226.

Brunsma, D. L. (2004). *The school uniform movement and what it tells us about American education.* Lanham, MD: ScarecrowEducation.

Burgess, A. (2004). *Cellular phones, public fears, and a culture of precaution.* Cambridge, UK: Cambridge University Press.

Burgess, A., Donovan, P., & Moore, S. E. H. (2009). Embodying uncertainty: Understanding heightened risk perception of drink "spiking." *British Journal of Criminology* 49: 848–862.

Burstein, P. (1991). Policy domains: Organization, culture, and policy outcomes. *Annual Review of Sociology* 17: 327–350.

Burstein, P. (1998). Bringing the public back in: Should sociologists consider the impact of public opinion on public policy? *Social Forces* 77: 27–62.

Burstein, P. (2006). Why estimates of the impact of public opinion on public policy are too high: Empirical and theoretical implications. *Social Forces* 84: 2273–2289.

Burstein, P., & Hirsch, C. E. (2007). Interest organizations, information, and policy innovation in the U.S. Congress. *Sociological Forum* 22: 174–199.

Burstein, P., & Linton, A. (2002). The impact of political parties, interest groups, and social movement organizations on public policy: Some recent evidence and theoretical concerns. *Social Forces* 81: 380–408.

Campion-Vincent, V. (2005). *Organ theft legends.* Jackson: University Press of Mississippi.

Ceobanu, A. M., & Escandell, X. (2010). Comparative analyses of public attitudes toward immigrants and immigration using multinational survey data: A review of theories and research. *Annual Review of Sociology* 36: 309–328.

Chalfen, R. (2009). "It's only a picture": Sexting, "smutty" snapshots, and felony charges. *Visual Studies* 24: 258–268.

Chambliss, D. F. (1996). *Beyond caring: Hospitals, nurses, and the social organization of ethics.* Chicago: University of Chicago Press.

Cherry, E. (2010). Shifting symbolic boundaries: Cultural strategies of the animal rights movement. *Sociological Forum* 25: 450–475.

Clarke, A. E., Shim, J. K., Mamo, L., Fosket, J. R., & Fishman, J. R. (2003). Biomedicalization: Technoscientific transformations of health, illness, and U.S. biomedicine. *American Sociological Review* 68: 161–194.

Cole, M., & Morgan, K. (2011). Vegaphobia: Deregatory discourses of veganism and the reproduction of speciesism in UK national newspapers. *British Journal of Sociology* 62: 134–153.

Conrad, P. (2007). *The medicalization of society: On the transformation of human conditions into treatable disorders.* Baltimore: Johns Hopkins University Press.

Cradock, G. (2011). Thinking Goudge: Fatal child abuse and the problem of uncertainty. *Current Sociology* 59: 362–378.

Dabney, D. (2010). Observations regarding key operational realities in a Compstat model of policing. *Justice Quarterly* 27: 28–51.

Daniels, J. (2009). Cloaked websites: Propaganda, cyber-racism and epistemology in the digital era. *New Media and Society* 11: 659–683.

Davis, P. W. (1994). The changing meanings of spanking. In J. Best (Ed.), *Troubling children* (pp. 133–153). Hawthorne, NY: Aldine de Gruyter.

de Vaus, D. A. (1986). *Surveys in social research*. London: Allen & Unwin.

DeGloma, T. (2009). Expanding trauma through space and time: Mapping the rhetorical strategies of trauma carrier groups. *Social Psychology Quarterly* 72: 105–122.

Del Rosso, J. (2011). The textual mediation of denial: Congress, Abu Ghraib, and the construction of an isolated incident. *Social Problems* 58: 165–188.

Dickson, D. T. (1968). Bureaucracy and morality: An organizational perspective on a moral crusade. *Social Problems* 16: 143–156.

Dobbin, F. (2009). *Inventing equal opportunity*. Princeton, NJ: Princeton University Press.

Doezema, J. (2010). *Sex slaves and discourse masters: The construction of trafficking*. London: Zed.

Donovan, B. (2006). *White slave crusades: Race, gender, and anti-vice activism, 1887–1917*. Urbana: University of Illinois Press.

Downs, A. (1972). Up and down with ecology—The "issue-attention cycle." *Public Interest* 28: 38–50.

Dundes, A. (1987). *Cracking jokes*. Berkeley, CA: Ten Speed Press.

Dundes, A., & Pagter, C. R. (2000). *Why don't sheep shrink when it rains? A further collection of photocopier folklore*. Syracuse, NY: Syracuse University Press.

Dunn, J. L. (2010). *Judging victims: Why we stigmatize survivors, and how they reclaim respect*. Boulder, CO: Lynne Reinner.

Eaton, M. (2010). Manufacturing community in an online activist organization: The rhetoric of MoveOn.org's e-mails. *Information, Communication and Society* 13: 174–192.

Ellis, B. (1991). The last thing said: The *Challenger* disaster jokes and closure. *International Folklore Review* 8: 110–124.

Ellis, B. (2001). *Aliens, ghosts, and cults: Legends we live*. Jackson: University Press of Mississippi.

Ellis, B. (2003). Making a Big Apple crumble: The role of humor in constructing a global response to disaster. In P. Narváez (Ed.), *Of corpse: Death and humor in folklore and popular culture* (pp. 35–79). Logan: Utah State University Press.

Erchak, G. M., & Rosenfeld, R. (1989). Learning disabilities, dyslexia, and the medicalization of the classroom. In J. Best (Ed.), *Images of issues: Typifying contemporary social problems* (pp. 79–97). Hawthorne, NY: Aldine de Gruyter.

Erikson, K. T. (1976). *Everything in its path: Destruction of community in the Buffalo Creek flood*. New York: Simon and Schuster.

Fassin, D., & Rechtman, R. (2009). *The empire of trauma: An inquiry into the condition of victimhood*. Princeton, NJ: Princeton University Press.

Fine, G. A. (1992). *Manufacturing tales: Sex and money in contemporary legends.* Knoxville: University of Tennessee Press.

Fine, G. A. (2007). *Authors of the storm: Meteorologists and the culture of prediction.* Chicago: University of Chicago Press.

Fine, G. A., Campion-Vincent, V., & Heath, C. (Eds.). (2005). *Rumor mills: The social impact of rumor and legend.* New Brunswick, NJ: AldineTransaction.

Fine, G. A., & Christoforides, L. (1991). Dirty birds, filthy immigrants, and the English sparrow war: Metaphorical linkage in constructing social problems. *Symbolic Interaction* 14: 375–393.

Fine, G. A., & Ellis, B. (2010). *The global grapevine: Why rumors of terrorism, immigration, and trade matter.* New York: Oxford University Press.

Fine, G. A., & McDonnell, T. (2007). Erasing the brown scare: Referential afterlife and the power of memory templates. *Social Problems* 54: 170–187.

Fine, G. A., & Turner, P. A. (2001). *Whispers on the color line: Rumor and race in America.* Berkeley: University of California Press.

Fischer, D. H. (1989). *Albion's seed: Four British folkways in America.* New York: Oxford University Press.

Foderaro, L. W., & Hu, W. (2010, October 1). Online musings point to student's state of mind before a suicide. *New York Times*, p. 17.

Freidson, E. (1986). *Professional powers: A study of the institutionalization of formal knowledge.* Chicago: University of Chicago Press.

Fujiwara, L. H. (2005). Immigrant rights are human rights: The reframing of immigrant entitlement and welfare. *Social Problems* 52: 79–101.

Fumento, M. (1990). *The myth of heterosexual AIDS.* New York: Basic Books.

Furedi, F. (2001). Bullying: The British contribution to the construction of a social problem. In J. Best (Ed.), *How claims spread: Cross-national diffusion of social problems* (pp. 89–106). Hawthorne, NY: Aldine de Gruyter.

Gallup. (2011). Trends A–Z. Retrieved from http://www.gallup.com/poll/trends .aspx.

Gamson, W. A. (1992). *Talking politics.* New York: Cambridge University Press.

Gamson, W. A., & Modigliani, A. (1989). Media discourse and public opinion on nuclear power: A constructionist approach. *American Journal of Sociology* 95: 1–37.

Gans, H. J. (1979). *Deciding what's news.* New York: Pantheon.

Gitlin, T. (1983). *Inside prime time.* New York: Pantheon.

Goedeke, T. L. (2005). Devils, angels, or animals: The social construction of otters in conflict over management. In A. Herda-Rapp & T. L. Godeke (Eds.), *Mad over wildlife: Looking at social conflict over wildlife* (pp. 25–50). Boston: Brill.

Goldstein, D. E. (2004). *Once upon a virus: AIDS legends and vernacular risk perception.* Logan: Utah State University Press.

Goss, K. A. (2006). *Disarmed: The missing movement for gun control in America.* Princeton, NJ: Princeton University Press.

Gould, D. B. (2009). *Moving politics: Emotion and ACT-UP's fights against AIDS.* Chicago: University of Chicago Press.

Gunter, V. (2005). News media and technological risks: The case of pesticides after *Silent Spring. Sociological Quarterly* 46: 671–698.

Gusfield, J. R. (1967). Moral passage: The symbolic process in public designations of deviance. *Social Problems* 15: 175–188.

Gusfield, J. R. (1981). *The culture of public problems: Drinking-driving and the symbolic order.* Chicago: University of Chicago Press.

Haines, H. H. (1984). Black radicalism and the funding of civil rights. *Social Problems* 32: 31–43.

Halfmann, D., & Young, M. P. (2010). War pictures: The grotesque as a mobilizing tactic. *Mobilization* 15: 1–24.

Hamilton, J. T. (2004). *All the news that's fit to sell: How the market transforms information into news.* Princeton, NJ: Princeton University Press.

Harris, S. R. (2010). *What is constructionism? Navigating its use in sociology.* Boulder, CO: Lynne Reinner.

Heath, C., Bell, C., & Sternberg, E. (2001). Emotional selection in memes: The case of urban legends. *Journal of Personality and Social Psychology* 81: 1028–1041.

Heller, J. (2008). *The vaccine narrative.* Nashville, TN: Vanderbilt University Press.

Herda-Rapp, A., & Godeke T. L., (Eds.). (2005). *Mad over wildlife: Looking at social conflict over wildlife* (pp. 73–96). Boston: Brill.

Hilgartner, S., & Bosk, C. L. (1988). The rise and fall of social problems. *American Journal of Sociology* 94: 53–78.

Holstein, J. A., & Gubrium, J. F. (Eds.). (2008). *Handbook of constructionist research.* New York: Guilford.

Holstein, J. A., & Miller, G. (Eds.). (2003a). *Challenges and choices: Constructionist perspectives on social problems.* Hawthorne, NY: Aldine de Gruyter.

Holstein, J. A., & Miller, G. (2003b). Social constructionism and social problems work. In J. A. Holstein & G. Miller (Eds.), *Challenges and choices: Constructionist perspectives on social problems* (pp. 70–91). Hawthorne, NY: Aldine de Gruyter.

Irvine, J. M. (2002). *Talk about sex: The battles over sex education in the United States.* Berkeley: University of California Press.

Jacobs, L. R., & Skocpol, T. (2010). *Health care reform and American politics: What everyone needs to know.* New York: Oxford University Press.

Järvinen, M., & Miller, G. (2010). Methadone maintenance as last resort: A social phenomenology of a drug policy. *Sociological Forum* 25: 804–823.

Jenkins, P. (1998). *Moral panic: Changing concepts of the child molester in modern America.* New Haven, CT: Yale University Press.

Jenkins, P. (1999). *Synthetic panics: The symbolic politics of designer drugs.* New York: New York University Press.

Jenkins, P. (2000). *Mystics and messiahs: Cults and new religions in American history.* New York: Oxford University Press.

Jenkins, P. (2001). *Hidden gospels: How the search for Jesus lost its way.* New York: Oxford University Press.

Jenkins, P. (2006). *Decade of nightmares: The end of the sixties and the making of eighties America.* New York: Oxford University Press.

Jenness, V. (1993). *Making it work: The prostitutes' rights movement in perspective.* Hawthorne, NY: Aldine de Gruyter.

Jenness, V., & Grattet, R. (2001). *Making hate a crime: From social movement to law enforcement.* New York: Russell Sage Foundation.

Jenness, V., & Grattet, R. (2005). The law-in-between: The effects of organizational perviousness on the policing of hate crime. *Social Problems* 52: 227–259.

Jerolmack, C. (2008). How pigeons became rats: The cultural-spatial logic of problem animals. *Social Problems* 55: 72–94.

Johnson, J. M. (1995). Horror stories and the construction of child abuse. In J. Best (Ed.), *Images of issues: Typifying contemporary social problems* (2nd ed., pp. 17–31). Hawthorne, NY: Aldine de Gruyter.

Keys, J. (2010). Running the gauntlet: Women's use of emotion management techniques in the abortion experience. *Symbolic Interaction* 33: 41–70.

Kiel, D. C., & Nownes, A. J. (1994). Political language, causal stories, and pesticide regulation. *American Review of Politics* 15: 491–506.

Kingdon, J. W. (1984). *Agendas, alternatives, and public policies.* New York: HarperCollins.

Kirk, S. A., & Kutchins, H. (1992). *The selling of DSM: The rhetoric of science in psychiatry.* Hawthorne, NY: Aldine de Gruyter.

Kitta, A. (2011). *Vaccinations and public concern in history: Legend, rumor, and risk perception.* New York: Routledge.

Kohm, S. A. (2009). Naming, shaming, and criminal justice: Mass-mediated humiliation as entertainment and punishment. *Crime Media Culture* 5: 188–205.

Kollmeyer, C. J. (2004). Corporate interests: How the news media portray the economy. *Social Problems* 51: 432–452.

Kubal, T. (2008). *Cultural movements and collective memory: Christopher Columbus and the rewriting of the national origin myth.* New York: Palgrave Macmillan.

Kurti, L. (1988). The politics of joking: Popular response to Chernobyl. *Journal of American Folklore* 101: 324–334.

Lafer, G. (2002). *The job training charade.* Ithaca, NY: Cornell University Press.

Langlois, J. (1983). The Belle Isle Bridge incident: Legend, dialectic and semiotic system in the 1943 Detroit race riots. *Journal of American Folklore* 96: 183–196.

Langlois, J. (2005). "Celebrating Arabs": Tracing legend and rumor labyrinths in post-9/11 Detroit. *Journal of American Folklore* 118: 219–236.

Lee, E. (2003). *Abortion, motherhood, and mental health: Medicalizing reproduction in the United States and Great Britain.* Hawthorne, NY: Aldine de Gruyter.

Leon, C. S. (2011). *Sex fiends, perverts, and pedophiles: Understanding sex crime policy in America.* New York: New York University Press.

Leon-Guerrero, A. (2011). *Social problems: Community, policy, and social action* (3rd ed.). Los Angeles: Pine Forge.

Lewis, M. (2010). *The big short: Inside the doomsday machine.* New York: Norton.

Lin, Y-C. J. (2011). *Fake stuff: China and the rise of counterfeit goods.* New York: Routledge.

Link, M. W., Battaglia, M. P., Frankel, M. R., Osborn, L., & Mokdad, A. H. (2007). Reaching the U.S. cell phone generation: Comparison of cell phone survey results with an ongoing landline telephone survey. *Public Opinion Quarterly* 71: 814–839.

Lipsky, M. (1980). *Street-level bureaucracy: Dilemmas of the individual in public services.* New York: Russell Sage Foundation.

Lipsky, M., & Smith, S. R. (1989). When social problems are treated as emergencies. *Social Service Review* 63: 5–25.

Liu, K-Y., King, M., & Bearman, P. S. (2010). Social influence and the autism epidemic. *American Journal of Sociology* 115: 1387–1434.

Lofland, J. (2003). *Demolishing a historic hotel: A sociology of preservation failure in Davis, California.* Davis, CA: Davis Research.

Loseke, D. R. (2003). *Thinking about social problems* (2nd ed.). Hawthorne, NY: Aldine de Gruyter.

Lowe, P. K., & Lee, E. J. (2010). Advocating alcohol abstinence to pregnant women: Some observations about British policy. *Health, Risk and Society* 12: 301–311.

Lowney, K. S. (1999). *Baring our souls: TV talk shows and the religion of recovery.* Hawthorne, NY: Aldine de Gruyter.

Lowney, K. S., & Best, J. (1995). Stalking strangers and lovers: Changing media typifications of a new crime problem. In J. Best (Ed.), *Images of issues: Typifying contemporary social problems* (2nd ed., pp. 33–57). Hawthorne, NY: Aldine de Gruyter.

Lowney, K. S., & Best, J. (1996). What Waco stood for: Jokes as popular constructions of social problems. *Perspectives on Social Problems* 8: 77–98.

MacCoun, R. J., & Reuter, P. (2001). *Drug war heresies: Learning from other vices, times, and places.* New York: Cambridge University Press.

Mackinem, M. B., & Higgins, P. (2008). *Drug court: Constructing the moral identity of drug offenders.* Springfield, IL: Charles C. Thomas.

Malloy, T. F. (2010). The social construction of regulation: Lessons from the war against command and control. *Buffalo Law Review* 58: 267–354.

Maratea, R. (2008). The e-rise and fall of social problems: The blogosphere as a public arena. *Social Problems* 55: 139–160.

Marin, R., & Dokoupil, T. (2011, April 25). Dead suit walking. *Newsweek*, pp. 30–36.

Martin, D. (2010). Identity management of the dead: Contests in the construction of murdered children. *Symbolic Interaction* 33: 18–40.

Maurer, D. (2002). *Vegetarianism: Movement or moment?* Philadelphia: Temple University Press.

McAdam, D. (1983). Tactical innovation and the pace of insurgency. *American Sociological Review* 48: 735–754.

McAdam, D. (1994). Culture and social movements. In E. Laraña, H. Johnston, & J. R. Gusfield (Eds.), *New social movements: From identity to ideology* (pp. 36–57). Philadelphia: Temple University Press.

McAdam, D., & Rucht, D. (1993). The cross-national diffusion of movement ideas. *Annals of the American Academy of Political and Social Science* 528: 56–74.

McCarthy, J. D., & Zald, M. N. (1977). Resource mobilization and social movements. *American Journal of Sociology* 82: 1212–1241.

McCombs, M. (2004). *Setting the agenda: The mass media and public opinion.* Cambridge, UK: Polity.

Miller, G., & Holstein, J. A. (Eds.). (1997). *Social problems in everyday life: Studies of social problems work.* Greenwich, CT: JAI Press.

Mills, C. W. (1959). *The sociological imagination.* New York: Oxford University Press.

Monahan, B. A. (2010). *The shock of the news: Media coverage and the making of 9/11.* New York: New York University Press.

Mooney, P. H., & Hunt, S. A. (2009). Food security: The elaboration of contested claims to a consensus frame. *Rural Sociology* 74: 469–497.

Murray, C. A. (1994). *Losing ground: American social policy, 1950–1980.* New York: Basic Books.

National Highway Traffic Safety Administration. (2011, April 1). Traffic fatalities in 2010 drop to lowest level in recorded history. Retrieved from http://www.nhtsa.gov/NHTSA-05-11.

Nelson, B. J. (1984). *Making an issue of child abuse: Political agenda setting for social problems.* Chicago: University of Chicago Press.

Nichols, L. T. (1997). Social problems as landmark narratives: Bank of Boston, mass media and "money laundering." *Social Problems* 44: 324–341.

Nichols, L. T. (2003). Voices of social problems: A dialogical constructionist model. *Studies in Symbolic Interaction* 26: 93–123.

Nichols, L. T., Nolan, J. J., III, & Colyer, C. J. (2008). Scorekeeping versus storytelling: Representational practices in the construction of "hate crime." *Studies in Symbolic Interaction* 30: 361–379.

Noy, D. (2009). When framing fails: Ideas, influence, and resources in San Francisco's homeless policy field. *Social Problems* 56: 223–242.

Oberlander, J. (2003). *The political life of Medicare.* Chicago: University of Chicago Press.

Offit, P. A. (2008). *Autism's false prophets: Bad science, risky medicine, and the search for a cure.* New York: Columbia University Press.

Oring, E. (1987). Jokes and the discourse on disaster. *Journal of American Folklore* 100: 278–286.

Ostertag, S. F. (2010). Processing culture: Cognition, ontology, and the news media. *Sociological Forum* 25: 824–850.

Pawluch, D. (1996). *The new pediatrics: A profession in transition.* Hawthorne, NY: Aldine de Gruyter.

Pearson, G. (1983). *Hooligan: A history of respectable fears.* London: Macmillan.

Perez, V. W. (2010). The rhetoric of science and statistics in claims of an autism epidemic. *Advances in Medical Sociology* 11: 203–221.

Pfohl, S. J. (1977). The "discovery" of child abuse. *Social Problems* 24: 310–323.

Pielke, R. A., Jr. (2007). *The honest broker: Making sense of science in policy and politics.* New York: Cambridge University Press.

Polletta, F., and Lee, J. (2006). Is telling stories good for democracy? Rhetoric in public deliberation after 9/11. *American Sociological Review* 71: 699–723.

Preves, S. E. (2003). *Intersex and identity: The contested self.* New Brunswick, NJ: Rutgers University Press.

Ravitch, D. (2003). *The language police: How pressure groups restrict what students learn.* New York: Vintage.

Reinarman, C. (1994). The social construction of drug scares. In P. A. Adler & P. Adler (Eds.), *Constructions of deviance* (pp. 92–104). Belmont, CA: Wadsworth.

Reinarman, C., & Levine, H. G. (1995). The crack attack: America's latest drug scare, 1986–1992. In J. Best (Ed.), *Images of issues: Typifying contemporary social problems* (2nd ed., pp. 147–186). Hawthorne, NY: Aldine de Gruyter.

Rodriquez, J. (2011). "It's a dignity thing": Nursing home care workers use of emotion. *Sociological Forum* 26: 265–286.

Rohlinger, D. A. (2006). Friends and foes: Media, politics, and tactics in the abortion war. *Social Problems* 53: 537–561.

Rosenberg, I. B. (2009). Height discrimination in employment. *Utah Law Review* 2009: 907–953.

Rossi, P. H., Lipsey, M. W., & Freeman, H. E. (2004). *Evaluation: A systematic approach* (7th ed.). Thousand Oaks, CA: Sage.

Rudy, D. R. (1986). *Becoming alcoholic: Alcoholics Anonymous and the reality of alcoholism.* Carbondale: Southern Illinois University Press.

Saguy, A. C. (2003). *What is sexual harassment? From Capitol Hill to the Sorbonne*. Berkeley: University of California Press.

Saguy, A. C., Gruys, K., & Gong, S. (2010). Social problem construction and national context: News reporting on "overweight" and "obesity" in the United States and France. *Social Problems* 57: 586–610.

Saguy, A. C., & Riley, K. W. (2005). Weighing both sides: Morality, mortality, and framing contests over obesity. *Journal of Health Politics, Policy and Law* 30: 869–921.

Saletan, W. (2003). *Bearing right: How the conservatives won the abortion war*. Berkeley: University of California Press.

Sample, L. L., & Kadleck, C. (2008). Sex offender laws: Legislators' accounts of the need for policy. *Criminal Justice Policy Review* 19: 40–62.

Santa Ana, O. (2009). Did you call in Mexican? The racial politics of Jay Leno immigrant jokes. *Language in Society* 38: 23–45.

Sasson, T. (1995a). African American conspiracy theories and the social construction of crime. *Sociological Inquiry* 65: 265–285.

Sasson, T. (1995b). *Crime talk: How citizens construct a social problem*. Hawthorne, NY: Aldine de Gruyter.

Schneider, A. L., & Ingram, H. M. (1993). Social constructions of target populations: Implications for politics and policy. *American Political Science Review* 87: 334–347.

Schneider, A. L., & Ingram, H. M. (Eds.). (2005). *Deserving and entitled: Social constructions and public policy*. Albany: State University of New York Press.

Schudson, M. (2003). *The sociology of news*. New York: Norton.

Schuldt, J. P., Konrath, S. H., & Schwarz, N. (2011). "Global warming" or "climate change"? Whether the planet is warming depends on question wording. *Public Opinion Quarterly* 75: 115–124.

Schwartz, B. (2009). Collective forgetting and the symbolic power of oneness: The strange apotheosis of Rosa Parks. *Social Psychology Quarterly* 72: 123–142.

Schwartz, H. (2011). *Making noise: From Babel to the Big Bang and beyond*. Cambridge: MIT Press.

Schwartz, J. (2010, October 3). Bullying, suicide, punishment. *New York Times*, p. WK1.

Scotch, R. K. (2001). *From good will to civil rights: Transforming federal disability policy* (2nd ed.). Philadelphia: Temple University Press.

Segovia, F., & Defever, R. (2010). The polls—trends: American public opinion on immigrants and immigration policy. *Public Opinion Quarterly* 74: 375–394.

Shibutani, T. (1966). *Improvised news: A sociological study of rumor*. Indianapolis, IN: Bobbs-Merrill.

Shiller, R. J. (2008). *The subprime solution: How today's global financial crisis happened, and what to do about it*. Princeton, NJ: Princeton University Press.

Shostak, S., Conrad, P., & Horwitz, A. V. (2008). Sequencing and its consequences: Path dependence and the relationships between genetics and medicalization. *American Journal of Sociology* 114: S287–S316.

Shwed, U., & Bearman, P. S. (2010). The temporal structure of scientific consensus formation. *American Sociological Review* 75: 817–840.

Silver, I. (2006). *Unequal partnerships: Beyond the rhetoric of philanthropic collaboration.* New York: Routledge.

Silver, I., & Boyle, M-E. (2010). Constructing problems by promoting solutions: Corporate advertisements about U.S. poverty. *Journal of Poverty* 14: 347–367.

Sloan, J. J., Jr., & Fisher, B. S. (2011). *The dark side of the ivory tower: Campus crime as a social problem.* New York: Cambridge University Press.

Snow, D., & Benford, R. (1988). Ideology, frame resonance, and participant mobilization. *International Social Movement Research* 1: 197–217.

Snow, D., & Benford, R. (1992). Master frames and cycles of protest. In A. D. Morris & C. M. Mueller (Eds.), *Frontiers in social movement theory* (pp. 133–155). New Haven, CT: Yale University Press.

Snow, D. A., Rochford, E. B., Jr., Worden, S. K., & Benford, R. D. (1986). Frame alignment processes, micromobilization, and movement participation. *American Sociological Review* 51: 464–481.

Sobieraj, S. (2011). *Soundbitten: The perils of media-centered political activism.* New York: New York University Press.

Sousa, A. C. (2011). From refrigerator mothers to warrior-heroes: The cultural identity transformation of mothers raising children with intellectual disabilities. *Symbolic Interaction* 34: 220–243.

Spector, M., & Kitsuse, J. I. (1977). *Constructing social problems.* Menlo Park, CA: Cummings.

Spencer, J. W. (2011). *The paradox of youth violence.* Boulder, CO: Lynne Reinner.

Staller, K. M. (2006). *Runaways: How the sixties counterculture shaped today's policies and practices.* New York: Columbia University Press.

Starr, P. (1982). *The social transformation of American medicine.* New York: Basic Books.

Stein, R. (2004, March 10). Obesity passing smoking as top avoidable cause of death. *The Washington Post,* p. A1.

Stone, D. A. (1989). Causal stories and the formation of policy agendas. *Political Science Quarterly* 104: 281–300.

Strang, D., & Meyer, J. W. (1993). Institutional conditions for diffusion. *Theory and Society* 22: 487–511.

Suarez, E., & Gadalla, T. M. (2010). Stop blaming the victim: A meta-analysis on rape myths. *Journal of Interpersonal Violence* 25: 2010–2035.

Taylor, V. (1989). Social movement continuity: The women's movement in abeyance. *American Sociological Review* 54: 761–775.

Tetlock, P. E. (2005). *Expert political judgment: How good is it? How can we know?* Princeton, NJ: Princeton University Press.

Toulmin, S. E. (1958). *The uses of argument.* Cambridge, UK: Cambridge University Press.

Tuchman, G. (1978). *Making news: A study in the construction of reality.* New York: Free Press.

Turow, J. (1997). *Breaking up America: Advertisers and the new media world.* Chicago: University of Chicago Press.

Tyson, N. d. (2009). *The Pluto files: The rise and fall of America's favorite planet.* New York: Norton.

U.S. Census Bureau. (1975). *Historical statistics of the United States: Colonial times to 1970.* Washington, DC: U.S. Government Printing Office.

Uggen, C., & Shinohara, C. (2009). Sexual harassment comes of age: A comparative analysis of the United States and Japan. *Sociological Quarterly* 50: 201–234.

Useem, B., & Zald, M. N. (1982). From pressure groups of social movement: Organizational dilemmas of the effort to promote nuclear power. *Social Problems* 30: 144–156.

Vasterman, P. L. M. (2005). Media-hype: Self-reinforcing news waves, journalistic standards, and the construction of social problems. *European Journal of Communication* 20: 508–530.

Vaughan, D. (2006). The social shaping of commission reports. *Sociological Forum* 21: 291–306.

Walker, E. T., McCarthy, J. D., & Baumgartner, F. (2011). Replacing members with managers? Mutualism among membership and nonmembership advocacy organizations in the United States. *American Journal of Sociology* 116: 1284–1337.

Watts, D. J. (2011). *Everything is obvious: Once you know the answer.* New York: Crown Business.

Weidenbaum, M. (2009). *The competition of ideas: The world of Washington think tanks.* New Brunswick, NJ: Transaction.

Weisner, C., & Room, R. (1984). Financing and ideology in alcohol treatment. *Social Problems* 32: 167–184.

Welch, M. (2000). *Flag burning: Moral panic and the criminalization of protest.* Hawthorne, NY: Aldine de Gruyter.

White, L. (2000). *Speaking of vampires: Rumor and history in colonial Africa.* Berkeley: University of California Press.

Whittier, N. (2009). *The politics of child sexual abuse: Emotions, social movements, and the state.* New York: Oxford University Press.

Zegart, A. B. (2004). Blue ribbons, black boxes: Toward a better understanding of presidential commissions. *Presidential Studies Quarterly* 34: 366–393.

Index

Note: Page numbers in *italics* refer to illustrations and examples.

AA, *see* Alcoholics Anonymous (AA)
abeyance, 85
abolitionist movement, 69
abortion debates
  intensity of, 41
  media coverage and, 153
abortion experience, managing, 248
abortion issue
  allies, opportunities, and, 84
  framing of, 81
  "partial-birth" (third-trimester),
    campaign against, 69
  surveys on, 163–64
abortion rights movements, 67
Abu Ghraib, 212
activists as claimsmakers, 18, 20,
  64–95
  alliances and, 77
  case study of, *93–95*
  criticism of policy outcomes,
    267–69, 270
  framing and, 67–73, *90*, 91, 92
    cultural resources and, 73
    diagnostic frames, 68

    disputes within a movement over,
      72, 73
    feedback and reframing, 72,
      73, 74
    frame alignment, 70–72
    grotesque images and, 69
    integrity issues in, 73
    motivational frames, 68
    prognostic frames, 68–69
  insider claimsmakers, 65, *65*–66
    see also experts as claimsmakers
  opportunity structures and, 80–85,
    90, 92
    cultural opportunities, 79–80
    political opportunities, 81–85
  outsider claimsmakers, 64–65, *65*, 196
  ownership of a social problem, *see*
    ownership of a social
    problem
  principles, practicalities, and, *90*,
    90–92
  private policymaking and, 228–30
  resource mobilization and, 73–80,
    90, 91

administrative agencies, policymaking by, 191, 203
adolescent runaways, 201
adopters, 294–95, 296–97
agenda setting, 153–54, 193–94
AIDS
    alarmist warnings in the late 1980s about, 311
    contemporary legends relating to, 177–78
    identification of, 56
alcohol, pregnancy and, 260
Alcoholics Anonymous (AA), 101–2, 230, 239–40
alcoholism, 101–2, 211, 230
American Enterprise Institute, 115
American Psychiatric Association, 101
animal rights activists, 61–63
animals, case study on social problems claims about, 61–63
antiabortion movement, 66, 69, 78
antidrug campaigns, 324
antidrug policies, 261
antisparrow campaign, 306
apocalyptic rhetoric, 310–12
appellate courts, 191, 276–78
arenas for social problems, 129, 192
audience segmentation by the media, 137–38, 142
audiences for claims, 40–47, 58, 59, 320
    appealing to the broadest possible audience, 44–45
    creating a consensus, 44–45
    preaching to the choir, 43
    revising claims based on audience reaction, 45–47, 320
    as segmented, 42–43
    social problems marketplace and, 46–47, 47
autism epidemics, 123–26

battered child syndrome, 48–49, 102, 118–19
    see also child abuse
beneficiaries of social movements, 76
berdaches, 12
bias in media coverage, 127–28, 129–30
biomedicalization, 104
blogs, 140
Bogard, Cynthia, 288–89
Brady Center to Prevent Gun Violence, 86
Brookings Institution, 115
bullying
    homophobic, case study of mobilizing against, 93–95
    workplace, 298–99
bureaucratic hierarchies, 224

carrying capacity of media sources, 129, 137, 140
Carson, Rachel, 110
cases in social problems work, construction of, 231–37
case studies, 286–87
    on activists as claimsmakers, 93–95
    on claims, 61–63
    of claims across time and space, 315–17
    on expert claimsmakers, 123–26
    on media coverage, 157–59
    on policymaking, 218–20
    on policy outcomes, 283–85
    pros and cons of, 288
    on public reaction, 187–89
    on social problems work, 251–53
Cato Institute, 115
causal stories, 208–11, 212, 213
CBS News, 212
cell phones, 284–85, 292
Ceres, 13

Challenger
  commission on, 277
  jokes about, 181, 182
child abuse
  audience for claims about, 41
  battered child syndrome, 48–49,
      102, 118–19
  death caused by, 263
  domain of, 48–49
  as example of grounds of claims,
      32, 33
  policy responses to, 269
  sexual, 151, 302–4
  spanking as, 54–55
"Christian anarchists," 288
Civil Rights Act of 1964, 17
  human resource workers' role in, 238
  Johnson's signing of, 21
civil rights movement, 17–23, 85
  frames and, 66, 75–76
  history of tactical choices in, 82–83
  momentum in the early 1960s,
      81–82
  ownership and, 87
claimants, 40
claims, 18, 29–63
  audiences for, 40–47, 59, 320
    appealing to the broadest possible
        audience, 44–45
    creating a consensus, 44–45
    preaching to the choir, 43
    revising claims based on audience
        reaction, 45–46, 320
    as segmented, 42–43
    social problems marketplace and,
        46–47, 47
  case study on, 61–63
  cultural resources and, 54–57, 58, 59
  definition of, 14, 15, 18
  dynamics shaping and, 58
  evolution of, 48–53, 59

counterclaims, 51–53, 52
  domain expansion, 48–49, 50
  piggybacking, 49–51
  linked to ideologies, 53
  primary, 128
  rhetoric of, 30–40
    conclusions, 31, 31, 38–40
    grounds, 31, 31–36
    warrants, 31, 36–38, 39
  secondary, 128
claims across time and space, 286–317,
    325–26
  case study of, 315–17
  comparative research and, 287–92,
      291, 314
    bases for, 289–90, 291
    construction of social problems
        and, differences in, 291–92
  cycles in claimsmaking, *see* cycles in
      claimsmaking
  diffusion and, 292–99
    common language and, 295, 296
    globalization and, 299
    nonrelational channels and,
        295–96
    relational channels and, 295–96
    social arrangements and, 297–99
    successful, elements of, 294
    theorization and, 297
    transmitters and adopters in,
        294–95, 296–97
  progress and, problem of, 307–13
claimsmakers, 40
  activists as, *see* activists as
      claimsmakers
  definition of, 15
  dispossessed, 141
  experts as, *see* experts as claimsmakers
claimsmaking
  cycles in, 299–307, 314
    examples of, 302–3

claimsmaking (*continued*)
    in other societies, 304
    periods in U.S. history favoring
        claimsmaking, 306–7
    tensions along societal fault lines
        and, 304–6, 307
    definition of, 15–16
    as a social problems process stage,
        18, *19*, 20
    think tanks and, 115
claustrophobia, 100
climate change, 164
    see also global warming
cloaked Web sites, 139
coercion in social problems work, 241
collective memories, 301
Columbia, 277
commissions to examine policy outcomes,
    275–76, 277, 278
committee system, legislative, 198, 200
comparative research, 287–92, *291*, 314
    bases for, 289–90, *291*
    construction of social problems and,
        differences in, 291–92
Compstat model, 229
conclusions of claims, 31, *31*, 38–40
condensing symbols, 146
Congress of Racial Equality (CORE),
    17, 20, 66
    confrontational activities and, 87
    frames of, 76
conscience constituents, 76–77
consensus, crafting claims to create,
    44–45
constituents of social movements, 76, 78
constructionist approach
    misconceptions about, 16
    terminology of, 14–16
    uses of, 325–29
    see also social problems process
contemporary legends, 173–74, *175–76*,
    176–78, *179*

CORE, *see* Congress of Racial Equality
    (CORE)
counterclaims, 51–53, *52*, *58*
countermovements, 66–67
courts, appellate, 191, 276–78
crime
    on college campuses, 268
    focus groups and, 170
    hate, 201
    media coverage of, 145, 167
cults, 303
cultural opportunities to promote
    activists' claims, 79–80
cultural resources
    claims and, 54–57, *58*, 59
    framing and, 73
    packages drawing on, 146, *155*
cyberbullying, *93–94*
cycles in claimsmaking, 299–307, 314
    examples of, 302–3
    in other societies, 304
    periods in U.S. history favoring
        claimsmaking, 306–7
    tensions along societal fault lines
        and, 304–6, 307

Dateline NBC: To Catch a Predator, 151
dead-baby joke cycle, 180
death penalty, *39*
democracy, Israeli social issues and, 293
Democratic presidential nominating
    convention, *135*
depression, medicalization and, 105
*Diagnostic and Statistical Manual of Mental
    Disorders (DSM)*, 101
diagnostic frames, 68
dialog between claimsmakers and
    audience, 45
diffusion, 292–99
    common language and, 295, 296
    definition of, 294
    globalization and, 299

nonrelational channels and, 295–96
relational channels and, 295–96
social arrangements and, 297–99
successful, elements of, 294
theorization and, 297
transmitters and adopters in,
    294–95, 296–97
dignity in nursing homes, managing, 236
direct-mail fundraising, 77
disasters
    commissions on, 277
    jokes about, 181–82
discretion of social problems workers,
    226–28
discrimination
    based on weight, 6–7
    Civil Rights Act of 1964 on, 238
    forms of, 246–47
    against "handicapped" persons,
        203–4
    medicalization and, 100
    racial, 5–6
    sexual harassment, 291–92
    see also racism; sexism
dispossessed claimsmakers, 141
domain expansion for claims, 48–49, 50
drug addiction, 240
drug laws, 211, 213
DSM, see Diagnostic and Statistical Manual
    of Mental Disorders (DSM)

economic crisis, loan applications and,
    251–53
Eighteenth Amendment, 256
elephant jokes, 180
emergencies, programs in response to,
    261
emotion
    contemporary legends and, 173–74
    framing and, 69
entertainment media, 148–52, 151, 155
Environmental Protection Agency, 191

ethnicity, joke cycles and, 180, 189
ethnic tensions, contemporary legends
    and, 176–77
evaluation research, 271–75, 274, 278
experts as claimsmakers, 20, 96–126
    case study on, 123–26
    criticism of policy outcomes,
        267–69, 270
    influence of, 98
    medicalization and, 98–104, 112
        adopting medical vocabulary,
            101–2
        biomedicalization, 104
        consequences of, 99–100
        genetic research and, 105
        growth of, during twentieth
            century, 99–101
        ownership of social problems,
            102–4
        vocabulary of, 98, 100
    officials as, 116–19
    science and, see scientific experts
    shifting patterns of institutional
        influence, 98
    in social problems process, 119–22,
        121
    subjective interests and, 112–16, 115

Facebook, 325–26
feedback, 26–27, 73, 74, 320
feminism, 85, 279
Fetal Alcohol Syndrome, 260
financial collapse, loan applications and,
    251–53
FOAF (Friend Of A Friend), 173
focus groups, 168–72, 171
folklore, 172–83, 184
    contemporary legends, 173–74,
        175–76, 176–78, 179,
        188
    definition of, 172
    jokes cycles, 179–83

food security, disputes within apparent
  agreement about, 42
forecasting future problems, 312
forest certification, 79
foundations, policymaking by, 206
FOX News, 137
frame amplification, 71, 72
frame bridging, 70, 71–72
frame disputes, 72, 73
frame extension, 71, 72
frame transformation, 71, 72
framing, 67–73, 90, 91, 92
  cultural resources and, 73
  diagnostic frames, 68
  disputes within a movement over,
    72, 73
  feedback and reframing, 72, 73, 74
  focus groups and, 170–71
  frame alignment, 70–72
  grotesque images and, 69
  integrity issues in, 73
  master frame, 81
  motivational frames, 68
  ownership of a social problem and, 86
  prognostic frames, 68–69
France, 291–92, 295, 298
Friend Of A Friend (FOAF), 173
fundraising, 77–78

Gallup Poll
  on healthcare coverage, 219, 220
  on immigration, 187
gambling, 148, 150
gangs, concern about, 302, 303
gender
  changing expectations regarding,
    246–47
  contemporary legends and, 177
genetic research, 105
geography
  as basis for comparative research, 289
  diffusion of a claim, see diffusion

geographical concentrations of news
  workers, 136
globalization, diffusion and, 299
global warming, 108–10, 145, 164
government agencies
  officials of, as expert claimsmakers,
    116–19
  policymaking by, 191, 203
grotesque images, framing and, 69
grounds of claims, 31, 31–36
  basic recipe for establishing, 31–33
    example, 34
    naming the problem, 32
    statistics, 33
    typifying example, 32
  other rhetorical devices for
    establishing, 33–36
    challenge to older interpretations,
      35–36
    familiar type of problem, 35
    hearings, legislative, 200
    kind of people affected, 35
    range of people affected, 35
    worsening situation, 34–35
gun control, 86, 91

Handgun Control Inc, 86
Haredi community, 293
Hate Crimes Sentencing Enhancement
  Act, 201
Hate Crimes Statistics Act, 201
Head Start, 281
health care
  case study on, as a policy challenge,
    218–20
  insurance for, 221, 222, 230
  hearings, legislative, 200, 205
Heritage Foundation, 115
hermaphrodites, 12
homelessness
  comparison of, in two major cities,
    288–89

frames and, 207
  media portrayal of, 143
  policies of officials toward, 119
home loans, financial collapse and,
    251–53
homicide victims, 52
homophobia, 100
homophobic bullying, 93–95
homosexuality, medicalization and, 105
human resource workers, 238
Hurricane Katrina, 209

iconic narratives, 145
ideologies, 283
  claims linked to, 53
  predispositions and policy outcomes,
    278–82, 281
immigration, case study on public
    reactions to, 187–89
infotainment, 150
insider claimsmakers, 65, 65–66, 97,
    204
  see also experts as claimsmakers
intellectual property, protection of,
    284
Internet, 138–39, 140
intersex, 12
Islamophobia, 100
Israel, 293
It Gets Better Project, 94

Japan
  earthquake in 2011 in, jokes about,
    182
  sexual harassment in, 298
  tobacco smoking in, 297
Jenkins, Philip, 302–3
Johnson, Lyndon
  signing of Civil Rights Act and the
    Voting Rights Act, 21
  "war on poverty," 14
jokes cycles, 179–83, 188, 189

King, Martin Luther, Jr.
  bus boycott and, 17, 301
  as outsider claimsmaker, 66
Kingdon, John W., 195–98, 199,
    200–202, 208

landmark narratives, 144, 145
language
  diffusion and, 295, 296
  medical, see medicalization
  social construction and, 11
  of sociologists, 16
legalization of drugs, 211, 213
legal scholars, 276
legends, contemporary, 173–74, 175–76,
    176–78, 179
legislative bodies as policymakers, 190,
    276–77
  committee system, 198, 200
  competition for places on legislators'
    agenda, 193–95
  hearings and, 200, 205
  incremental nature of legislative
    reform, 201
  policy domains and, 192–93,
    198, 200–201
  policy stream model and,
      see policy stream model
libertarianism, 279
life expectancy, 307
loan applications, financial collapse
    and, 251–53
lobbyists, 193–95, 197, 203, 204

macrosociological approach, 222
MADD, see Mothers Against Drunk
    Driving (MADD)
March of Dimes, 88
Massachusetts, establishment of,
    96
master frame, 81
measles, 214, 216

media and media coverage, 127–59
  alteration of primary claims by, 128
  arenas for presenting social problems
      claims, 129
  audience segmentation, 137–38, 142
  bias issues, 127–28, 129–30
  carrying capacity of, 129, 137, 140
  case study on, 157–59
  changing forms of news media,
      137–39
  entertainment media, 148–52, 151,
      155
  feedback received by, 155
  impact of, 152–54
    agenda setting, 153–54
    on public opinion, 165–67
    structuring of the debate, 153
  Internet and, 138–39, 140
  of legislative hearings, 190, 200
  news work and workers, 130–36,
      135, 319
    balancing of coverage, 133–34,
        141
    complex stories and, 133
    constraints on, 128, 130
    geographical concentrations of, 136
    as primary claimsmakers, 134
    reporter beats, 131
    stories favored by, 131–32
  packaging of claims for, 128–29,
      134–36, 139–47
    audience segmentation and, 142
    changing media packages, 146–47
    condensing symbols, 146
    constructing packages in, 144–47
    cultural resources and, 146, 155
    issue ownership, advantages of,
        140–44
    landmark narratives and, 144, 145
  of scientific research, 106–7
  of social movements, 308

  as stage in the social problems
      process, 19, 20–21, 128,
      154–56, 155
medicalization, 98–104, 112
  adopting medical vocabulary, 101–2
  biomedicalization, 104
  case study on, 123–26
  consequences of
    providing a familiar frame for an
        issue, 99
    shifting of attention from social
        conditions shaping
        problems, 99
    shifting of responsibility from the
        individual, 99–100
  definition of, 98
  genetic research and, 105
  growth of, during twentieth century,
      99–101
  ownership of social problems, 102–4
  vocabulary of, 98, 100
medical model, 99
Medicare, 219, 220
methadone programs, 240
microsociological perspective, 223
Mills, C. Wright, 114, 150
misguided policies, 259–64
  emergencies, programs responding
      to, 261
  ironic consequences of, 261–62
  subverted by social program work,
      262
Mothers Against Drunk Driving
      (MADD), 89
motifs of contemporary legends, 174,
      175–76
motivational frames, 68

NAACP, see National Association for the
      Advancement of Colored
      People (NAACP)

Nader, Ralph, 110
naming the problem, 32
National Association for the
        Advancement of Colored
        People (NAACP), 65
    ownership and, 87–88
    resources of, 76
National Rifle Association (NRA), 65,
        86, 87, 91
National Right to Life Committee
        (NRLC), 84
National Weather Service, 226
National Women's Party (NWP), 84–85
Native American societies, 12
natural history of social problems
    definition of, 17–18
    stages of, 319, 18, 19, 20–23, 319,
        321, 322, 323
        claimsmaking, 18, 19, 20
        media coverage, 19, 20–21, 128,
            154–56, 155
        policymaking, 19, 21–22, 221
        policy outcomes, 19, 22–23
        public reaction, 19, 21, 183–86,
            185
        social problems work, 19, 22, 221
New Orleans, Hurricane Katrina and,
        209
news media, see media and media
        coverage
Nineteenth Amendment, 256
nonmembership advocacy organizations
        (NMAOs), 120
nonrelational channels, 295–96
novelty of news stories, 145, 300–301
NRA, see National Rifle Association
        (NRA)
NRLC, see National Right to Life
        Committee (NRLC)
nursing homes, managing dignity in, 236
NWP, see National Women's Party (NWP)

Obama, Barack, 219–20
Obamacare, 219–20
obesity, 6–7
objectivist definitions of social
        problems, 3–8
office folklore, 183
officials
    activist stances of, 203
    as expert claimsmakers, 116–19
opportunity structures, 80–85, 90, 92
    cultural opportunities, 79–80
    ownership of a social problem
        and, 86
    political opportunities, 81–85
organ thefts, contemporary legends
        relating to, 178
outsider claimsmakers, 64–65, 65,
        196
    see also activists as claimsmakers
ownership of a social problem,
        85–89, 90, 92
    advantages of, 85–89
    benefits for the owners, 90
    development of a broader set of
        interrelated concerns
        and, 87–88
    framing and, 86
    institutionalized, 103–4
    lobbying and, 195
    long-term, 87–88
    media coverage and, 140–44
    medicalization and, 102–4
    multiple owners, 86–87
    narrowly focused SMOs, 88
    opportunity structures and, 86
    political opportunities and, 86
    possibilities for evolution of
        establishment of new SMO to
            assume ownership, 89
        existing SMOs assume ownership
            of new issue, 89

ownership of a social problem (*continued*)
    no one assumes ownership,
        88–89
    resource mobilization and, 86

packages, definition of, 144
packaging of claims for the media,
        128–29, 134–36, 139–47
    audience segmentation and, 142
    changing media packages, 146–47
    condensing symbols, 146
    constructing packages in, 144–47
    cultural resources and, 146, *155*
    issue ownership, advantages of,
        140–44
    landmark narratives and, 144, 145
paranoia, social progress and, 310–11
Parks, Rosa, 301
pathologists, 263
pediatrics, 102–3
perfectibility, 309
performance standards, 227–30, *229*
pesticides, 210
Pfohl, Stephen, 102
pharmaceuticalization, 104
phobia, 100
pigeons, case study on claims about, *61*
piggybacking, 49–51
planets in the solar system, 12, 13
Planned Parenthood Federation of
        America (PPFA), 84
Pluto, 13
police departments, Compstat model
        and, 229
policy domains, 192–202, 203
    arenas compared with, 192
    definition of, 192
    policy stream model and, 195–202
        convergence of the three streams,
            198, *199*, 200–202
        policy proposal stream, 196,
            197, *199*

political stream, 196–97, *199*
    problem recognition stream, 195,
        199, 208
policymakers, 190
    activist stances of, 203
    pressures on, 202–8
    public opinion, responsiveness to,
        204, 205
policymaking, 190–220
    activist stances, 203
    by administrative agencies, 191
    by appellate courts, 191
    behind-the-scenes, 191, 202–3
    case study in, *218–20*
    by legislative bodies, *see* legislative
        bodies as policymakers
    in multiple arenas, 205–6
    by nongovernmental bodies, 191,
        206–8
    policy domains and, *see* policy
        domains
    pressures on policymakers, 202–8
    rhetoric of, 208–17
        causal stories and, 208–11, *212*,
            213
        "declaring war" on social
            problems, 214, *215*, *216*,
            216–17
        symbolic politics, 211, 213
    as stage in the social problems
        process, *19*, 21–22,
        221
    visible, 190–91, 204
policy outcomes, 255–85
    actors, evidence, evaluation, and
        original activists and experts,
            267–69
    rival activists and experts, 270
    social problems workers, 264,
        265, 266
    subjects of social problems
        workers, 266–67, *268*

case study on, 283–85
definition of, 255
ideological predispositions and,
        278–82, 281
impartial evaluations, search for,
        271–78
    appellate courts and, 276–78
    commissions and, 275–76, 277,
        278
    evaluation research and, 271–75,
        274, 278
new claims based on policy
        evaluation, 257–64
    critique of policy as excessive,
        258–59
    critique of policy as insufficient,
        257–58
    critique of policy as misguided,
        259–64
    persistence of troubling conditions,
        256
    range of, 255–56
    as stage in the social problems
        process, 19, 22–23
policy proposal stream, 196, 197, 199,
        216
policy stream model, 195–202
    convergence of the three streams,
        198, 199, 200–202
    policy proposal stream, 196, 197,
        199, 216
    political stream, 196–97, 199, 208
    problem recognition stream, 195,
        199, 216
political opportunities to promote
        activists' claims, 81–85,
        86
political stream, 196–97, 199, 208
polity, 65
polling, see public reaction
popular culture, 148, 149
popular wisdom, 169–70

population (statistical term), 162
position issues, 41, 86
poverty
    cultural diversity and, 55–56
    social construction and, 14
    as a social problem, 10
PPFA, see Planned Parenthood
        Federation of America
        (PPFA)
preaching to the choir, 43
predispositions, ideological, 278–82, 281
pregnancy, alcohol and, 260
presidential nominating conventions,
        135
primary claims, 128, 134
problem recognition stream, 195, 199,
        208, 216
pro-choice movement
    focus groups and, 170–71
    fundraising by, 78
    see also abortion issue
professional standards for social
        problems workers,
        227–30, 229
prognostic frames, 68–69
progress, claimsmaking and the problem
        of, 307–13
Prohibition, 211, 213, 256, 306–7
pro-life movement, 66, 78
    see also abortion issue
proliferation of social problems claims,
        310
proportion of social problems, progress
        and, 309–10
prostitution, case study of, 315–17
psychiatry and medicalization of social
        problems, 101
public reaction, 160–89
    case study on, 187–89
    focus groups and other interviews to
        assess, 168–72, 171
    folklore and, 172–83, 184

public reaction (*continued*)
  contemporary legends, 173–74,
    175–76, 176–78, *179*
  definition of, 172
  immigration and, 188
  jokes cycles, 179–83
  overview of, 160–61
  policymakers' responsiveness to,
    204, 205
  public opinion polls/surveys to
    assess, 161–68
    factors affecting public opinion
      and, 165–67
    impact of, 167–68
    impact of methods in
      interaction of pollster and
        respondent, 165
      representative samples,
        162–63
      simplifying of complex
        issues, 163–64
      wording of questions, 163, *164*
  as stage in the social problems process,
    19, 21, 183–86, *185*
Puritans
  establishment of colonial
    Massachusetts, 96
  view of children, 54–55

race
  changing expectations regarding,
    246–47
  contemporary legends and, 176–77
  joke cycles and, 180, 189
racism
  in popular culture, 149
  segregation and, 17–23
  as a social problem, 5–6
reality television, 151
Rehabilitation Act of 1973, 203
relational channels, 295–96

religion, Israeli social issues and, 293
representative sample, 162–63
reproductive health services programs,
    259–61
Republican presidential nominating
    convention, *135*
research, evaluation, 271–75, *274*
resource mobilization, 73–80, *90*, 91
  case study of, *94*
  ownership of a social problem
    and, 86
resources, *24*, 24–25
rhetoric, *24*, 25–26
  apocalyptic, 310–12
  of claims, 30–40
    conclusions, 31, *31*, 38–40
    grounds, *31*, 31–36
    warrants, 31, *31*, 36–38, *39*
  definition of, 25, 30
  of policymaking, 208–17
    causal stories and, 208–11, *212*,
      213
    "declaring war" on social
      problems, 214, *215, 216*,
      216–17
    symbolic politics and, 211, 213
risk, news stories about, 157–59
risk assessment, scientific authorities
    and, 110–11
risk society, 157
Roe v. Wade, 191
routines of social problems workers,
    235–37, 238
rumors, 174, 176–78
runaways, adolescent, 201

sample, polling, 162
sample survey, 162
satanic ritual abuse, concerns about, 295
Savage, Dan, *94*
school shootings, 142–44

scientific experts, 104–12
  disputes among, 107–10
    global warming example, 108–10
    over causes, 109
    over remedies, 109–10
  funding of research and findings of,
    112–13
  media's reporting on scientific
    research, 106–7
  risk assessment and, 110–11
  science as socially constructed, 106
  scientific evidence and, 106
  subjective interests of, 112–16, *115*
SCLC, *see* Southern Christian Leadership
    Conference (SCLC)
secondary claims, 128
segmentation, audience, 42–43
segregation, 17–23, 66
selective memories, 301
September 11, 2001, terrorist attacks
  commission on, 277
  construction of news after, 131
  focus groups and, 171
  focus on terrorism after, 80, 83
services provided by social problems
    workers, 241–42
sex crimes, legislators' understandings
    of, 194
sex education, 259–61
sexism
  diffusion and, 297
  identifying additional forms of, 48
  as a social problem, 4, 5, 8, 9
sex offender policies, 274
sexting, 284–85
sexual harassment, 291–92, 298
sexual trafficking, case study of,
    315–17
smart phones, 284–85
SMOs, *see* social movement organizations
    (SMOs)

SNCC, *see* Student Nonviolent
    Coordinating Committee
    (SNCC)
social conditions, 256
social construction, 10–14, 16
  definition of, 11
  as interactive process, 320–21, 322,
    323
  uses of constructionist stance,
    325–29
  see also constructionist approach;
      social problems process
social issues, 256
social movement organizations (SMOs),
    66
  alliances across, 77
  frames and, *see* framing
  narrowly focused, 88
  resource mobilization and, *see*
      resource mobilization
social movements, 66–67
  activists as claimsmakers, *see* activists
      as claimsmakers
  experts and, *see* experts as
      claimsmakers
  media coverage of, 308
  recruitment of members, 69–70
  selective memories of, 301
social problems, 256
  defining, 3–10
    claimsmaking process and, 15
    objectivist approach to, 3–8
    subjectivist approach to, 8–10,
      16, 319
  ownership of, *see* ownership of a
      social problem
  see also social problems process
social problems marketplace,
    46–47, *47*
social problems process, 3–28, 318
  complex system of, 322, 323–24

social problems process (*continued*)
  defining social problems, 3–10
    claimsmaking process and, 15
    objectivist approach to, 3–8
    subjectivist approach to, 8–10, 16
  expert claimsmakers in, 119–22, 121
  feedback and, 26–27
  model of, 319, 17–18, 19, 20–23,
      319, 321, 322, 323
    as oversimplification, 321
    stage five: social problems work,
      19, 22, 221
    stage four: policymaking, 19,
      21–22, 221
    stage one: claimsmaking, 18,
      19, 20
    stage six: policy outcomes, 19,
      22–23
    stage three: public reaction, 19,
      21, 183–86, 185
    stage two: media coverage, 19,
      20–21, 128, 154–56, 155
  new claims based on, *see* policy
      outcomes: new claims
      based on policy
      evaluation
  as ongoing, 320
  resources and, 24, 24–25
  rhetoric and, 24, 25–26
  social construction and, 10–14
social problems work, 221–53
  case construction and, 231–37
  case study on, 251–53
  categorizing problems of subjects,
      232–33
  classifying subjects by status
      categories, 233–34, 238
  coercive, 241
  deciding on relevant aspects of the
      case, 233
  definition of, 222
  everyday, 246–49
  judging the seriousness of the
      problem, 233
  observers and, 234
  as stage in the social problems
      process, 19, 22, 221
  by "street-level" bureaucrats, 222
  work-related considerations, 235
social problems workers, 222–31, 250
  bureaucratic hierarchies and, 224
  case construction and, 231–37
  cultural expectations of, 223
  decision making by, 225, 226, 227
  degree of discretion, 226–28
  evaluation of policy outcomes by,
      264, 265, 266
  expectations of, 223
  institutional rules affecting, 224
  in the middle, 224–25, 225
  oversight of, response to, 243–46
    control over information about
        activities, 244–45
    efforts to limit outsiders'
        authority over activities,
        245
  performance standards for, 227–30,
      229
  realities for, on-the-job, 230–31
  routines of, 235–37, 238
  subjects of, *see* subjects of social
      problem workers
  supervisors' expectations of, 243
Social Security, 210
sociological imagination, 114, 150–51
solar system, 12, 13
Southern Christian Leadership
    Conference (SCLC),
    17, 20, 76
spanking, 54–55
spiked drinks, contemporary legends
    and, 176–77

stalking, 89
standards, performance, 227–30, 229
statistics
    to establish grounds for a claim, 33
    policy outcomes and, 269, 270
stereotypes, 180, 189
Stone, Deborah A., 208
Stonewall riots, 301
Student Nonviolent Coordinating
            Committee (SNCC),
            17, 20, 66
    confrontational activities and, 87
    resources of, 76
subjectivist definitions of social
            problems, 8–10, 16,
            319
subjects of social problem workers,
            222–23, 237–43
    case construction and, 231–37
    classifying, 233–34
    coercion of, 241
    evaluation of policy outcomes by,
            266–67, 268
    repeaters, 242
    resistance of, 242–43
surveys, see public reaction
symbolic politics, rhetoric of, 211

talk shows, 148, 149–50
TANF, see Temporary Assistance to
            Needy Families (TANF)
target populations, 209–10
technological change, case study on
            policy outcomes and,
            283–85
television, see media and media
            coverage
Temporary Assistance to Needy
            Families (TANF), 281
terminology of constructionist
            approach, 14–16

terrorism, see September 11, 2001,
            terrorist attacks
theorization and, 297
"thinking dirty," 263
think tanks, 114, 115, 120
time as basis for comparative research,
            289
tobacco smoking, 297
To Catch a Predator, 151
topical joke cycles, 181
traffic fatalities, 215
transmitters, 294–95, 296–97
trauma domain, expansion of, 50
troubling conditions, 318
    as basis for comparative research,
            289
    definition of, 15–16
    persistence of, 256
twelve-step programs, 102, 148, 239–40
typifying example, 32

UFO abductions, social construction of,
            12–13
unemployment of college-educated
            white males, 34
urban legends, see contemporary
            legends

vaccinations
    autism and, 123–24
    for measles, 214, 216
valence issues, 41, 42, 133
variants of tales, 173
vegaphobia, 100
vegetarianism, 44
violence, television and, 152
voting rights, 307–8
Voting Rights Act of 1965, 17, 21

Walt Disney Company, 47
warrants of claims, 31, 31, 36–38, 39

war rhetoric, 214, *215, 216*, 216–17
weather forecasting, 226
Web sites, cloaked, 139
weight, discrimination and, 6–7
welfare programs
    criticism of, 261–62
    differences in the ways politicians
        talk about, 210

women's movement
    framing of issues involving
        victimization, 74
    new wave of feminist activism, 85
    stalking and, 89
workplace bullying, 298–99
worsening situation a grounds for a
    claim, 34–35